Mark Hopkins and the Log

WILLIAMS COLLEGE, 1836-1872

THE BICENTENNIAL EDITION

WITH AN APPENDIX BY THE AUTHOR
Williams College 1793-1993: Three Eras, Three Cultures

BY FREDERICK RUDOLPH

WILLIAMS COLLEGE
WILLIAMSTOWN, MASSACHUSETTS
1996

ALSO BY FREDERICK RUDOLPH

- The American College and University: A History

- Essays on Education in the Early Republic (editor)

- Curriculum: A History of the American Undergraduate
  Course of Study Since 1636

- Perspectives: A Williams Anthology (editor)

Originally published:
New Haven: Yale University Press, 1956
Under the direction of the Department of History
in Yale Historical Publications, Miscellany 63.

This edition published by Williams College, 1996

Second Printing 2005

ISBN 0-915081-03-2

Printed in the United States of America

To D. D. R.

Preface to the Bicentennial Edition

Until the publication of *Mark Hopkins and the Log* in 1956 both Mark Hopkins and the Williams over which he presided were more firmly fixed in academic mythology than in scholarly understanding. James A. Garfield's defense of Hopkins at an 1871 meeting of New York alumni became not just an aphorism for sentimentalizing an era in the college's history. It also allowed Hopkins and his era to escape serious study. The aphorism said it all: "The ideal college is Mark Hopkins on one end of a log and a student on the other."

When my Yale graduate school mentor, Ralph Gabriel, wondered in 1949 whether a scholarly exploration of the aphorism might be an appropriate dissertation subject, I welcomed his inspired suggestion. (I had had to give up an earlier topic, the appeal of totalitarian philosophies and methods to American business leaders during the Great Depression, when I discovered that a graduate student was pursuing the subject elsewhere.) The dissertation was completed in 1953. Turning it into a book took three years. By 1955 the manuscript had been reduced by at least a third, and it would benefit from further cutting before it was published. While the Yale faculty readers of the dissertation thought that it was publishable, the question of by whom engaged me in extended conversations and correspondence that led eventually to its appearing as a publication of the Yale Department of History.

Getting there was not easy. Originally all the Yale readers thought that the book should be a Williams publication and that the Yale history department should husband its limited resources for books without alternative hopes. Friends at Williams advised that I not ask the college to publish the book, perhaps taking their cue from one of the Yale readers (a Williams alumnus) who thought "the account . . . not very flattering to the college." Ralph Gabriel's view, on the other hand, was that it "helps to build up the dignity of the institution." In any case, I did not ask and thus the book was not considered for Williams sponsorship and I was perhaps spared rejection.[1]

A few trade publishers expressed an interest in the manuscript, but listened to their business offices when it came time to decide whether to publish it. In the end, the Yale University Press brought

out the book in an edition of 1500 copies in April, 1956, the author
being required to provide the then customary subsidy of a 3/8 share
of the cost of publication. A third of the printing was gone within
days of publication, thanks to the promotional efforts of the College
Book Store in Williamstown with the cooperation of the college's
Alumni Office. By mid-October only 367 copies remained, and in
January 1957, the Yale Press decided to order a second printing of
1000 copies. In 1968 the book went out of print. I purchased from the
Yale Press 185 sets of unbound sheets of the book, had them bound,
and over the years made them available to local bookstores.[2]

The initial response of the Williams community forty years ago
triggered the necessity of the second printing, but for twenty-five
years the book has essentially not been available and, indeed, has
been unknown to generations of students and alumni. This new
edition, sponsored by the Society of Alumni in its 175th year, makes
the book available once more, other than in secondhand bookstores
where a copy was recently offered for $28.50.

A new edition allows errata from the first edition to be removed
and provides an opportunity to say something about the critical
response to the book as well as to address questions raised by its
portrait of Hopkins and the college during his administration.

In the *Mississippi Valley Historical Review* (now the *Journal of
American History*) Thomas Le Duc, author of a study of Amherst
that was also a Yale dissertation directed by Ralph Gabriel, recognized that the book "analyzed the disparity between the secular
interests, social and intellectual, of the students and the traditional
preoccupation of the college with personal religion." He pointed out
that the "emphasis on the students as forces of innovation" conveyed
an accurate picture, as did the analysis of the old curriculum that
revealed its "intellectual aridity and inadequacy."[3] In the *Journal of
Higher Education* Wilson Smith, who had been a student of Richard
Hofstadter's at Columbia, referred to one chapter as "the best available study of the origins and aims of college fraternities before the
Civil War" and another on "the development of the cult of the alumnus" as "a unique contribution to our growing body of critical literature on the nineteenth-century American middle class."[4]

Where reviewers and correspondents had trouble was in the
book's evaluation of Mark Hopkins. Robert Samuel Fletcher, a sometimes acidic professor of history at Oberlin and author of a history
of that institution, in the *American Historical Review* expressed the
extreme, and I believe inaccurate, view that "Professor Rudolph . . .
has not said that Mark Hopkins was pretty much of an old fraud,
but he has provided us with the data from which that conclusion

may readily be drawn."[5] William W. Brickman of New York University in *America* saw the matter more clearly: "He has marshaled enough evidence to show that Hopkins was an influential teacher and molder of men, if not the pedagogical paragon that he has been made out to be."[6]

Some reviewers and readers had difficulty distinguishing between what Le Duc called a "masterful . . . dissection of the Mark Hopkins myth" and what others regarded as debunking.[7] Samuel E. Allen, a retired Williams English professor, in *The Berkshire Eagle* got it right when he wrote that the book harbored no intention to debunk: "Every point in it is based on reliable documents; the object is to present the picture clear and true."[8] Claude M. Fuess, former principal of Phillips Andover Academy, in the *Saturday Review* thought that the book was "obviously an attempt to sift out fact from myth," adding, "If Mark Hopkins is 'debunked,' the process is as merciful as it is successful . . . . Out of Rudolph's honest book a man emerges although not by any means the unblemished hero of tradition."[9] John Walton of Johns Hopkins in the *Baltimore Sun* concluded that although the book "preserves the integrity of Mark Hopkins, the log and the student . . . the portrait that emerges [of Hopkins] is not altogether flattering."[10]

Perhaps the most astute reading of the book came from someone who had not read it but who had had it read to him. After having heard the book read to him by Professor Richard A. Newhall, his successor as chairman of the Williams history department, Professor Theodore Clarke Smith wrote me in August 1957:

> Those features of the Williams College of 1820-1872 and of Mark Hopkins himself as a person which arose from the Calvinistic religious habits and phraseology of that period are described with absolute accuracy, but without a particle of respect or sympathy . . . . On the contrary, those chapters which chronicle the ways in which the students and alumni paved the way for modern Williams are written with no . . . [less] objectivity as to fact but with unmistakable zest . . . . Your treatment of Mark Hopkins is objective, kindly and thoroughly appreciative of his personality and teaching gifts. There is nothing [here that is] like debunking.[11]

Smith was right. Without being sentimental or filiopietistic the book could have been as sympathetic to Hopkins and his age as it clearly was to the age that was replacing it. It may not convey an adequate appreciation of the greatness that his contemporaries attributed to him. On the other hand, I do not agree with Claude Fuess's judgment expressed in a letter to Lewis Perry, retired principal of Phillips Exeter Academy and a Williams alumnus, that the book "destroyed the reputation of Mark Hopkins." I prefer Perry's view that while the book "takes off a little from the glamour of Mark Hopkins' reputation," Fuess's judgment was, as Perry told him, "just an Amherst man's attitude."[12]

* * *

Mark Hopkins and the Log led to a career as a teacher at Williams College and as a scholar of American higher education. A Guggenheim Fellowship in 1958-59 allowed me to move from the micro to the macro in *The American College and University: A History* (1962). A commission from the Carnegie Foundation for the Advancement of Teaching resulted in *Curriculum: A History of the Undergraduate Course of Study Since 1636* (1977). Both of these books in recent years have been published in new paperback editions. I retired from teaching in 1982 and, as Mark Hopkins Professor of History emeritus, edited an anthology of Williams documents, *Perspectives: A Williams Anthology*, which the college published in 1983.

* * *

To this new edition of *Mark Hopkins and the Log* there is appended a 1993 essay of mine, "Williams College 1793-1993: Three Eras, Three Cultures," an overview of the college's history that began as a contribution to the Class of 1942's fiftieth reunion book and then was developed into a contribution to the bicentennial faculty lecture series. It is included here as an opportunity to relate Mark Hopkins's Williams to the college's two hundred years and the world that shaped and was shaped by it.

* * *

Without the support of my former student, Chester K. Lasell, Secretary of the Society of Alumni, and the expert and energetic skills of Thomas W. Bleezarde, Editor of Alumni Publications, this new edition would not have been possible. I am grateful to them and to Sylvia Kennick Brown and Lynne K. Fonteneau-McCann of the Williams Archives, where I was able to piece together the story this new preface tells.

F.R.

Williamstown, Massachusetts
September 1996

Notes

Material cited below is in Frederick Rudolph Papers, Williams College Archives, Box 10: "Mark Hopkins and the Log (1956)."

1. Leonard W. Labaree, dissertation reader's notes, Yale Department of History, Spring, 1953; Ralph H. Gabriel to author, July 4, 1956.

2. This summary is based on correspondence in folder marked "Hopkins and Log" in Box 10.

3. Thomas Le Duc, *Mississippi Valley Historical Review.* 43 (Dec., 1956), pp. 492-493.

4. Wilson Smith, *Journal of Higher Education,* 28 (Apr., 1957), p. 229.

5. Robert Samuel Fletcher, *American Historical Review,* 62 (Jan. 1957), p. 410.

6. William W. Brickman, *America,* 99 (Apr. 27, 1957), p. 128.

7. Thomas Le Duc, *Mississippi Valley Historical Review,* 43 (Dec., 1956), pp. 492-493.

8. Samuel E. Allen, *The Berkshire Eagle* (Pittsfield, MA.), Apr. 28, 1956.

9. Claude M. Fuess, *Saturday Review,* 39 (July 21, 1956), p. 28.

10. John Walton, *Baltimore Sun,* May 2, 1956.

11. Theodore Clarke Smith to author, postmarked Aug. 8, 1957.

12. Lewis Perry to author, June 18, 1956.

Preface

THE UNITED STATES is a nation of small colleges. Nowhere else in the world is the countryside so generously sprinkled with liberal arts institutions of a thousand students, a few hundred more or less. These little colleges in the country—or what was once the country—are important enough to the American educational pattern to distinguish it from those of other nations in the modern world. And one of these small institutions in northwestern Massachusetts, Williams College, has become in the folklore of American education a symbol of what Americans have often meant by a college education.

"The ideal college is Mark Hopkins on one end of a log and a student on the other," James A. Garfield is reported to have said one December night in 1871, at a New York meeting of the Williams alumni. In time his remarks came to be looked upon by many as the most satisfactory definition of what an American college ought to be. No one can properly address himself to the question of higher education in the United States without paying homage in some way to the aphorism of the log and to Mark Hopkins, who presided over Williams College from 1836 to 1872. Denis Brogan, friendly British observer of American life, has suggested that today's American college is more in harmony with the Mark Hopkins Hotel in San Francisco than with the Williams of Mark Hopkins' day.* When the United States government issued a series of postage stamps honoring American educators in 1940, it singled out Hopkins to represent the small liberal arts college. In the company of the great Eliot of Harvard, of a pioneer like Booker T. Washington of Tuskegee, or of a friend of the common schools like Horace Mann, Mark Hopkins was not out of place. His name long since had become synonymous with an American educational ideal.

More Americans seemingly are acquainted with Garfield's aphorism than they are with its meaning: few have understood how important to Mark Hopkins' college were the students on the other end of the log. Their role in giving shape and purpose

---

* See D. W. Brogan, *The American Character* (New York, Knopf, 1944), pp. 143–4. The San Francisco hotel, by the way, is named for another Mark Hopkins, the great California railroad builder.

to the 19th-century college was extraordinarily vital. The aphorism, while doing justice to the desirability of inspired teaching
and to the irrelevance of material surroundings and equipment,
gives no adequate impression of the degree to which the total
collegiate experience was a reflection of undergraduate initiative
and enterprise.

This study has attempted to recapture not only the story of
Hopkins and the log, and of the thirty-six years at Williams when
the Hopkins legend was putting down its roots—it has attempted
to get at its meaning as well. The history of Mark Hopkins' administration at Williams College is, in one way, an inspection of
those years on an American college campus when many of the
directions of the 20th-century college were being set. Mark Hopkins and others who were fashioning the Williams of their own
time did not know how or to what degree they were shaping the
future. This story of the creative years of higher education in
19th-century America is an attempt to recover Hopkins, his college, and its students from mythology and to suggest the degree
to which they and their contemporaries on other college campuses
cast shadows upon our own time.

Some colleges ventured into uncharted waters, as did Oberlin
with coeducation—or resisted longer than others the disquieting
impact of new institutions: Greek letter fraternities made their
first appearance at Williams in 1833 but not until 1852 at Ken-
yon. Evangelical religion maintained its hold at some places
longer than at others. And some institutions, like Harvard and
Yale, developed into universities, where the pursuit of learning
gained a prestige that it had not known at the typical small liberal arts college. Yet, when the returns were all in, the Williams
pattern, not the Yale or Harvard pattern, was a more typical
manifestation of American education. The following chapters,
focusing attention upon Williams College, which has been the
symbol of an ideal, thereby may shed light upon the history of
the many colleges of which it was a fair representative.

My excursion into Mark Hopkins' world was first encouraged
by Professor Charles R. Keller, chairman of the Williams College Department of History, who has been a source of friendly
encouragement and assistance during the preparation of this
work. I gladly acknowledge the advice and inspiration of Professor Ralph H. Gabriel of Yale University, under whose guidance the original study was undertaken as a doctoral dissertation
at Yale University, where it was awarded the John Addison

Porter Prize in 1953. I am indebted to President James P. Baxter, 3rd, and the trustees of Williams College for permitting me to work in the archives and manuscript collections of the college. To the entire staff of the Williams College Library I owe a debt of gratitude, but especially to Miss Ethel Richmond of Bennington, Vermont, who, for more than twenty-five years built and cared for the Williamsiana collections of the library. In addition to Professors Gabriel and Keller, Leonard W. Labaree, George W. Pierson, David M. Potter, and Robert C. L. Scott read the manuscript, and their suggestions have been most helpful. Professor Luther S. Mansfield gave the proof a critical and beneficial reading.

I would also like to acknowledge the assistance of Miss Rena Durkan, Amherst College Library; Miss Marion Douglas, Westfield, N.J.; Herbert C. Gutman, University of Wisconsin; Mrs. Henry Hopkins, Shaftsbury, Vt.; Mrs. Arthur Howe, Plymouth, N.H.; Miss Annette Kar and Miss Ruth Kronmiller, both of the Collection of Regional History, Cornell University; John S. Lawrence, Manchester, Mass.; The Rt. Rev. W. Appleton Lawrence, Bishop of Western Massachusetts, Springfield; Lewis Perry, Boston; Mrs. Zara Jones Powers, Sterling Memorial Library, Yale University; Stephen T. Riley, Massachusetts Historical Society; Mrs. Sidney D. Ross, Williamstown; Samuel A. Scoville, New Haven, Conn.; Miss Mildred M. Smith, Adams, Mass.; George V. Thompson, Oberlin College; Mrs. Howard Van Horn, Williamstown; and Karl E. Weston, Williamstown.

As for my wife, although I am certain that she would balk at following the example of one Williams alumnus of the 19th century who named his daughter Markita, I am equally certain that she has traveled as far toward such a step as any man could reasonably expect.

F. R.

Williamstown, Massachusetts
September 1955

Contents

Illustrations

Abbreviations

AL	Amos Lawrence
HL	Hopkins Letters (MSS in Williams College Library)
HP	Hopkins Papers (MSS in Williams College Library)
LC	Library of Congress
MH	Mark Hopkins
MHS	Massachusetts Historical Society
SML:YU	Sterling Memorial Library, Yale University
SOA	Society of Alumni
TR	Trustees' Records (MS minutes of meetings, Admissions Office, Williams College)
WCL	Williams College Library

Part One: MAN

1. *"The Ideal College Is . . ."*

IN 1836 WILLIAMS COLLEGE was looking for a president again.
The little college in the northwestern corner of Massachusetts was
in a characteristic fix: for the third time since the election of the
first president in 1793 the board of trustees was being called upon
to make the management of a wilderness institution sound attractive, and once more it was failing.

In the past, as many men had refused the position as had accepted, and it always would be a matter of debate which group was
more distinguished. Now, Absalom Peters, a Dartmouth man of the
Class of 1816 and secretary of the American Home Missionary Society, was being appropriately polite and flattering, but the answer
was "no" just the same.[1] As the search continued, the Williams corporation decided to stop looking so far afield.

"If the boys want him, let them have him," one trustee is supposed to have responded to the suggestion of the senior class that
there was a suitable prospect on the grounds.[2] The rest of the board
acquiesced, and without fanfare Mark Hopkins, professor of moral
philosophy and rhetoric, was elected to the presidency on August
17, 1836. The thirty-four-year-old professor had been performing
some of the functions to which the retiring and ailing president,
the Reverend Edward Dorr Griffin, was no longer equal, and he was
known to enjoy eating chestnuts and drinking root beer with the
undergraduates. But surely he was a man of no surpassing promise,
regardless of the opinion of the thirty members of the senior class.
In submitting to the seniors' recommendation, however, the Williams governing body ushered the college into an era that found
its way into the lore of American education. In brief, it launched a
legend.

Of all the problems and prospects which lay before the new president of Williams College and on which the legend was to build, the
one that Mark Hopkins could do the least about was geographic.
Ebenezer Fitch, the first president, had complained of this Massa-

1. MH, *A Discourse Delivered at Williamstown June 29, 1886, on the Fiftieth
Anniversary of His Election as President of Williams College* (New York, Scrib-
ner's, 1886), p. 15; Calvin Durfee, *Williams Biographical Annals* (Boston, Lee and
Shepard, 1871), p. 84.

2. *Williams Review, 2* (1872), 185–6. Arthur Latham Perry, *Williamstown and
Williams College* (Williamstown, Mass., privately printed, 1899), p. 496.

chusetts region that it was "a mere desert as to furnishing scholars
for any college," and the complaint would be heard again.[3] Early
friends of the college had responded that there would be less sin at
a country institution than at a place like New Haven or Cambridge; and in the 19th century, spokesmen for Williams made as
much as they could of its low student death rate and alumni longev-
ity.[4] But in 1836 Americans had not yet swarmed into cities, there
to long for the simple pleasures of the country. Not until the railroad and the automobile improved accessibility and made the aesthetic exploitation of the countryside a possibility did Williams
move out from under the shadow of uncertainty over enrollment
which an abundance of natural assets placed upon it.

A range of mountains and a quiet river will compensate for many
of the shortcomings of an American college in the 20th century.
In 1836, however, Williams was suffering from the embarrassments
inherent in *two* mountain ranges—the Taconic to the west and the
Hoosac, capped by Mount Greylock, the highest point in Massachusetts, five miles to the east—and *two* rivers, the Hoosic, running
from the south through Williamstown into New York, finally unit-
ing with the Hudson about ten miles north of Albany; and the
Green, named for the color of its waters, which entered the Hoosic
from the south at Williamstown. In time, the mountains and the
waters were put to appropriate collegiate use. Room was found for
both in undergraduate songs. The Green River, it was said, assumed
a brighter greenness whenever a new freshman class entered. And
the first path up Greylock was constructed in 1830 by Williams
students, who erected a small observatory on the top when they got
there. This complex of mountains and rivers, nevertheless, im-
pounded the college into one of the least accessible valleys in the
state.

A crude road, no better and no worse than most American roads
of the time, ran through Williamstown for east-west travel, but the
demands which the Hoosac Mountains placed upon man, horse, and
carriage discouraged all but the most enterprising travel, in summer or winter. A north-south road leading from Sheffield, near
the Connecticut border in southern Berkshire County, was so hilly
—and in season so muddy—that in 1836 travelers from Connecticut bound for Vermont usually left the road at Great Barrington

3. Fitch to Abel Flint, May 10, 1815; in "A President's Letters," ed. Charles R.
Keller, *Sketch, 10* (1941), 20–1, 32–3.
4. TR, *1*, 29; May 23, 1792. Senate Document No. 19, *Massachusetts Legislative
Papers* (1842), p. 8.

and detoured to the north by way of Albany. To Williams College
the road was a symbol of the slender thread which connected it with
the outside world, a world which really did not care very much
whether Williamstown and Williams College survived at all.

Sometimes the Commonwealth of Massachusetts, whose authority
was centered in Boston a hundred and thirty-five miles from
Williamstown, acted as if it did not care even about Berkshire
County. This vast western wilderness of almost a thousand square
miles, sparsely inhabited by a yeomanry who tilled a meager soil,
was in every way remote from the state government. Not only distance but habit, occupation, and custom separated mercantile Boston from agrarian Berkshire. In the decade before the founding of
Williams College disgruntled debtor farmers of western Massachusetts had risen in revolt against the Commonwealth. The rebellion of Daniel Shays and his band of farmers did not succeed:
the last remnants of his forces were swept out of Williamstown
early in 1787; but their protest and their failure exposed the gulf
which lay between the aspirations of Berkshire and those of Boston,
a gulf which the Commonwealth permitted to widen during the first
half of the 19th century. Finding no encouragement in their state
legislature, the people of Berkshire built their own railroad in 1838.
The connection from Pittsfield, the county seat, however, was not
with Boston but with Albany, the capital city of neighboring New
York.

In turn, Berkshire tended to neglect its college. Williamstown
was obviously closer to Pownal, Vermont, and Petersburg, New
York, than it was to the political and social center of the county,
the southern Berkshire communities of Pittsfield, Stockbridge,
Lenox, and Great Barrington. And Berkshire was poor. The last
county of the Commonwealth to be settled, it had drawn heavily
for its early inhabitants from veterans of the French and Indian
Wars, moving westward from eastern Massachusetts and northern
Connecticut. For many of these would-be farmers and their de-
scendants Berkshire became little more than a staging area for
further westward movements. During the fifty years before 1830
emigration from the county was continuous; in 1820 population
statistics registered an actual decline, and during the following
decades the small villages and townships steadily lost population.[5]
When the Erie Canal was opened in 1825, a college holiday was

5. The best source of information on early Berkshire is *A History of the County
of Berkshire, Massachusetts*, ed. David Dudley Field, Pittsfield, Samuel W. Bush,
1829.

declared at Williams, but Berkshire cultivators of wheat and rye, already discouraged by cold summers and grasshoppers, were soon losing their markets to western competition, a competition which drew them ever westward to more fertile lands or drove them into subsistence farming at home.[6]

Distance and poverty, which contributed heavily to Berkshire's neglect of Williams, also drew the county into stronger commercial ties with New York City and with the neighboring Hudson River communities of Albany, Troy, and Hudson. With these blossoming urban centers southern Berkshire exchanged its butter, cheese, pork, potatoes, marble, sheep, and apples for iron, wheat, flour, and manufactured goods. In this exchange of trade, made possible by the navigability of the Hudson, Berkshire found the means of a moderate economic life. When southern Berkshire turned to manufacturing, its markets continued to lie to the south and the west, to areas beyond the Commonwealth. As these ties, so natural and so necessary, were strengthened, Williamstown suffered what later generations, respectful of its unspoiled charm, might be pleased to call a kind of salutary neglect. Growth came less precipitately to Williamstown—what growth there was. Between 1800 and 1850 the population rose hardly at all—from 2,086 to 2,626.[7]

The price for so little change and so clear a divorce from the economic and social developments taking place elsewhere in the county was paid by Williams College; for whatever had been the aspirations of the original trustees of the institution, in 1836 Williams was clearly in no position to lay claim to success as a regional college. In 1829 more than thirty sons of Berkshire County were attending colleges other than Williams; the same year, when the enrollment at Williams stood at ninety-seven, only twenty-five students were from the county, and of these, fourteen were from Williamstown.[8]

The founders were not to blame. At first the college had been able to draw upon surrounding communities in New York and Vermont for its students; and although as a region the tri-state area formed at the northwestern corner of Massachusetts was artificial, it *was* a region as far as higher education was concerned in 1793. In that year there were no colleges at all in Vermont and none in New York except in New York City. By 1836, however, true regional colleges had been founded: Union, Rensselaer Poly-

6. Albert Hopkins to Harry Hopkins, Oct. 24, 1825; HL, 2. Field, p. 87.
7. *Vital Records of Williamstown, Massachusetts, to the Year 1850* (Boston, New England Historic Genealogical Society, 1907), p. 8.
8. Field, p. 173.

technic Institute, Colgate, Middlebury, Hamilton, and the University of Vermont. In addition, Amherst College now lay between Williamstown and Cambridge, drawing students from communities in the Connecticut Valley, southern Berkshire County, and northern Connecticut, all of which had once been prime sources of the Williams enrollment. In Connecticut, sectarianism had destroyed the educational monopoly enjoyed by Yale and indirectly by Williams; Methodists now went to Wesleyan and Episcopalians to Trinity. Everywhere piety and learning had found new and eager friends.

Enrollment was not the only casualty caused by the location: endowment also suffered. In 1842 the legislature of the Commonwealth, asked by the trustees of the college to come to its aid, remarked that Williams was "not so situated as to attract the gaze of cities." It was, the legislators said, secluded "from the eyes of the wealthy." [9] In forty years, it was true, the only man of wealth in Berkshire County to contribute at all heavily to the funds of Williams College was Woodbridge Little of Pittsfield, whose gift of $2500 in 1811 and legacy of $3200 in 1813 constituted the "charity" funds of the college.[10] Williams was not alone in a heartless world, but geography had indeed placed it beyond the purview of the men upon whom it depended for students and funds.

Colonel Ephraim Williams, for whom the college was named, had not intended that students should be difficult to recruit or endowments almost impossible to build. For that matter, he had not intended to found a college. Enroute with his regiment of Massachusetts militia to join battle with the French and Indians at Crown Point, the Colonel had tarried long enough in Albany to write his last will and testament on July 22, 1755. By this will he bequeathed his residuary estate—amounting to approximately

9. Senate Document No. 19, p. 8.
10. TR, *1*, 205–7; Sept. 3, 1811. Durfee, *Williams Biographical Annals*, p. 100.
Financial aid to undergraduates was referred to as charity. In 1866 the college catalogue announced, for the first time, the existence of scholarship funds as well as the charity fund, although the difference between them was only a matter of nomenclature. Beginning with the catalogue for 1870 no distinction was made, the word "charity" was abandoned, and all aid, including that from the Woodbridge Little fund, was distributed in the form of scholarships. Despite the change in nomenclature, need was still a requisite for financial assistance. Although the connotation of "scholarship" seemed to suggest that intellectual capacity and promise were being rewarded, no scholarship divorced from financial need was established at Williams until late in the century. In 1895 the board of trustees used a $20,000 legacy to establish scholarships which were awarded to the recipients of highest grades in the entrance examinations and in the examinations of the sophomore, junior, and senior year. Performance, not need, was the only criterion. TR, *3*, 407, 412, 417; May 9, June 24, and Oct. 24, 1895.

$5800—for the founding and support of a free school in West Township, where for some years he had commanded a detachment of militia at Fort Massachusetts, farthest outpost of the province. The will stipulated that West Township, then in dispute between Massachusetts and New York, must fall within Massachusetts and that the name of the township must be changed to Williamstown, if the free school was to be established at all.

On September 8, 1755, Colonel Williams led his troops into ambush and was himself killed; in 1765 the name of the township was changed to Williamstown; and in 1785 the executors of the will petitioned the legislature of Massachusetts for authority to carry out its provisions and were granted a charter which recognized Williamstown as a part of Massachusetts and appointed nine residents of Berkshire County to become "the Trustees of the donation of Ephraim Williams, Esq., for maintaining a Free School in Williamstown." In 1790 the nine trustees authorized the erection in Williamstown of the four-story red brick building which came to be known as West College. The next year, on October 11, they elected Ebenezer Fitch, senior tutor at Yale and a graduate in the Class of 1777, to become preceptor of the free school.

On October 26 fifteen scholars were admitted to the free school, thus fulfilling the terms of the Colonel's will and realizing his ambition to provide for the scholastic relief of the neighborhood which had provided him with a band of devoted soldiers. In the thirty-six years between his death and the opening of the school, the residual estate had grown to a little over $9,000. The Williamstown area, not freed from the menace of Indians until 1760, was inhabited in 1790 by close to 1800 settlers. They welcomed the school, which might have carved out a comfortable career for itself in the life of the town had not the trustees been more ambitious than Ephraim Williams. For it was their idea, not his, to abandon the community school—their idea, not his, to establish a college to which were invited "young gentlemen from every part of the Union [to] resort for instruction in all the branches of useful and polite literature." [11] When the state legislature acceded to their petition of 1792 for a college charter, certainly no wrongdoing was contemplated. The arguments of the board were impressive enough: food would be cheap because farmers in the region lacked markets elsewhere; the new institution would not compete with Harvard, then the only college in the Commonwealth, but with Dartmouth and Yale, where boys from Berkshire had been inclined to go;

11. TR, *1*, 29; May 23, 1792.

students from Vermont and New York would benefit by the diffusion westward and northward of the "best habits and manners" of Massachusetts. Capitulating to these urgings, the legislature of the Commonwealth, on June 22, 1793, transformed the neighborhood school into Williams College.

Their bold decision to plant a college in the wilderness betrayed the intentions of the founder; yet their vision was fed by the same sort of dreams that had led Ephraim Williams to see a school and a comfortable community where only a military outpost had stood. Perhaps the trustees and the legislature were not altogether wrong in believing that the infant United States needed college-educated men as much as it needed a yeomanry instructed in the three R's. They would be remembered for their foresight, but in the decades after 1793 they had reason to acknowledge that the soil they had chosen was stubbornly uncongenial.

So uncongenial, in fact, that during much of its history prior to 1836 the trustees of Williams spent more time and energy in trying to close the college than in keeping it open. As ambitious as they had been in 1792 to have a college where Ephraim Williams had desired a school, they were among the first to admit that perhaps they had made a mistake. In 1815 they sent six of their number into Hampshire County to canvass the clergy there on the advisability of transferring the college to the Connecticut Valley.[12] In 1818 they rejected the proposal of Noah Webster that they join the Amherst Academy in creating a new college at Amherst.[13] The next year, however, they petitioned the Commonwealth for permission to remove the college to Northampton, revealing at the same time a willingness to leave what remained of Ephraim Williams' legacy and dreams behind them in Williamstown.[14] Among those who spoke before the Senate in February 1820 in opposition to the board was President Josiah Quincy of Harvard, who scolded the Williams trustees for thinking "themselves guardians of science and literature all over the world." [15] With Quincy's blessings, the legislature dismissed the pleas of the Williams board and sent the trustees back to Williamstown to run the college for which they had been given a charter in 1793.

The next year, 1821, President Zephaniah Swift Moore, who

12. Keller, p. 20. At its meeting of Sept. 5, 1815, the board of trustees voted that removal was "inexpedient at the present time and under existing circumstances." TR, *1*, 244.

13. TR, *1*, 298–300; Sept. 2 and Nov. 2, 1818.

14. TR, *1*, 302–19; June 22 and Nov. 2, 1819.

15. MS of Quincy's speech, WCL.

had succeeded Ebenezer Fitch in 1815, took matters into his own hands. Convinced that almost everything about Williams was impossible—its location, its funds, its enrollment—he led a group of fifteen students over the mountains into the Connecticut Valley. There he became their president once again, at the new college known as Amherst. In the same year at least five students transferred to Union, two members of the board became charter trustees of Amherst, and the Williams enrollment declined to 48, rising to 131 in 1824 and then, under the impact of the chartering of Amherst College by the Commonwealth in 1825, declining to 86 in 1828. By the fall of 1836 enrollment had returned to only 119, despite the determination with which Edward Dorr Griffin, with the help of an impressive series of religious revivals, had demonstrated that a college in the Massachusetts wilderness was possible, if not altogether believable.

In 1820 the legislature of Massachusetts determined, presumably for eternity, the legal status of Williams College. The ambitious dream of 1793 would be encouraged. Yet since the college would remain, so would the problems of enrollment, finance, and accessibility from which the trustees had hoped to find relief at Northampton in 1819. Thus far Williams had survived in part because the financial operations of a small college were relatively simple. If the expenditure for salaries could be equaled by receipts for tuition charges, the college could at least stand still. In 1836, for instance, tuition charges equaled salaries almost exactly: salaries at $4100 were but $50 more than the charges.[16] Repairs to college buildings, fuel for the heating of classrooms, chapel, and dormitories, funds for the operation of the college library—these were provided for by fees and pro-rata charges to the undergraduates.

Williams needed more money not so much in order to stay open as to meet emergencies, to add professorships, to increase scientific equipment and library acquisitions, and to provide a cushion for frequently unpaid tuition bills. A meager endowment, composed largely of the Woodbridge Little donation and small appropriations from the Commonwealth, was devoted almost exclusively to the payment of tuition charges of "charity" students. If for any reason tuition receipts or contemplated state bounties failed, there was no place to turn except to a public that had been reluctant or unable to support the college adequately.

In the past the public had sometimes responded on a rescue-

16. TR, *2*, 182–3; Aug. 18, 1836.

operation basis. A lottery, authorized by the Commonwealth, furnished funds essential to the opening of the free school. A subscription of $17,000, much of it never paid, was the answer of Berkshire to the threat of removal in 1819. And in 1828 President Griffin was able to erect a three-story chapel and classroom building with funds contributed largely by residents of the Connecticut Valley who were impressed by the work being done at Williams in the cause of religion. For the normal operation of the college—the payment of faculty salaries, for instance—Williams depended essentially upon its ability to attract students.

In 1833, when enrollment once again declined, Mark Hopkins, in his third year as professor of moral and intellectual philosophy, wrote to his brother Harry, "The Trustees have just found out that they are spending all their money and say that they must diminish our salaries . . . probably 1 or 200 dollars." [17] The salary retrenchment put into effect that year, reducing the president from $1400 to $1,000 and the five professors from $800 to $700, was only partially caused by a decline in enrollment. The habit of feeling sorry for poor students, for which the faculty seems to have been primarily responsible, also took its toll of funds that might have been available for faculty salaries. The $900 saved in 1834 was partly dissipated by a remission of over $500 in term bills, a laudable gesture, to be sure, though perhaps made necessary because the bills were in fact uncollectable.[18] Generosity of this sort helped to reduce the importance of faculty salaries among the financial obligations of the trustees. The professors themselves acquiesced, with a kind of Christian good will, in the knowledge that a noble work was being done for God and man; and in the process the erection of plant and the subsidization of needy students took precedence over the payment of faculty salaries. Much later, when the Christian calling of teaching became a purely secular profession, other factors operated to keep the professors in the state of constant impoverishment which an earlier religious environment had dictated. In 1836 it was just as well for Mark Hopkins' peace of mind that he had decided that Williams was a place in which he would never grow rich, although he thought that he might manage to "live without trouble." [19]

There was, however, a point below which faculty salaries could not go without serious damage to self-respect, even among devoted

17. Sept. 14, 1833; HL, 5.
18. TR, 2, 160–1; Aug. 19, 1834.
19. MH to Harry Hopkins, Aug. 21, 1831; HL, 5.

Christians, as was attested by a series of bitter letters written by Ebenezer Fitch after his resignation from the Williams presidency.[20] Also, if salary was to be inadequate, compensation had to be found in satisfactory tools—books, laboratories, classrooms—and in willing students. Thus far, despite almost annual appeals to the state legislature, appeals which had availed the college a life-saving $53,000 by 1836, Williams was not yet in a financial position that warranted any optimism.[21] Men could argue that the college would receive all the money that it could profitably use, once the enrollment was stabilized and the caliber of Williams graduates recognized as superior; or they could argue that before the college could attract students in sufficient quantity to provide that stability, money would have to be found to provide the buildings and facilities necessary to attract them. In either case, something had to be done.

Some problems, however, had been solved. An unprofitable connection with the Berkshire Medical Institution in Pittsfield, entered into in 1822 in anticipation of some nebulous gain to the college, was dissolved in 1836.[22] The last medical degrees awarded by Williams were voted upon at the board meeting which elected Hopkins (himself a graduate of the Pittsfield institution in 1829) to the Williams presidency. In addition, political animosities which at an earlier time had placed the college in considerable disrepute had largely been dissipated. A Pittsfield newspaper may have been exaggerating when it declared in 1806 that no self-respecting Republican would have any connection with Williams College, but there can be no doubt that Ebenezer Fitch's efforts to make the college a bastion of conservatism were detrimental during the period from 1801 to 1813, when Berkshire County was represented by Jeffersonians in the House of Representatives.[23] By 1836, however, a calmer view of political dissent prevailed at Williams: Jacksonians were not being removed from the college platform, as is reported to have happened to one Jeffersonian during the tenure of Fitch.

20. Fitch to Mason Cogswell, Aug. 2, 1816; photostatic copy, WCL, Howe MSS. Fitch to Daniel Noble, Oct. 15, 1816; WCL, Misc. MSS, *8*. TR, *2*, 297, Sept. 2, 1818; and 307–8, Aug. 21, 1819.

21. The record of state aid is found in TR, *1*, 16–17, 67, 163, 181, 189, 195, 217, 220, 227, 229, 294–5; *2*, 24, 52, 70, 82, 111, 114–15.

22. TR, *2*, 21–2, Sept. 3, 1822; 27–9, Nov. 19, 1822; 174, Aug. 17, 1836.

23. *Pittsfield Sun*, Sept. 20, 1806; cited in James H. Stone, "Williams College circa 1800: A Study of Its Kind of Liberalism and Conservatism," course paper, Williams College, 1947. *Biographical Directory of the American Congress 1774–1949*, Washington, Government Printing Office, 1950.

To be free of the medical school and of a clearly manifest political partisanship was obviously an advantage to the new president of Williams College. For many small favors, too, Mark Hopkins could be thankful. Ebenezer Fitch had been the one to worry about where Williams was to find a bell, that most necessary item of college equipment. He had been the one to ask a New Haven bookseller to remind President Timothy Dwight of Yale to select a few titles so that Williams might have a library. Under President Griffin an orderly procedure for awarding honorary degrees had been established. A system of bookkeeping was instituted in the treasurer's office in 1830, and a method was found for eliminating chronic absentees from the board of trustees.[24] Rules, regulations, and customs had experienced a growth of over forty years. Some were of local origin; most were imports from New Haven, products of the collegiate experience of that overwhelming Yale influence represented in the first board of trustees, the first president, and the first faculty of the college.[25]

By 1836 much had already been accomplished in the way of establishing an operating procedure. Of even greater importance, the reputation of the college for safe and successful religious inspiration warranted generous expectations for the future. Religion had pursued an uneven career at Williams, as elsewhere on the American college campus, but the moments of brilliance and promise had been frequent. The Williams of 1836 found inspiration in the religious practices which had been transferred from Yale by Ebenezer Fitch, in the compulsory morning and evening prayers, in Saturday morning lessons for seniors on the meaning of the Westminster Catechism.[26] It found evidence of religious success in the chapel which Edward Dorr Griffin had built, in the alumni who battled for Christ in little churches throughout the land, in the

24. See Fitch to Mason F. Cogswell, Oct. 16, 1793; WCL, Misc. MSS, 6. Fitch to Isaac Beers, June 12, 1798; WCL, Misc. MSS, 8. TR, 2, 52, 63, 120. A bookkeeping system was established at the meeting of the board of trustees on Aug. 31, 1830: TR, 2, 111–13. The first trustee to be removed for being absent from three consecutive annual meetings was Joseph Lyman: TR, 2, 135; Sept. 4, 1832.

25. Of the twelve trustees who presided when the college was opened, seven were Yale alumni, one was a Princeton alumnus, and the other four were not college men. Fitch, as well as six of the first seven tutors, were Yale alumni; one of them, Jeremiah Day (1796–98) was president of Yale 1817–46. The early alliance is best symbolized by the experience of Thomas Robbins, son of a Yale alumnus and Williams trustee, who was awarded B.A. degrees by both Williams and Yale in 1796 as the result of work at both colleges.

26. See the 1795 edition of *The Laws of Williams College*, as well as Calvin Durfee, *Sketch of the Late Rev. Ebenezer Fitch, D.D., First President of Williams College* (Boston, Massachusetts Sabbath School Society, 1865), p. 59.

memories of revivals, anxious tears, and impassioned oratory. Williams, after all, was the place from which card playing and gambling were banished, however temporarily, by the revival of 1806; the place where, in 1812, an hour of prayer was substituted for ball playing; where, in 1826, penitent undergraduates fervently remembered iniquitous Boston in their daily prayers.[27]

Religion at Williams, however, found its apotheosis not in these commonplace manifestations of Congregational evangelism but in a haystack to which five Williams undergraduates retired from a nearby grove in the summer of 1806, seeking shelter for their prayers and conversations from a sudden thunderstorm. Under this haystack was born the impulse which inspired the great adventure of American foreign missions.[28] Soundness of doctrine, devotion to purpose, dignity of conduct—but most of all, the symbol of the haystack: these formed the inheritance upon which Mark Hopkins might hope to build a firmer college. As president of Williams he assumed as a primary responsibility the obligation to lead young men, willing and unwilling, toward the kind of public profession of Christian faith which he had himself made in 1826.[29] A visiting clergyman reported in the fall of 1836 that he found Williams College "healthful and prosperous," and a majority of its students "setting examples of fidelity and zeal." [30] Hopkins would see, to the best of his ability, that reports from Williamstown gave evidence that Williams College still bore the impress of the haystack.

Such, in effect, was the message of the inaugural address which he delivered to a respectable gathering of town folk and college alumni, faculty, and students, assembled in the Congregational meeting house on September 15, 1836. Situated at the western end of the village, the meeting house stood on a slight eminence which permitted it to look across to the east, where, along a crude dirt road, were clustered a few clapboard dwellings, a few stores, and the college. On such a day as this the large frame Mansion House, across the street, was busier than usual catering to the needs of visitors who knew it as Williamstown's finest lodge and tavern. The village itself—eighty or so houses, a cotton factory, a

27. Chester Dewey to Albert Hopkins, Nov. 14, 1840; WCL, "Williams College Autographs," 2. Alvan Hyde to his son Alvan, July 17, 1812; cited in *Memoir of Rev. Alvan Hyde, D.D. of Lee, Mass.* (Boston, Perkins, Marvin, 1835), p. 171. Edward Dorr Griffin to [?], Feb. 2, 1826; WCL, Misc. MSS, 8.

28. The story of the Haystack Meeting is told well in Perry, *Williamstown and Williams College,* pp. 352-70.

29. MH to Samuel H. Miller, Apr. 20, 1826; WCL, Misc. MSS, 8.

30. *Quarterly Journal of the American Education Society, 9* (1836), 195-6.

Williams College, *ca.* 1842, seen from the south. Far left: Congregational meeting house; middle left, first large building: West College. The cluster of buildings to the right includes South College, the Observatory, East College, and Griffin Hall.

tannery or two, a post office, the general stores, the college—was crowded on this important day with farmers and their wives who had come in from outlying districts, where most of the town's two thousand inhabitants lived in simple frame houses set in poplar and willow groves, overlooking the meadows, orchards, and grazing lands which supported them.

For most of the people of Williamstown, whether they lived in the village or in the fields beyond it, the Congregational meeting house was their place of worship, but on an occasion such as the inauguration of the president of the college even the few Baptists and Methodists, members of the only other organized denominations in town, willingly joined in celebrating a day so important to the town. All men could share with pride the view from the meeting house hill. How few were the American communities that could point to buildings as solidly constructed and finely designed as the three red brick buildings which Williams College had planted along the main street, down the road from the meeting house! First there was the four-story West College, the original college building, standing on a second eminence and as conspicuous from a distance as the meeting house itself. At the end of a raised gravel walk which led from the West College down a small hollow up to a third eminence was perched the East College, similar to West in design except that in 1798 the college could not afford to duplicate West's four stories. East was a three-story dormitory. Across the road from East, however, was the largest and most magnificent building of all, the red brick chapel patterned after the work of Charles Bulfinch at the Andover Theological Seminary and carefully erected in 1828 under the direct supervision of President Griffin himself.

These college buildings may have seemed incongruous in a setting that included cows and pigs which roamed at will throughout the village, but they suggested, as perhaps no other group of buildings could have, that within the valley, men were ready to challenge an abundant nature for primacy. Among such men was the new president of the college, who, for the next thirty-six years, shouldered its burdens, pursued its dreams, fought its battles, and fashioned a happy and useful career.

To some in his audience the address which Mark Hopkins delivered at his inauguration may have seemed prosaic. Certainly his manner and his expectations were modest. "I enter upon [this office] with no excitement of novelty," he said, "with no buzz of expectation, with no accession of influence to the college from

abroad, and with no expectation of pleasing every body." [31] Few
could disagree. Hopkins lacked the renowned "abdominal dignity"
which the portliness and magnificent height of Griffin had contributed to the Williams commencement platform. The professor
was hardly known outside the college family. But this much could
be said in his favor: he was a graduate of the Class of 1824, for
which he had been the valedictorian, and the alumni would like
that; and he was a native of Stockbridge, the village in the southern
part of the county which had contributed all four members of the
first graduating class in 1795, and Berkshire would like that. Moreover, the tall, awkward man on the platform spoke with an obvious
sincerity. Stiff as he was, unskilled as he was in the manners of
accomplished oratory, he spoke with a cautious conviction and
wisdom not altogether expected of so young a man. Perhaps it was
the slight stoop to his shoulders, the Ciceronian profile, the receding
hairline, or the deep-set brown eyes sheltered by shaggy brows—
but, whatever it was, the new president of Williams College looked
much older than he really was.

When he spoke, people listened, perhaps because they mistook
appearances for experience, probably because they saw in this
spare, massive son of a Berkshire farmer a proper leader for
the college whose career had been so insecure. Those who knew of
the circumstances under which he entered Williams certainly had
reason to believe that he would understand what the neighborhood
expected and what was in fact possible. Hopkins himself had gone
to Williams because it was near and because he was poor. His
mother had supposed that he would go to Yale, and his Uncle
Sewall Hopkins of Clinton, New York, had hoped that he would
go to Hamilton. Mark, instead, entered the junior year at Williams in 1822, admitted at once to advanced standing by virtue of
schooling at his Uncle Jared Curtis' academy in Stockbridge and
at the academies in nearby Lenox and in Clinton. Then twenty years
old, he had earned the funds necessary for his college preparation
by working as a farm hand for his Uncle Sewall and by teaching in
the village school at Richmond in Berkshire County. In search of
money enough to put himself through college, he left the modest
Hopkins farm in Stockbridge in 1820 and went to Virginia, where
as Yankee schoolmaster in a family school he achieved the economic
independence which permitted him to go to Williams. Desirous of
being near his family, fearful of the higher cost of living in New

31. MH, *An Inaugural Discourse, Delivered at Williams College, September 15,
1836* (Troy, N. Tuttle, 1836), p. 29.

Haven, Hopkins chose to be a poor boy at a poor college. His inaugural address in 1836 suggested that under him Williams would continue to be a suitable college for western Massachusetts farm boys. "I have no ambition to build up here what would be called a great institution," the new president told his audience. "The wants of the community do not require it. But I do desire, and shall labor that this may be a *safe* college." [32] Mark Hopkins would do what was expected of him.

The Williams which he envisioned for his inaugural audience would educate young men to the degree that a college could. Professors, after all, could do very little to counteract the accidents of birth, wealth, and environment. But they would do what they could in the classroom, and the college would see to it that a whole set of important influences was brought to bear on the young men: "opportunities and inducements for physical exercise, a healthy situation, fine scenery, proper books, a suitable example on the part of instructors, companions of correct and studious habits, and above all, a good religious influence." For Mark Hopkins these influences were considerably more important than the classroom. Instruction, he reminded his audience, merely formed the intellect; influence molded the moral character.

"The true and permanent interests of man," he remarked, "can be promoted only in connection with religion; and a regard to man as an immortal, accountable and redeemed being, should give its character to the whole course of our regulations, and the spirit of our instruction." For this reason, if for no other, "We are to regard the mind, not as a piece of iron to be laid upon the anvil and hammered into any shape, nor as a block of marble in which we are to find the statue by removing the rubbish, nor as a receptacle into which knowledge may be poured; but as a flame that is to be fed, as an active being that must be strengthened to think and to feel—to dare, to do, and to suffer." Seldom had the spirit of the humane studies been conveyed so well.

"Evil is in the world, and must be met," the new president warned. "Youth must be kept from the fascination of the serpent, till we have shown him its fangs." Williams had known a harsh and trying past; its future, as was that of all higher education in America, was once more under attack. Health faddists and advocates of manual training objected that colleges were destroying the physical vigor of young men and preparing them for no practical occupation. The rising tide of democracy objected that colleges were aristocratic,

32. *Ibid.*, pp. 29–30.

intent on transforming boorish ill-mannered undergraduates into a ruling class.[33] But the new president of Williams College was not discouraged. He had a job to do, and so did his college. To youth, he pledged, it would show the serpent's fangs.

33. *Ibid.,* pp. 6–7, 30, 7, 16, 18–23.

2. "Mark Hopkins on One End . . ."

In 1826, after a year of tutoring at Williams College, Hopkins wrote to a classmate: "I am for the most part the same good for nothing being as when you knew me, with vigor enough to go through the routine of any situation . . . but without that energy either of body or mind, which would be requisite for my doing anything greatly to benefit myself or others." [1] Hopkins may have judged himself correctly, but he certainly miscalculated the role that he would assume in the life of generations of college students. An absence of energy, physical or intellectual, would not prevent him from wielding a powerful influence upon his age. History would pronounce his verdict of 1826 premature and wrong.

Nearly ninety years later—after Hopkins' career had run its course, after he had come to symbolize a concept of teaching and an era in the history of American higher education—one of his former students and faculty colleagues at Williams turned in his own report on the Mark Hopkins he had known. John Bascom, reviewing a career that already was becoming distorted by the adulation and exaggeration of legendry, was in complete agreement with Hopkins' youthful analysis of himself. Hopkins, said Bascom, "rarely did anything which was not required of him by the circumstances in which he was placed. . . . His lazy, reposeful strength rendered him indifferent to diligence and slightly scornful of it." [2]

The immaturity of Mark Hopkins in 1826 and the embittered cantankerousness of John Bascom at the end of life led, in both instances, to an overemphasis upon qualities which, while costly in their way, would not deny to Hopkins a warm place in the hearts of men. Although the history of Williams under Hopkins abundantly testifies that those qualities existed to a very real degree, he was fashioned of other materials as well, materials which, in proper combination, could more than compensate for an apparent indolence of mind and manner.

Although Bascom might have disagreed, Hopkins received a certain compensation in the good fortune of being born, on February

1. MH to Samuel H. Miller, Apr. 20, 1826; WCL, Misc. MSS, 8.
2. John Bascom, *Things Learned by Living* (New York, G. P. Putnam's Sons, 1913), pp. 102, 119.

4, 1802, in a small cottage on a modest farm which lay within the bounds of the old Stockbridge Indian Mission. Stockbridge was just the place for a child born at the dawning of the 19th century to steep himself in the traditions, customs, and thought of Puritan New England. As every schoolboy knows, 19th-century democracy in the United States expected presidential candidates to be born in log cabins. It was just as necessary that guardians of the old virtues—what else were college presidents?—be born and reared in the shadow of a safe and solid village like Stockbridge.

Archibald Hopkins and his wife, Mary Curtis, were not the social equals of people like the Sedgwicks and the Dwights, who figured so prominently in the political and intellectual life of the community. In the ancestry which Mark and his two young brothers, Harry and Albert, inherited from their parents, however, were men and women of equally substantial stature. The family tree could boast no wealth, no men of property or commercial success. But a history of accomplishment was recorded in the names of John Sergeant, first missionary to the Indians of western Massachusetts; Colonel Mark Hopkins, pioneer lawyer of Berkshire County; and Samuel Hopkins, the eminent divine who had created a system of theology upon which hell-and-damnation orthodoxy was ready to rest its case.

Here were men who had fought a wilderness in order that the dream of Plymouth might be transplanted to the West, men who had found a wasteland and transformed it into a legacy of Congregational meeting houses, plowed fields, village schools, courtrooms, and sound religious doctrine. That legacy of simple institutions enabled the men and women of Mark Hopkins' childhood to work, play, live, and worship in harmony. Everywhere their world was permeated by the wrathful God to whom Mary Hopkins herself could not surrender, unable as she was to find in her own heart the fear and the sense of sin necessary to qualify as a Christian. Nonetheless, she led her son Mark along the way to religious conviction, teaching him to pray and to read out of *Pilgrim's Progress* before he was five years old. Mark learned to respect the institutions of agrarian New England, first at his mother's knee in the little cottage, later in the fields beside his father and brothers, and then in the village schoolhouse and the Congregational meeting house. In those institutions he recognized the work of a free people in covenant with God.

In the century that lay ahead, a century in which old institutions

faltered and crumbled, he would defend the old way with a vigor
that would have surprised John Bascom, had he been willing to
recognize it. His devotion to New England virtues led others to
trust him as a proper teacher for their sons. His faith in New England institutions helped to make a revolutionary age less harsh and
less bewildering for many men and women—whether he was addressing them from the platform of the Lowell Institute or from the
pages of his published lectures and sermons. Hopkins' most challenging opportunity, however, lay in the Williams classroom. As a
public figure he did impressive work for the old ways, but his most
telling triumphs occurred in the minds and hearts of literally thou-
sands of young men. In the classroom he displayed his greatest
talents, teaching with a freshness and charm that were not ordinary
at the time. His students, too, caught some of the enthusiasm which
he held for an age that was being buffeted by change.

To be sure, Hopkins did not always exhibit the gusto with which,
in his maturity, he defended the old way against the new. In 1830,
a few months before he was appointed to his professorship at Williams, he confided to his brother Harry, "I am sure that . . . I
should not desire to live over the same life that I have lived." [3] The
despondency of that year, however, was not altogether a reflection
upon New England institutions, except in the sense that at the
bottom of his uneasiness about the past lay an unhealthy preoccupation with his religious future. [4] After 1830 he found a way to
accommodate religious conviction with a happier view of man and
God than had been permitted by the old dispensation. Until he
found his way out of the melancholy appropriate to the old religion, however, he suffered from headaches, loss of weight, and
frequent exhaustion. In the grip of gloom and religious uncertainty, it was understandable that he should review his past with a
sense of disappointment. Certainly it seemed as if his life thus far
had lacked direction or especial promise.

Before he was thirty years old he had tasted all of the careers
then considered desirable for ambitious and educated young men.
As a youth, he had read to a blind clergyman of the vicinity the
weighty theological works of Samuel Hopkins. During 1819 he
studied law with Charles Sedgwick. Even before entering Williams

---

3. From New York, Mar. 6, 1830; HL, 4.
4. A thread of despondency, tied to his religious worries, runs through Hopkins'
early letters. See the letter to his mother on Dec. 5, 1822 (HL, 2) and those to his
brother on Nov. 28 [1833?] (HL, Misc. Vol.) and Apr. 17, 1830 (HL, 4).

College in 1822 he had tried his hand at teaching. After his graduation in 1824 he taught at the Stockbridge Academy, then for two years as tutor at Williams, later at the Pittsfield Gymnasium of Chester Dewey, and as recently as 1828 at a select school for girls in New York. In 1830 he was training to be a doctor. His schooling at the Berkshire Medical Institution, at the Northern Dispensary in Greenwich Village where he lived in 1829, and with private doctors in New York was as complete as was possible at the time. But the long apprenticeship, the necessary poverty, and the struggle for recognition which were required of a young doctor filled Mark Hopkins with discouragement. "If I had money it would be pleasanter living here than in the country," he wrote from New York to his father in 1828.[5] But the "competition is prodigious." In December of the next year he informed his brother Harry, "I am doing little better than wasting my time. . . . As for delving along and having classes to hear . . . I don't like to think of it." [6] Few men were ever as ripe for escape from confusion and despair as was Hopkins in August 1830, when Williams College asked him to return to his native soil.

From the first, Edward Dorr Griffin was not happy at the proposal from one of his trustees that Mark Hopkins, a physician, be appointed to the professorship of moral and intellectual philosophy. Hopkins, who was not ordained until the morning of his inauguration to the presidency of Williams, was not even licensed to preach, and although his trustee neighbor from Stockbridge, Henry Dwight, might speak with praise of Mark's impressive Master's oration at the commencement of three years before, President Griffin's memory was even longer. He never had relished the trick which Mark had played upon him during his senior year. The young student had tampered with quotation marks in his metaphysical essay, ascribing to the eminent Scotch theologian, Adam Reid, his own portions of the essay and leaving unquoted lengthy selections from Reid. Griffin had fallen victim to the ruse, castigating the young Hopkins for the nonsense being passed as original theological thought, praising him for the wisely selected quotations. Griffin did not know that at the commencement exercises the same year the surprisingly brilliant oration delivered by one of the dullards of the class had also been the work of Mark Hopkins, but he did know that the young man was to be viewed with suspicion. The voice of Henry Dwight—the voice of Stockbridge and Berk-

5. Feb. 26, 1828; HL, *3*.
6. Dec. 14, 1829; HL, *4*.

shire—prevailed, however, when the board chose Hopkins to fill the professorship of philosophy.[7]

The struggling doctor did not hesitate to leave New York for the certainties of home ground. He welcomed the opportunity to turn his back upon the city, to return to a way of life the customs and institutions of which he clearly understood. Playmates of his Stockbridge childhood, among them the talented brood of the Reverend David Dudley Field, were already beginning to carve a career for themselves in the city. Hopkins could not reverse the tide which filled the cities with ambitious country boys like these, but he rejected it for himself. For fifty-seven years after 1830 he remained in the country, teaching the seniors at Williams College how to meet the demands of a new and marvelous century with the wisdom and faith of the ages.

In that half century he achieved a reputation that rested squarely upon the inclinations which had taken him back to Williams in 1830. He became a kind of provincial Puritan, a conscience and a voice of warning for an age that was merrily abandoning itself to materialism. He welcomed the progress which the century so proudly acclaimed, but he tempered his optimism with frequent pronouncements upon the decline of the old virtues. He invited a widening audience to get rich—an invitation that was unnecessary in 19th-century America—but he showed it how to get rich "religiously." A country boy in the president's chair of a country college could achieve the success that came to Hopkins only by fulfilling a deep-felt want of the times. It was an age, after all, when country boys and country colleges were going out of fashion. Stockbridge and its simple institutions were losing favor, as men turned to the city and to the life which the city demanded.

During his presidency of Williams the old ways—the farmhouse, the fields, the firm religious faith, the one-room schoolhouse, the Congregational meeting house—were being undermined by forces let loose by urban democracy, immigration, the rising mill towns, and material plenty. However lustily and aggressively 19th-century Americans appeared to grasp at the new order, they could not altogether surrender a past in which their minds and attitudes and habits had been molded. In Mark Hopkins they found not only a comforting spokesman for the past but also one who was willing to embrace the material marvels of a changing world. In

7. The relations between Griffin and Hopkins are treated in Perry, *Williamstown and Williams College*, pp. 469–71, 492–3; and in Franklin Carter, *Mark Hopkins* (Boston, Houghton, Mifflin, 1892), pp. 11, 17.

him, if they heard or read him aright, his audiences could find a
guide to the very best of both the old and the new.

In 19th-century New England a good Puritan was not obliged
to believe in the total depravity of man or the wrath of a merciless
God. Proper Puritans, of whom Mark Hopkins was one, reefed the
sails of old doctrine and made allowance for the winds of human
goodness blown their way by the French Revolution. In the hands
of Hopkins and others the old views of Jonathan Edwards were
accommodated to the democratic beliefs and material aspirations
with which Americans more and more optimistically faced the
future. The faith and zeal of the old-time religion were of course
not abandoned, but God became more merciful and man more
capable of goodness. For all of the concern with doctrine, however,
it was not doctrine which defined a 19th-century New England
Puritan. He was defined more by his outlook, by the little things
he did and did not do, by the priorities he placed upon his time
and energy.

In Hopkins an inherited provincialism and a deeply-held Puritanism were probably combined in equal measure. Certainly it
would be difficult to determine which was more responsible for the
fact that he had no fault to find with New England weather. As
John Bascom said, a man who could find no fault with New England's climate was irrevocably committed to the entirety of New
England life.[8] Hopkins did not hesitate to claim for its ways a
success achieved at no other time or place in history. He saw New
England's greatness in the equality with which her people enjoyed
the right to work, the security they possessed as the results of their
own labor, the learning they diffused so widely in their common
schools—above all in "the religious element infused into society
by the Pilgrim Fathers" and "the cultivation of reverence towards
God and the State, without a nobility in the state, and without
forms in religion." [9]

However pervasive, the Puritan way was but one approach
which Americans had taken to the problems of living; along the
banks of the Hudson, the Delaware, and the James, Americans had
planted other values and other institutions; but for Mark Hopkins
life began and ended in Berkshire County, Massachusetts. Brief

8. John Bascom, "Mark Hopkins," *Collections of the Berkshire Historical and
Scientific Society, 3* (1899), 171.

9. MH, "A Sermon, Delivered at Pittsfield, August 22, 1844, on the occasion of
the Berkshire Jubilee," in *The Berkshire Jubilee, Celebrated at Pittsfield, Mass.
August 22 and 23, 1844* (Albany, E. P. Little, 1845), p. 49.

excursions beyond her boundaries—to Virginia to teach school, to New York to study medicine—only confirmed his belief that the Berkshire way was essentially sound. After 1800, New England was in the process of attaining a social maturity in which the restraints of Puritanism were no longer so necessary for social cohesion as they were in the earlier stages of her development.[10] Relaxation of restraint, in manners and morals and religious observation, paralleled New England's arrival at social maturity. In the case of Mark Hopkins, however, the mold was so deeply set that relaxation, if it came at all, came painfully.

If he wrote letters on the Sabbath evening, a habit which some of his correspondents might not understand, he informed them that "we still adhere to the old Puritan custom of keeping Saturday night." [11] When in 1859 he received an invitation to preach in the Harvard chapel, he declined, unwilling to lend his name to the institution which had strayed from the old faith into the byways of Unitarianism.[12] He agreed with the assertion of Amos Lawrence, one of the college's benefactors, that the thought of Margaret Fuller, Ralph Waldo Emerson, and Theodore Parker was characterized by "fooleries . . . talkativeness & vanity . . . transcendental vagaries." [13]

It was characteristic of him to report in 1847 concerning a religious conference which had taken him away from Williamstown: "Saturday was given up to the dreadfully laborious business of pleasure and sightseeing." [14] He was unlikely to display any untoward enthusiasm or emotion, in his person or in his letters. "We are all well," he might write, "and though not as happy as we ought to be, which I suppose few persons are, yet that we are not happier

10. See the provocative analysis of Puritanism in Marcus Lee Hansen, *The Immigrant in American History* (Cambridge, Mass., Harvard University Press, 1940), pp. 97–128.

11. MH to AL, Dec. 29, 1844; MHS, MH–AL MSS.

12. MH to Mary Hubbell Hopkins, Dec. 21, 1859; HP, *1*.

13. AL to MH, Mar. 31, 1852; MH to AL, Apr. 5, 1852: MHS, MH–AL MSS. Lawrence looked to Hopkins to counter the influence of what he called "the 'Jack O' Lantern' philosophy of these geniuses, like Emerson." Lawrence had no reason to fear for the soundness of the Williams president. Hopkins, after all, had written to his wife from Boston on Aug. 31, 1837, "I have just returned from Cambridge where I have been today to hear an oration and poem before the Phi Beta Kappa Society. . . . The oration was interesting to me. It was Mr. Emerson . . . and was a genuine piece of Germanism, with a great deal of truth . . . in it, and some nonsense" (HP, *1*). Just how much nonsense Mark Hopkins found in "The American Scholar" he did not say, but it was enough that he found it, and early recognized the enemy.

14. MH to Mary Hubbell Hopkins, May 20, 1847; HP, *1*.

is our own fault." [15] During his first trip to Europe in 1861, in the
letters in which he detailed his journeys to his children at home
perhaps the most revealing observation of all was in a letter to his
son Harry. "In passing the Appenines," he wrote in July, "we
came upon country precisely like that in N[ew] Ashford"—a small
community on the county road between Williamstown and Pittsfield.[16] In 1863, when Mark was attending a religious meeting at
Saratoga, he wrote to his wife:

> I have been down to the spring and drank three tumblers of
> the water finding it difficult to get any there was such a crowd.
> They are there of all sorts. The ladies came down without any
> bonnets looking shockingly after the dissipation of the night
> before, and the whole scene is in striking contrast with the danc-
> ing rooms of the evening before. The truth is there are a great
> many miserable specimens of humanity in this world.[17]

Hopkins combined with his Puritanism an almost inbred distrust
of the world beyond the narrow confines of Berkshire County, where
Puritan ways remained almost untarnished by new and foreign
ideas. The circle of his acquaintances expanded as his own reputation and that of the college increased, but his friendships were
few. He seldom associated or corresponded with other college
presidents, educators, or moral philosophers. Beyond Berkshire
County his correspondents were old college friends like John Morgan at Oberlin, college benefactors like Amos Lawrence, and associates in religious enterprises like Ray Palmer, the Congregational hymn writer.

Isolation from developments elsewhere stemmed undoubtedly in
part from the geographical liabilities of Williamstown. At the basis
of his provincialism, however, was his own certain conviction that
he had already found all the truth that was necessary, both for
himself and for the Williams students who, in so many instances,
became his agents. A man must be dissatisfied with what he knows
or what he is or where he is before he becomes a searcher after un-
discovered truth or before he pioneers in new directions. Hopkins
was perhaps that happiest of creatures—an eminently satisfied
man, who felt no compulsion to conquer great horizons in order
to lead a useful and rewarding life. He was animated by no un-

15. MH to AL, Aug. 4, 1845; MHS, MH-AL MSS.
16. MH to his son Henry, July 15, 1861; MS in possession of Mrs. Henry Hopkins, 1952.
17. Aug. 11, 1863; HP, *1*.

satiated ambition, no unanswered questions, no far-ranging visions.

Remarkably self-contained as he was, Hopkins suffered, and his college suffered, because self-sufficiency in isolated Williamstown was clearly prohibitive of the kind of growth which would have given both him and his college an intellectual stature that they lacked. Yet the advantages which accrued to Hopkins and to Williams by reason of the fact that he virtually stood still were impressive. Men clearly knew and approved of where Mark Hopkins stood—two hundred miles, two centuries and a half from Plymouth —but on Plymouth Rock just the same.

A teacher and college president who chose to stand upon Plymouth Rock was not expected to assume the mannerisms or the habits of a scholar. Learning of more than the most ordinary sort was a tool which he could most easily dispense with in fashioning a career, especially on an American college campus in the middle decades of the 19th century. Hopkins, as a matter of fact, won a place in the history of American education, not because he was learned but in part because he considered himself and his task as beyond the realm of learning—in that nobler area where the souls of men, especially young men, were touched with moral truth.

As teacher or as college president, Hopkins never suffered any real embarrassment because of the fact that he had decided to push aside the claims which learning might have placed upon him. Undoubtedly a dislike for demanding exertion contributed to his readiness to allow others on his faculty to assume the scholar's robes. But primarily he could look for support to a religious and educational tradition which had found its strength not in intellect but in piety. His triumph as one of the old-time college presidents must be attributed, in no small degree, to the success with which he refused to permit learning to assume an ascending importance in his life.

This success was clearly demonstrated by the alumni of the college at their annual dinner in New York in February 1870. "I am free to confess there are things in metaphysics I don't understand," said the grand old man who had been teaching philosophy at Williams for forty years. "Nay," he continued, "there are many writers on metaphysics of whose meaning I have not the faintest glimmer." [18] The alumni cheered and applauded, laughing with their "Prex," the man who had given meaning to their undergraduate classroom experience. Their applause and their laughter

18. *Williams Quarterly, 17* (1870), 219.

were a tribute to their reverence for Mark Hopkins, but they were, as well, evidence that learning had very little to do with that reverence.

Forty years earlier Hopkins had thought that he might ease the transition from medicine to metaphysics by reading the work of Immanuel Kant. He therefore stopped long enough in Albany, on his way from New York to his new professorship at Williams, to purchase a copy of Kant in translation. Unable to make "head, tail, or body" of the few paragraphs he attempted to read, he closed the book and thereafter opened it only to exhibit "specimens of nonsense" to his classes in rhetoric.[19] Discovering as he went along in his teaching that learning was not really essential for success as a moral philosopher, he made no further effort to study any of the German philosophers. Generations of college students would not notice the difference. Mark Hopkins, with or without Kant—what did it matter? For the essence of his message was not to be found in German philosophers, in the original or translation. Hopkins was a great teacher, not an encyclopedia of great books.

"It is now long since I have read anything but newspapers," he wrote to Ray Palmer in 1862, admitting that in time of war he felt he must read newspapers.[20] Certain that a knowledge of God was possible, he set himself up as an opponent of the skepticism of David Hume, and he was undisturbed when one of his professors, unable to find the works of the Scottish philosopher in Williamstown, discovered that Hopkins had never read Hume.[21] Darwin's *Origin of Species* had hardly appeared before Hopkins launched a counterattack in the college chapel, an attack that later encompassed Thomas Huxley and continued until Hopkins' death. Darwin and Huxley, it should be observed, were also among the authors Hopkins did not read.[22] In spite of that, he was more than adequately equipped to perform the role he had chosen for himself. What he needed was a reservoir of faith, an abiding conviction, a capacity for transferring his confidence in God's rule to others—and these he had in abundance.

He of course paid a price for his attitude toward learning. In the classroom and on the public lecture platform he sometimes did

19. MH to Ray Palmer, Jan. 27, 1863; WCL, Hopkins-Palmer MSS. See also G. Stanley Hall, *Life and Confessions of a Psychologist* (New York, Appleton, 1923), p. 169.

20. Apr. 14, 1862; WCL, Hopkins-Palmer MSS.

21. Arthur Latham Perry, "Recollections and Diaries," typescript of MSS in possession of Perry family, *1*, 174 ff.

22. *Ibid.* Cf. Carter, *Mark Hopkins*, p. 154.

not know whether what he said was new or old. When critics of his published lectures commented upon the unoriginality of his thought, he was at a loss to understand the charge.[23] Yet criticism of this sort left him essentially unmoved. Referring to his *Lectures on Moral Science*, published in 1862, he admitted that "at times I was inclined to regret my want of learning and opportunity for research, especially my want of German literature, but I saw distinctly that the system must go straight through and could not be much modified whatever others had said." [24]

The advantages of being unread and unashamed, indeed, far outweighed the disadvantages. He could endear himself to a man of affairs like Amos Lawrence by recounting the story of "a professor whose friends, remarking on his small library, answered that [if he] had . . . as many books as they, he would know as little." [25] He could endear himself to students, upon whose time and energy he placed very little demand, much less, for sure, than did some other members of his faculty. He could endear himself to alumni, many of whom agreed with him that tendencies in the world to exalt the intellect ran counter to the maintenance of a sound Christian outlook. That he held to the old faith at a time when scholarship and learning were becoming matters of concern to American higher education contributed a tragic touch to his last years at Williams. The tragedy of those years, however, was greatly overshadowed by the devotion which Americans could so readily muster for a college president who, true to the old faith and to their own sense of values, kept learning in its place.

Keeping learning in its place did not require that Mark Hopkins find room near the top of his scale of values for wealth. As a Puritan, of course, he could not have denied to man the rewards of his own labor. As president of a college badly in need of funds, he could not have ranted against privileged wealth like a Jacksonian Democrat. Hopkins was a Puritan. He was a Whig. He was an American. On the subject of wealth he said what was expected of a man bearing such designations.

First as a college professor and then as a college president, he refused material success for himself. In no sense, however, did he ever subscribe to the notion that poverty is the best of man's estates. He had suffered the deprivations of a Berkshire farm in his child-

23. MH to Ray Palmer, Nov. 18, 1862; WCL, Hopkins-Palmer MSS.
24. MH to Palmer, Mar. 7, 1863; WCL, Hopkins-Palmer MSS.
25. MH to AL, Feb. 3, 1846; MHS, MH-AL MSS.

hood and youth; he had seen something of people who enjoyed
the physical and mental comforts of wealth. Poverty might keep
a virtuous school, but the delights reputedly found there were not
to his liking. "Go on, and may the Lord prosper you more and
more" was his reaction to his brother Harry's first success in
business.[26] "Father and Mother . . . have enough of everything
except money and enough of that for them" was his verdict upon
the home in which he had been reared.[27] Give up your scientific pursuits with Louis Agassiz and take a money-making job with the
Lawrence interests—this was his advice to David Ames Wells, a
promising graduate of the college in 1850.[28] To his friend and
benefactor, Amos Lawrence, he confided: "If I had been told once,
when I was poor, and shy, and proud, and perhaps a little jealous
of the influence and pretension so apt to be connected with wealth,
that I should come to feel towards one in your position as I do
towards you, it would hardly have seemed credible. But," he concluded, "the feelings have their own laws, and will work themselves
out in spite of obstructions." [29]

The obstructions of which Mark Hopkins spoke were not so
great as he suggested. For wherever he went he carried with him
some of the sense of awe and silent respect for material accomplishment which was to be expected of an American country boy. Whenever he left Williamstown on college or related business, he delighted in writing back to his wife, Mary Hubbell Hopkins, about
the successful men of affairs whose paths he crossed. Almost gleefully, he anticipated a breakfast with David Dudley Field at which
Senators Charles Sumner and Salmon P. Chase were to be guests.[30]
From Nahant, summer resort for fashionable Boston, he wrote
with unconcealed respect in 1864 that at the Amorys' he had met
"Mrs. Green, the widow of Gardner Green . . . who was . . . a
daughter of the famous painter Copley and sister of Lord Lynd-
hurst." [31] And from Boston in 1867, where he was delivering his
third set of lectures at the Lowell Institute, he wrote with
unabashed enthusiasm of a dinner at the home of Judge Daniel
Wells:

26. Nov. 18, 1838; MHS, Hopkins Family MSS.
27. MH to Harry Hopkins, Sept. 14, 1833; HL, 5.
28. Wells to MH, Feb. 12, 1849; Apr. 22, 1850; and Apr. 29, 1850: HP, 5. Wells
decided against Hopkins' advice and later became a leader of the free trade movement.
29. July 7, 1844; MHS, MH-AL MSS.
30. "[Sumner] is quite a lion here now. . . . I should like to see these people,"
he wrote on May 14, 1855; HP, 1.
31. July 18, 1864; HP, 1.

We had 1st four raw oysters on the shells with ½ a lemon on each plate. I should say by the way that we were waited on by a man taller than I am with white gloves and a white cravat and black swallow-tail coat suit as it is necessary for people to have to attend weddings in. Then came two kinds of soup—white and dark. I took the dark because it was next to me and the lady served it. Then came at one end salmon, and the other spiced oysters lying on the shells. . . . Then beef with olives, and partridges. . . . Then roast ducks—two kinds. . . . with these potatoes, oyster plant and celery cooked in butter. What was next I am not sure, but think it was ice cream (chocolate). Then charlotte russe. Then splendid pears and . . . grapes. No before that dry toast and butter—and just where the lettuce came in I cannot say. Then lemon biscuit. Then nuts, and then sweet meats. As to the wines I can say nothing as I did not taste them.[32]

Reports of this sort were clearly intended to be of interest to his wife Mary, as they would surely have been to many country housewives. Allusions to men of affairs and their material blessings were, however, too persistent in Hopkins' letters, too often couched in admiring language, to be looked upon as merely innocent and idle chatter meant to appease an absent wife. He exhibited, for instance, a readiness to emulate such men, within the limits of his meager income. When he bought a one-horse carriage in 1845, his conscience was at first not perfectly at ease, "lest I should have run into a little extravagance." Accordingly, he sought a kind of mental absolution in attributing the purchase to the influence of Amos Lawrence.[33] His salary as president, which rose from $1200 in 1836 to $3,000 at the time of his retirement in 1872, was barely adequate for rearing a large family. Fees for lectures, proceeds from their sale in published form, and gifts from wealthy patrons, however, permitted him to dabble, although apparently not too successfully, in western lands and bank stocks. "You need not suppose that philosophers have so little skill in money matters as poets," he chided his hymn-writing friend Ray Palmer.[34]

32. Dec. 5, 1867; HP, 1.
33. MH to AL, June 6, 1845; MHS, MH-AL MSS.
34. Feb. 15, 1873; WCL, Hopkins-Palmer MSS. In a previous letter, Jan. 29, Hopkins had asked Palmer to pick up and forward to him a dividend on $1,000 of stock in a Chatham, N.Y., bank. Hopkins' involvement in western lands is made apparent in the following letters: Hazen Cheney to MH, Jan. 31, 1860; HP, 4. MH to one of his sons, Apr. 16, 1861; HP, 2. R. McClelland to MH, Feb. 24, 1863; HP, 8.

A one-horse carriage, some western mortgages, a few shares of bank stock—these represent the short distance which Hopkins traveled along the road of material success. But he did not need a fortune in order to respect wealth. He held as firmly as did the founders of New England the conviction that men not only required property but were obliged to use it as a trust committed to their care by God. But he never boldly pressed the claim of wealth upon his students, as did some practitioners of the Gospel of Wealth. His approach, though it entertained the essential promise of material rewards, was indirect. "Incidental advantages are always best secured," he said again and again, "by aiming at the highest possible results." [35] For Hopkins the highest possible result of human endeavor was, of course, Christian salvation, from which might be derived such incidental advantages as worldly material blessings. He realized that many of his listeners were inclined to reverse the order of his own system of priorities. Many 19th-century Americans seemed to act, at any rate, as if they could be saved by wealth rather than by surrender to God. Hopkins insisted that quite the opposite was true.

"Seek ye first the kingdom of God, and . . . all these things shall be added unto you" was the text from Matthew which he chose for one of his most typical baccalaureates. "Why should not he who attains the kingdom of God and his righteousness, have all other things added?" he asked, assuring the graduating class of 1857 that those who did seek God would receive the fullest share of material blessings—health, wealth, pleasure, and fame. Be prudent, be energetic, be honest, be righteous, he urged, and inevitably you will be wealthy. "You are at liberty, my friends, to pursue wealth, and pleasure, and fame, as far as you please, provided that pursuit be not incompatible with the attainment of a higher good." [36]

In his inaugural address Mark Hopkins expressed the hope that he might preside over a "safe" college. Safety, in his terms, con-

35. MH, *The Sabbath and Free Institutions: A Sermon, Delivered before the American and Foreign Sabbath Union. May 1847* (Boston, T. R. Marvin, 1847), p. 17.

36. MH, *Higher and Lower Good: A Baccalaureate Sermon, Delivered at Williamstown, Mass. August 4, 1857.* (Boston, T. R. Marvin and Son, 1857), p. 19. The same theme is introduced in *Receiving and Giving: A Baccalaureate Sermon, Delivered at Williamstown, Mass. August 15, 1852,* Boston, T. R. Marvin and Son, 1852; *Self-Denial: A Baccalaureate Sermon, Delivered at Williamstown, Mass. August 3, 1856,* Boston, T. R. Marvin and Son, 1856; and *Nothing to Be Lost: A Baccalaureate Sermon, Delivered at Williamstown, Ms. July 29, 1860,* Boston, T. R. Marvin and Son, 1860.

sisted of sound religious teaching, the absence of doctrinal innovation, and the predominance of piety over intellect. If the college
were to maintain a reputation for safety, however, its president
must also be safe in matters other than the merely religious. Hopkins seldom felt obligated to control any inclinations within himself to step beyond the bounds of safety. As a friend of property
and wealth he could hardly have been expected to show any enthusiasm for the propertyless democracy of the cities, where danger
to the old foundations lurked in every shadow. No critic of higher
education in 19th-century America ever had occasion to accuse him
of harboring a radical thought or uttering an unpopular sentiment.
On the most explosive issue of his day—the issue of Negro slavery
—he was cautious, circumspect, and compromising.[37] He walked
a path dictated by the outlook and aspirations of the solid
middle class New England citizenry in whose midst he had been
reared.

When he stepped upon the public platform to battle against
rum, Romanism, or transcendentalism, he assumed the role of the
righteous defender. On such occasions he spoke less with the fervor
of an advocate than with the conviction of a man propounding a
few observations on matters already clearly settled. In the 1850's,
long after he had joined the ranks of those in Massachusetts who
were troubled by the ascendancy of Roman Catholicism in the citadel of Congregational orthodoxy, he permitted the publication of
one of his anti-Popery discourses, convinced that there was nothing
controversial about what he said.[38] His Congregational audiences
could only nod their heads in approval when he sarcastically
charged against transcendentalism that its advocates "believe in
God—but then all things are God. . . . They believe in inspira-

37. For the development of Hopkins' attitude toward slavery see MH to AL,
Sept. 23 and Oct. 20, 1850, Apr. 5 and 16, 1852; and AL to MH, Mar. 31, 1852: MHS,
MH-AL MSS. Also, nine letters, 1857–58, from Elihu Burritt, founder of the National Compensated Emancipation Society, to Hopkins, who served as a vice-
president of the organization; HP, 6. Hopkins' version of his role in the society is
recounted in his letter to Erastus Fairbanks, Sept. 24, 1857, in Vermont State
Papers, 81, 10. His views on whether the freedmen should be permitted to vote, a
masterpiece of straddling, are contained in a letter to A. C. Paige, Oct. 18, 1865;
HP, 9.

38. MH, A Discourse, Delivered before the Congregational Library Association,
in the Tremont Temple, Boston. May 29, 1855 (Boston, T. R. Marvin, 1855), p. 2.
Earlier anti-Catholic sermons are A Sermon, Delivered before the Pastoral Associa-
tion of Massachusetts, in Park Street Church, Boston. May 30, 1843, Boston, Tap-
pan and Dennet, 1843; A Sermon before the American Board of Commissioners for
Foreign Missions, at the Thirty-sixth Annual Meeting, Brooklyn, N.Y. Sept., 1845,
Boston, Crocker and Brewster, 1845; A Sermon, Delivered at Plymouth, on the
Twenty-second of December, 1846, Boston, T. R. Marvin, 1847.

tion—but then all good books are inspired." [39] Experience taught
them, too, that Hopkins was right when he saw in liquor-consuming
men and novel-reading women a waste of talents and a dissipation
of ambition.[40]

In his day those who would be safe sought refuge not in the
mysticism of an Emerson but in the clear call to faith of a Mark
Hopkins, who offered salvation and material success to those who
would learn the message of Christ and surrender to his God.
Safety lay in spurning reform and reformers, hopefully agreeing
with Hopkins that nothing but the religion of Christ could eradi-
cate the evils with which reformers dabbled piecemeal. The reformers and the mystics, to be sure, led busy lives during the first
half of the 19th century, spawning organization after organization designed to serve a noble cause, erecting here a model factory
and there an agrarian utopia. But, in the end, none of them came
as close as did Hopkins to being a representative man of the age.
Nineteenth-century America did not belong to transcendentalism
or to reform; it belonged to the men and women who agreed with
Mark Hopkins that the world was full of reformers crying "Lo
here! and lo there! whom we are not to go after or follow." [41]

Hopkins' attitude toward reform was reflected in his own construction of the most pervasive idea of the age—the optimistic idea
of unrelenting, inevitable progress. A belief in progress permeated
19th-century attitudes, dissipating in large measure, as far as
religion was concerned, the gloom of an earlier day and substituting
for it a hopeful but cautious expectation of endless human achievement under God. Hopkins was too much a man of his century, too
much impressed by its material achievements, not to subscribe to
the notion that a law of progress was at work in the world. Because
he was a cautious man and a deeply religious man his reservations
on the prospects of progress were inevitable. He could not abandon
himself to the secularism and materialism which most men accepted

39. MH, *Faith, Philosophy, and Reason: A Baccalaureate Sermon, Delivered at
Williamstown, Ms. August 18, 1850* (2d ed. Boston, T. R. Marvin and Son, 1859),
pp. 21–2.

40. Hopkins' first recorded temperance address was delivered before the Stockbridge Agricultural Society in 1827. See Perry, *Williamstown and Williams College*,
pp. 476–7. A British observer's reactions to Hopkins' efforts on that occasion is
contained in Basil Hall, *Travels in North America, in the Years 1827 and 1828*
(Edinburgh, Cadell and Co., 1829), *2*, 82. In *The Connexion between Taste and Morals: Two Lectures* (Boston, Dutton and Wentworth, 1841) Hopkins registered his
opposition to the whole catalogue of dissipations—theater-going, intemperance,
and novel-reading.

41. For a typical sermon on reform see MH, *A Sermon before the American
Board of Commissioners for Foreign Missions* (above, n. 38), esp. pp. 5, 10.

as progress. Nor could he escape the mood of optimism with which his countrymen were busily creating a great nation. In characteristic fashion he found room for the old faith and the new hope in his own projection of the idea of progress, a combination of optimism characteristic of the day with a pessimism appropriate to an awareness of the world's sins. It was a tribute to the contagiousness of Hopkins' own outlook on his age that in the theological seminaries his former students were known as "cheerful" Christians.[42]

In 1843 when Williams College was fifty years old, and again in 1876 when the United States had passed its first century, he told the alumni of his college, "I believe in a law of progress for the race." The evidence, on both occasions, he found in material prosperity, in American inventiveness and initiative, in stable government and sound schools, in all the manifold "appliances of civilization." [43] Recurring to his old law of high aim and incidental advantage, he warned, however:

> The true idea of progress . . . involves a recognition of the true end of man as a social being. . . . This end I suppose to be, the upbuilding and perfection of the individual man in everything that makes him truly man. . . . The germ of all political and social well-being is to be found in the progress of the individual towards the true and highest end for which he was made.[44]

In machinery he saw the evidence, as well as the weapons, of progress, but he asked the graduating class of 1858: "Tell me what is to be done with the leisure that . . . machinery . . . is beginning to give, and will yet give more fully to the race, and I will tell you what the destiny of the race will be. . . ." [45] In democratic institutions he saw the ultimate in human organization, but he also cautioned, "What we must have is a *people*, and not a rabble." For Hopkins, the capacity of the American people for democratic government was still an open question.[46] The advantage of his position,

42. Carter, *Mark Hopkins*, p. 320.
43. MH, *The Law of Progress: A Centennial Discourse, before the Alumni of Williams College* (North Adams, Mass., James T. Robinson and Son, 1876), pp. 5, 10.
44. MH, *An Address, Delivered before the Society of Alumni of Williams College, at the Celebration of the Semi-centennial Anniversary. August 16, 1843* (Boston, T. R. Marvin, 1843), p. 13.
45. MH, *Eagles' Wings: A Baccalaureate Sermon, Delivered at Williamstown, Ms. August 1, 1858* (Boston, T. R. Marvin and Son, 1858), p. 14.
46. MH, *The Sabbath and Free Institutions: A Paper Read before the National Sabbath Convention, Saratoga. Aug. 13, 1863* (New York, Edward O. Jenkins, 1863), p. 5.

as far as his own fame mattered, lay in the opportunity it gave him to become a kind of collective conscience for a society somewhat uneasy in its possession of a remarkable and sudden material progress. There were Jeremiahs in 19th-century America, men like Henry Thoreau who uttered grim pronouncements on the age and crawled into the seclusion of a cabin on Walden Pond. There were men who worshiped at the altar of material progress, like Cornelius Vanderbilt, who with inveterate optimism created an empire of steamships and railroads. The nay-sayers and the yea-sayers had their following, to be sure, but so did Mark Hopkins. If he could wholeheartedly say neither "nay" nor "yea," many Americans could understand why. Their optimism, like his, was tempered by a cautiousness grounded in the knowledge that the story of God's struggle with man was of ancient origin.

The world beyond Berkshire discovered Mark Hopkins in January 1844, when he delivered a series of twelve lectures before the Lowell Institute in Boston, taking as his subject "The Evidences of Christianity." "I come, not to dispute, but to exhibit truth," he told his listeners, who apparently found in his solid conviction welcome support for their own inherited beliefs.[47] Lowell Lectures were new in 1839, and when Hopkins delivered his first series in 1844, attendance at them was more or less expected of fashionable, intellectual, and religious Boston. He provoked no sectarian controversy, as he might have done in that Unitarian citadel. Instead of attacking Unitarianism, he attacked "the religion of Mohammed, unsustained by miracles or by prophecies, propagated by the sword, encouraging fatalism, and pride, and intolerance, sanctioning polygamy, offering a sensual heaven." [48] The few Mohammedans of Boston may have protested; the Brahmins, on the other hand, vigorously applauded, in large measure because he appealed to them not as the Congregationalists or the Unitarians or the Episcopalians which they were, but as Christians, and because he helped them to renew a faith that was being buffeted by skepticism, naturalism, and intellectualism.

In brief, the big, tall Puritan from Berkshire was something of a success—perhaps because Boston had not realized before that a man could be Christian without being overbearingly sectarian; perhaps because the carefully reasoned and fully elaborated ex-

47. MH, *Lectures on the Evidences of Christianity, before the Lowell Institute. January, 1844* (Boston, T. R. Marvin, 1846), p. 13.
48. *Ibid.*, p. 70.

position and pleasant delivery of Hopkins provided them with the kind of religious lift they badly needed; or perhaps because it was a revelation to them that a clear head on an adequately attractive body could hail from the hinterlands. For whatever reason, their discovery of Hopkins in January 1844 led to his discovery by an ever-widening audience.[49] His students had known for some time that Mark Hopkins was not an ordinary man; now, others would also take notice.

Although he had lectured occasionally before, after the success of 1844 Hopkins became a platform lecturer as well as a college president. That he was discovered at a time when the lyceum and other instruments of popular instruction were in the ascendancy certainly contributed to the widening of his audience. Eight years after his first lectures, he was able to write to his wife from Boston with pardonable pride that he was drawing a full house—two thousand people.[50] And three times again, in the winters of 1860–61, 1867–68, and 1871–72, he repeated on the Lowell platform the success of earlier years, avoiding controversy, confirming progress, blessing wealth, and reaffirming the old faith.

His annual lecture tours took him well beyond Berkshire into the Connecticut Valley in 1844, to eastern Massachusetts in 1846, to western New York in 1850, to Chicago, Detroit, and Cleveland in 1855. He received invitations to speak at college commencements, at annual meetings of religious organizations, in fact almost anywhere that a sound and effective Christian speaker might be in demand. New honors came his way. Honorary degrees from Dartmouth in 1837 and Harvard in 1841 and his election to membership on the American Board of Commissioners for Foreign Missions in 1836 had been more or less automatically bestowed upon him as president of Williams College. But after 1844, elections to positions of responsibility, and the efforts of churches and educational institutions to wean him away from Williams, testified to his own popularity. In 1848 he was elected to the board of visitors of the Andover Theological Seminary, in 1849 to the Massachusetts Board of Education, in 1857 to the presidency of the American Board of Commissioners for Foreign Missions. New responsibilities gave him new audiences, as did membership in the various arms of evangelical Congregationalism which now asked him to address

49. See Perry, *Williamstown and Williams College*, pp. 591 ff. For a short and useful account and list of the Lowell Lectures to 1898 see Harriette Knight Smith, *The History of The Lowell Institute*, Boston, Lamson, Wolffe, 1898.
50. Dec. 13, 1852; HP, *1*.

them—the American Bible Society, the Society for Promotion of Collegiate and Theological Education at the West, the American Home Missionary Society, and the American Education Society.

The fresh force which his Lowell lectures gave to old ideas recommended them warmly to friends of Christian orthodoxy, and when they were published, as each series was, they soon found their way into use as textbooks in colleges, seminaries, normal schools, Sunday-school classes, and evening discussion groups.[51] Noah Porter at Yale and Andrew Peabody at Harvard used the lectures in their own classrooms.[52] From Bates College in Maine to Mills Seminary in California, from Iowa College at Grinnell to Straight University at New Orleans, the published lectures of Mark Hopkins performed a vital service for Christianity and added new prestige to their author and to the college over which he presided.

The preparation and delivery of these lectures seldom interfered with his responsibilities as teacher, educator, and college administrator. To a very great extent the published lectures were the same ones he had first prepared for the Williams classroom, and the textbooks, after all, were lectures in book form. Hopkins enjoyed his popularity, but he was also proud of the fact that he had not exerted himself greatly to secure it, or diverted himself from his primary responsibilities as teacher and college president.

The burdens were heavy, varied, and unpredictable. A 19th-century New England college appeared to be quite capable of running along automatically. Problems of discipline, curriculum, and procedure did arise, however. Alumni, students, and faculty did not always agree upon the emphases placed upon such diverse matters as religion, athletics, fraternities, and natural science. A recent alumnus might want the president of the college to marry him and his bride at the summit of Petersburg Mountain. A student might ask for leave of absence because his grandmother was dead, and since the student had asked for leave the previous year for the same reason, the president had to pursue the matter (and discover that the grandmother was dead, all right—in fact had been dead for fifteen years). The mail—not heavy, to be sure, had to be attended to, as did frequent requests for names of promising students capable of becoming teachers at academies and

51. The 1861 lectures were published as *Lectures on Moral Science,* Boston, Gould and Lincoln, 1862; the 1867 lectures, as *The Law of Love and Love as a Law; or, Moral Science, Theoretical and Practical,* New York, Scribner, 1869; and the 1871 lectures as *An Outline Study of Man; or, the Body and Mind in One System,* New York, Scribner, Armstrong, 1873.
52. Porter to MH, Feb. 18, 1863; Peabody to MH, Dec. 2, 1862: HP, *8.*

female institutes, invitations to give lectures or to exchange pulpits with neighboring clergymen, promises from alumni and friends of the college to drop into the president's house at commencement time, sermons to prepare, students to discipline, funds to raise, faculty to placate, and classes to meet.

With it all, even if his duties sometimes seemed to deny that it was so, Mark Hopkins was a husband, a father, and a son. Because he left Williamstown no more often than was necessary, he did not become, as busy men so often do, a remote and distant member of his family. Time spared from his presidential duties was spent with his family rather than with his books. He welcomed each of the ten children—five boys and five girls—whom Mary bore him between 1833 and 1853 with pride and with the solemn hope that they would find salvation. When, after two girls, his first son was born on Thanksgiving Day 1837, he hurriedly wrote to his father in Stockbridge, referring to the difficulties of preparing a dinner that day, "You know how it is—if you have a poor dinner, somebody is always sure to come. . . . I am glad for your sakes as well as for my own that it is a boy." [53] In the absence of the family doctor, Mark was called back into medical practice at the birth of Alice in 1846. No wonder that soon after the delivery he wrote to Amos Lawrence, "Six children of my own, and a hundred and sixty of other peoples. . . . My only ground of hope is that as I have been most mercifully and unexpectedly sustained and prospered hitherto, so there is One who is able to give me strength equal to my day." [54]

Good humor pervaded his relationships with his family. "What shall I do?" he asked his wife Mary in a letter from Stockbridge, where he was visiting his mother in 1842. "I cannot sleep nights." "It is not however for want of bedfellows," he continued, describing the heated sticks wrapped in cloth which his mother put into his bed as a defense against the Berkshire winter. "Mother has to go up and fix the bed about as much as she did when I was four years old. I let her do pretty much as she is a mind to as it gives her pleasure." [55] When his wife Mary, leaving him alone for the first time, went to Troy in 1833 to buy furniture for their new home, he wrote to her, "It is so still that I can hear every frog that jumps within a mile of me." [56] Thirty-seven years later he was still as

53. Nov. 30, 1837; MS letter in possession of Mrs. Henry Hopkins, 1952.
54. May 30, 1846; MHS, MH-AL MSS.
55. Jan. 6, 1842; HP, *1*.
56. Apr. 22, 1833; HL, *4*.

lonely in her absence, but more dependent. "If you must insist on
my wearing shirts with separate collars and wrist-bands," he wrote
her, "I have made up my mind to have a special set made otherwise
in case of your absence. I have dispensed with the wrist-bands and
perhaps shall with the collars." [57]

He was a proud father, an understanding father. He wrote of
his three-month-old son in 1844 as being "in fine condition, and as
likely as any boy I know of his age to be President of these United
States." [58] Twenty years later the boy, one of three sons of Mark
Hopkins to serve under Grant in the Civil War, was a captain in
the Union forces, and his father wrote to him, "I used to speak to
you in my letters about your spelling. Will it do any good if I recur
to it. . . . Let me put down a few words as they come—leter—de-
taled—positon—bieneal—desmised—suprised—ammusing. . . .
In writing to me you need not mind and I hesitate to say anything
lest you should write less and feel constrained about it." [59] As for
the war and the participation of his three sons in it, he accepted
their going stoically, disturbed at the threat to Christian morality
implicit in military service, confident that they would avoid temptation, but aware just the same that they were boys. To one he wrote,
"I should like to know how many more of our young officers must
be taken prisoners through the agency of beautiful and accomplished secesh young ladies who can play on the piano. . . . You
did not get caught it seems, but I am surprised at it." [60]

That his children—eight of whom grew to maturity—gave him
some heartaches there can be no doubt. Lawrence, for whom Hopkins secretly desired a career in the church, became a vice-president
and receiver for many midwestern railroads, a successful man of
affairs. Archie turned to law and renouncing the orthodox faith
of his father asked in an article he wrote for a free-thought magazine, "Are All the Teachings of the New Testament Infallible and
for All Time?" His response was a determined "I think not." [61]
After a series of failures in business and the death of his wife, young
Mark remarried two weeks after his father's death and left for
Europe, where he turned to novel writing and sculpture. Of the
boys, Henry most nearly approximated what Mark Hopkins desired of a son: he found a career in the church and in time himself

57. Apr. 25, 1870; HP, *1*.

58. MH to AL, July 29, 1844; MHS, MH-AL MSS.

59. MH to Lawrence Hopkins, Apr. 11, 1864; HP, *2*.

60. MH to Lawrence Hopkins, Mar. 9, 1864; HP, *2*. See also letters of the following dates to Lawrence Hopkins: Mar. 16, Mar. 24, and Apr. 4, 1864: HP, *2*.

61. *Free Thought Magazine, 14* (1896), 206.

became president of Williams College. Of the girls, Alice and Caroline married well; Mary Louisa and Susie remained spinsters. Susie, continuing to live at home, became a comfort to Mark and his wife in their old age.

If there were heartaches, however, there was also a kind of compensation in that larger family of sons, the Williams alumni body, so many of whom respected and revered him as a son so seldom does his father. In 1886, a year before his death, Mark Hopkins leafed through the catalogues and the records of the college and discovered that he had taught all but 31 of the 1726 Williams alumni then living. The college was approaching its centennial, and of all its graduates, living or dead, only a quarter of them had not sat before him in a Williams classroom.[62] His sons were indeed plentiful. They were everywhere.

62. MH, *A Discourse Delivered at Williamstown June 29, 1886*, p. 6.

3. "Of a Log . . ."

IN THE DAYS of Mark Hopkins, what was an American college? Was it a full-time Sunday school, perhaps on its way to becoming a success school? Was it a log upon which a professor and a student exchanged ideas? Or was it perhaps more than either? Nineteenth-century undergraduates probably came as close to accuracy as anyone when, returning from a vacation, they exclaimed, "College is back!" [1] We are the college, they said in effect, and no one seems to have accused them of arrogance. According to other points of view, the college might be defined as its buildings, or even its president. In time, organized alumni groups came to act as if they were the college, and an occasional faculty member was known to nurse pretensions of indispensability and delusions of power. Hardly anyone, however, seriously suggested that the college was its curriculum.

In truth the small liberal arts college of the 19th century was more expert at finding substitutes for a curriculum than in developing one, and these substitutes, not the curriculum itself, gave most of the small colleges their particular fame and flavor. Energetic students found one substitute in a well-developed extracurriculum. Necessity, tradition, and circumstance created another out of the "old-time college president."

Early American colleges transplanted to the New World, as best they could, the curricular concepts which had long prevailed in the English universities. As a result, even a small country institution like Williams offered a course of study based upon a traditional program of Latin, Greek, mathematics, and moral and intellectual philosophy. Williams inherited its notions on matters of curriculum from Yale, which had in its turn learned of such things from Harvard. Back of Harvard were Cambridge and Oxford. Early in the national experience, to be sure, it became clear to some Americans that the educational needs of a frontier society went beyond the traditional. [2]

In 1779 electives in the modern languages and sciences were

1. For an example of "college" used in this sense see *Vidette, 2* (Apr. 24, 1869), 1.
2. Of particular value in understanding the old curriculum are Louis Franklin Snow, *The College Curriculum in the United States,* New York, Teachers College, Columbia University, 1907; and George P. Schmidt, "Intellectual Crosscurrents in American Colleges, 1825–1855," *American Historical Review, 42* (1936), 46–67.

introduced into the curriculum at William and Mary. In 1802 Union College permitted students not headed for the learned professions to substitute French for Greek. Deviations from the old curriculum were nevertheless infrequent and inconsequential. Most American colleges of the day were indebted to Yale or to Princeton for their curricular systems. Since these institutions did not veer significantly from the classical curriculum, neither did the overwhelming majority of small colleges which accepted them as models. In 1828 the faculty of Yale College issued a report on the proper course of study for an American liberal arts college.[3] On this report Yale and most American colleges for another half century were willing to rest their case for the classics, mathematics, and intellectual and moral philosophy. At Williams the atmosphere for forty years after 1828 was never seriously charged with controversy on the subject of curriculum, so complete was the respect in which the Yale position was held. Rejecting the suggestion that American colleges should adjust themselves "to the business character of the nation," the Yale professors described the main purposes of a college education as the disciplining of the mind, the formation of a "proper *balance* of character," and the provision of an adequate substitute for "*parental superintendence.*" The classics, they announced, would remain as the core of the curriculum, effectively disciplining all of the mental faculties—memory, judgment, reason, taste, and fancy. Mathematics would continue to "sharpen the intellect, to strengthen the faculty of reason, and to induce a general habit of mind favorable to the discovery of truth and the detection of error." Small doses of the physical sciences would provide training in induction and probability; logic and mental philosophy would give experience in thinking; and as a concession to practicality, rhetoric and oratory would equip the young Yale graduate with the means of exerting his influence over others. As for the modern languages, the Yale faculty would continue to look upon them as an "accomplishment."

Despite its adherence to the old curriculum and to the Yale rationale, Williams experienced during the presidency of Mark Hopkins a gradual whittling away of the domination which the classics and mathematics had traditionally enjoyed. The natural sciences strengthened their feeble hold. French, which from 1828 had been lumped with Hebrew and fluxions as a one-term optional study in junior year, slowly widened its range, becoming a required

3. Published as "Original Papers in Relation to a Course of Liberal Education," *American Journal of Science and Arts, 15* (1829), 297–351.

three-term study in 1868.⁴ German appeared as an optional study in 1846, and achieved a position of respectability in the curriculum of 1868. A term of history and of political economy had been transplanted from Yale when the college was founded, but under the guidance of two able professors, Joseph Alden (1835–52) and Arthur Latham Perry (1853–91), history and political economy encroached upon the old subjects. In 1843, for the first time, a term in junior year was devoted to American history. Under Perry the domain of the historical and political studies was enlarged to include five terms, from the third term of sophomore year through the first term of senior year, covering a variety of subjects which ranged from the historical evidences of Christianity to a course on international law.

Notwithstanding these clear indications that the college had bowed to the incessant demands from its public that education be somehow made practical, in 1872 it had not yet abandoned the core curriculum inherited from Yale in 1793. When Mark Hopkins stepped down from the presidency of Williams in 1872, the freshman year was still devoted to Latin, Greek, and mathematics. In the sophomore year the intrusion of new subjects had caused a reduction of time allowed for the old subjects from three terms to two; in the junior year also, Latin and Greek suffered a loss of one term. Oratory and rhetoric continued to be a part of the instruction in all four years. The total cost of curricular innovation to the ancient subjects was, therefore, one term of mathematics and two terms each of Latin and Greek.

The price was very small. It represented the distance which Mark Hopkins himself was willing to go in adapting the Williams curriculum to the demands of a nation whose respect for the practical was everywhere apparent. In no sense, however, was he doggedly hostile to curricular change. For instance, he eagerly welcomed the natural sciences into the course of study at Williams, certain that they materially contributed to man's understanding of himself and of God's world. If it had been financially possible, he said, he would have found room for art and music, convinced as he was that man's aesthetic sense had long been neglected.⁵ He harbored no doubts of the essential correctness of concentration in the classics

4. The arrival and departure of courses in the Williams curriculum have been charted by reference to the appropriate numbers of *Catalogue of the Officers and Students of Williams College,* issued annually, as well as various editions of *The Laws of Williams College,* issued irregularly since 1795.

5. MH, *An Address, Delivered in Boston, May 26, 1852, before the Society for the Promotion of Collegiate and Theological Education at the West* (Boston, T. R. Marvin, 1852), p. 15.

and mathematics, although he suspected that the tendency had been to emphasize the classics to the exclusion of other desirable areas of study. Early in his presidency he had voiced a willingness to add an agricultural department to the college, as a means of making Williams attractive and useful to neighboring farmers. The main tendencies of his educational thinking, however, coincided with the purposes of the Yale report of 1828. When President Francis Wayland of Brown voiced his pleas for curricular reform in the 1850's, Hopkins exhibited little interest, revealing his distrust of all reform schemes and announcing his intention to stick to the traditional curriculum, secure in the knowledge that it offered everything that was essential to fulfill the college's primary object.[6] "It is the object of the College," said Mark Hopkins, "to make men." [7]

A curriculum alone could not make men, and for that reason Hopkins and most of his contemporaries among college presidents were little inclined to excite themselves about curricular matters. As makers of men, rather than as instructors in practical skills, they had already evolved a workable and productive scheme of education, based upon a tried course of study, a community of feeling between student and faculty, a reasonable system of discipline, and, most of all, the senior's year of study with the president of the college. In such a scheme Christian influence far transcended in importance the utility of subject matter. Besides, while many of the new subjects might help a man make money, there was little assurance that they would contribute to the formation of his character.

Hopkins stated his own position frequently, but seldom as precisely as in an address of 1852:

By a liberal education, I mean that which has for its object the symmetrical expansion, and the discipline of the human powers,

6. MH to AL, May 20, 1850; MHS, MH-AL MSS: "I fear Dr. W. will go too far & practically break up all regular & prescribed courses of study. I agree substantially with President Sparks on that subject." The choice between Wayland and Jared Sparks, president of Harvard, was an easy one for Mark Hopkins. Wayland had succumbed to the democratic notion that a college education should be sufficiently elective to prepare young men for the "practical" vocations; Sparks, in his inaugural address at Harvard in 1849, announced that he would keep the university safe for the old prescribed curriculum.

7. MH, *Colleges and Stability: A Discourse, Delivered in Marietta, Ohio, Nov. 8, 1868, at the Quarter-century Anniversary of the Society for the Promotion of Collegiate and Theological Education at the West* (reprinted from the proceedings of the society, n.d.), p. 16.

—the cultivation of man as man. . . . Such an education is
distinguished . . . by the fact that knowledge and power are
gained without reference to any specific end to which they are
to be applied. . . . Education, conducted on these principles,
is, indeed, regarded by some as not practical. But what can be
more practical than to make a true man? I distrust that practi-
calness that would take from the man, to add to his possessions.[8]

Williams, in company with other American colleges, had developed an impressive arsenal of weapons for making men out of boys.
Unrelenting revivals, unheated dormitories, and underpaid professors made their own small contribution toward helping the college fulfill its major objective. But the heaviest burden for ac-
complishing the college's purpose rested upon the shoulders of the
president. In his course for seniors, known almost everywhere as
"moral and intellectual philosophy," the full force of a mature mind
and personality was turned upon a variety of subjects considered
essential to the making of men. Nor were the prospects of the senior
year lost upon the students themselves. "The coming year," a
Williams senior wrote in 1861, "is fraught with responsibility and
yet pleasure. It must tell heavily on our after lives. . . . We are
treated, like, and feel like, men now and must quit ourselves like
men. Soon the greatest mind in New England will take and train
us." [9]

Similar letters were undoubtedly written by seniors at other
American colleges, for in conception there was nothing unique
about the senior year at Williams under Hopkins. This curricular
capstone, as one historian has said, "became as common a feature of
the average American college as the president's house and the
treasury deficit." [10] The fame which attached itself to the senior
year at Williams had been equaled at Yale by Timothy Dwight,
at Transylvania by Horace Holley, and at Union by Eliphalet
Nott. Transplanted from the universities of 18th-century England
and Scotland, the course in moral and intellectual philosophy embraced the tough problem of how to reconcile man's newly emanci-
pated reason and natural law with the old theology and Christian
law.

8. MH, *An Address, Delivered in Boston, May 26, 1852*, pp. 7-8.
9. Samuel C. Armstrong to Mrs. C. C. Armstrong, Sept. 14, 1861, in "Personal
Memories and Letters of General S. C. Armstrong," ed. Helen W. Ludlow (typescript in possession of Mrs. Arthur Howe), p. 99.
10. George P. Schmidt, *The Old Time College President* (New York, Columbia
University Press, 1930), p. 109.

The tortuous methods by which this problem was solved, in an age innocent of psychology and scarcely acquainted with the complexities of the human mechanism, cannot be made readily understandable. Not surprisingly, however, the efforts of these self-proclaimed philosophers led to the discovery that human reason, when applied to nature and man's consciousness, simply reaffirmed the old truths. When William Paley and Joseph Butler, the English predecessors of Hopkins and Wayland and Nott in America, had finished their work, religious conviction and Christian ethics rested not only upon the word of God but upon the verification which man's reason found in nature. This comforting Christian message, masquerading as philosophy, dominated the man-making course of the senior year in American colleges of Hopkins' era. At Williams, as a later-day occupant of Hopkins' chair has pointed out, preconceived theological views and evangelistic purposes combined to deprive the course of anything resembling earnest philosophical investigation.[11]

What provided the course with an intrinsic appeal, apart from the fact that it was taught by the president, was its universality of subject matter. "It embraces man in his unity, and God in his sovereignty" was a student's accurate description of what he labeled "the key-stone of the whole arch of the college studies." [12] At the semicentennial celebration of the college in 1843 Hopkins took time to tell the alumni what he was doing. "We take up first the physical man, and endeavor to give . . . an idea of every organ and tissue of the body," he explained, and went on to describe the systematic route which led the Williams senior through the byways of mental faculties, grounds of belief, logic, and emotion, to the ultimate destination—the moral government of God.[13] The route was circuitous, to be sure, permitting Hopkins to impart his opinions and advice on many subjects. By the end of the senior year, a Williams student knew exactly where the president of his college stood on such matters as bodily hygiene, physical exercise, the rights of property, the responsibilities of suffrage, and the duties of marriage and parenthood. Into the warp and woof of this complex fabric known as philosophy were woven aesthetics, ethics, economics, politics, and theology.

Diverse as the subject matter may have seemed, an artificial

11. James Bissett Pratt, "Mark Hopkins as a Philosopher"; WCL, Pratt MSS.
12. *Vidette, 6* (Mar. 23, 1872), 137.
13. MH, *An Address, Delivered before the Society of Alumni of Williams College, at the Celebration of the Semi-centennial Anniversary,* p. 31.

unity was placed upon it by the enthusiasm and serenity with which Mark Hopkins revealed his own convictions. In addition, however, there was an inherent unity, based upon Hopkins' own schematic construction of the role of man in relationship to his world. Unity was imposed upon the course by the harmony which Hopkins believed to exist between nature and revelation, by the universal reach of God's laws and the universal character of Christianity. Although the course was everywhere accepted as philosophy, it was, both in purpose and practice, a mixture of Congregational orthodoxy and personal opinion. That it succeeded in conveying to the seniors of Williams College a strong and practical Christian message there can be no doubt.

"If the human constitution was made by the divine being," Hopkins told a class of seniors in 1837, "it was made for certain ends. To discover these ends is the science of moral philosophy." [14] Almost thirty years later he was reaffirming his earlier approach to moral studies. "If to avoid utilitarianism," he wrote to Ray Palmer, "it is necessary to have a theory requiring man to act with no regard to what is useful and implying that God has made a universe that is of no use then I am a utilitarian." [15] A sublimated utilitarian, he has been called, but regardless of kind he made of moral philosophy a practical search for the practical way of doing things in a practical Christian world.

Probably as important as any one element in contributing to Hopkins' fame as a teacher was his ability and willingness to make his classes something more than exercises in memory, recitation, and regurgitated "truth." He took seriously his own dicta on the characteristics of good teaching, first publicly announced at his inauguration to the presidency of Williams in 1836. On that occasion he said:

> It is far easier for a teacher to generalize a class, and give it a lesson to get by rote, and hear it said, and let it pass, than it is to watch the progress of individual mind, and awaken interest, and answer objections, and explore tendencies, and, beginning with the elements, to construct together with his pupils, so that they shall feel that they aid in it, the fair fabric of a science with which they shall be familiar from the founda-

14. MS lecture notes of Francis W. Tappan; WCL.
15. Jan. 20, 1863; WCL, Hopkins-Palmer MSS. In 1869 Hopkins' utilitarianism led to an interesting—at that time—dispute with President James McCosh of Princeton. The controversy is treated at length in Carter, *Mark Hopkins*, pp. 160–79.

tion to the topstone. . . . Every man who is educated at all,
is, and must be, self-educated. . . . It is for the want of understanding this properly, that extravagant expectations are
entertained of instructors. . . . Young men will not set themselves efficiently at work until they feel that there is an all-
important part which they must perform for themselves, and
which no one can do for them. . . . It is easy to see what it is
that constitutes the first excellence of an instructor. It is not his
amount of knowledge, nor yet his facility of communication,
important as these may be; but it is his power to give an impulse
to the minds of his pupils, and to induce them to labor. For this
purpose, nothing is so necessary as a disinterested devotion to
the work, and a certain enthusiasm which may act by sympathy
on the minds of the young.[16]

Hopkins succeeded in meeting his own requirements. In the otherwise almost arid classrooms of Williams his instruction was ex-
ceptional and effective.

William Dwight Whitney, for instance, had hardly begun his
instruction under Hopkins when he wrote to his cousin in the fall
of 1844: "The Prex. is the greatest teacher entirely that was ever
suffered to appear on this earth." [17] In November 1855 James A.
Garfield wrote into his journal: "Today and yesterday I have done
about what I ought to do in four days. . . . But this mighty Dr.
Hopkins is so infinitely suggestive." [18] The next month he wrote
to a friend: "We have been walking in the strong clear light of
Dr. Hopkins['] teachings which lead us deeper down into the heart
of things than anything we have had before. He is a real sky-
clearer, a cloud-compelling Jupiter." [19] Samuel Chapman Armstrong, writing to his family in 1862, declared, "Prex makes a man
think, and think quickly too." [20]

Hopkins' own enthusiasm for his work, the all-encompassing
nature of the subject he taught, and even his magnificent physical
frame created a classroom atmosphere from which such student
tributes might come. Yet it was his method of teaching which led

16. MH, *An Inaugural Discourse*, pp. 8–12.
17. Whitney to D. W. Marsh, Oct. 28, 1844; SML:YU, Whitney MSS.
18. Theodore Clarke Smith, *The Life and Letters of James Abram Garfield* (2
vols. New Haven, Yale University Press, 1925), *1*, 96.
19. Garfield to Amos S. Hayden, July 17, 1854; in Arthur H. Merritt, "Two Unpublished Letters of James A. Garfield Written while a Student at Williams College," *New York Historical Society Quarterly, 31* (1947), 137–8.
20. Jan. 4, 1862; in "Personal Memories and Letters of General S. C. Armstrong,"
p. 120.

students like Whitney, Garfield, and Armstrong to the conclusion
that their own mental powers were being magnificently expanded
under the president's tutelage. "What do *you* think?" was the
disarming and at that time unique question with which he frequently punctuated his classes. Students, unaccustomed to being
asked what they thought, experienced a sense of growth merely in
the presence of the question. Furthermore, Hopkins did not insist
that students agree with him. He did not care whether they had
paid much attention to the textbook or whether they had committed
any of it to memory. He did not push abstruse points to their
furthest refinement, preferring to deal in generalities which would
leave his students free to explore for the refinements themselves.
He introduced a bit of novelty into his teaching by pioneering in
the use of visual classroom aids: in 1841 he enlivened his discussion
of anatomy with a lifesize model of a man made by the French
physician, Louis Auzoux.[21] In 1845 he added a skeleton to his
classroom equipment, and in the 1870's he began to make extensive
use of the blackboard to illustrate the main outlines of his "moral
system." [22]

He never took attendance and would have preferred that the
dullards in the class stayed away; since they generally attended,
he chose instead to ignore them. The students themselves he knew
as intimately as was possible, calling upon them in their rooms,
conversing with them freely about their problems in his study and
on the college walks. "Your instruction . . . appears to have been
a turning point to me" was the verdict of E. P. Roe, who after
leaving Williams wrote best-selling novels in which were imbedded
a homely Christian message.[23] Hopkins carried this fatherly concern into the classroom; the questions which he asked did not follow
an alphabetized class list but were directed wherever he thought
they might do the most personal good. He turned his classes into
friendly disputations, in which his students were his fellow companions in the search for "truth." His criticism, although sometimes sarcastic, was friendly and frequently touched with humor.
After quietly listening to a student object to the extension of the
Fifth Commandment to include members of the college faculty,
for instance, he remarked, "Hence we see that a father who has an
unruly son whom he knows not what else to do with is sure to send

21. See above, n. 13. Carter, *Mark Hopkins,* pp. 64–8. TR, *2,* 224; Aug. 16, 1842.
I am indebted to Professor Chester Dale of Ohio State University for pointing out
that Hopkins' use of the manikin made him a pioneer in the use of visual aids.
22. MH to AL, Oct. 14, 1845; MHS, MH-AL MSS. MH to Ray Palmer, Jan.
13, 1874; WCL, Hopkins-Palmer MSS.
23. E. P. Roe to MH, June 6, 1880; HP, *5.*

him to Williams College." [24] On another occasion he asked a student in what respect he thought that God's system on earth could be improved, the student already having indicated that he was not at all certain that man lived under the best possible system of divine government. Young James H. Canfield responded, "Certainly, I would kill off all the bedbugs, mosquitoes, and fleas, and make oranges and bananas grow farther north." Hopkins cheerfully agreed.[25]

The senior year, under Hopkins' guidance, became a memorable experience to most of his students because they felt that they were treated as the intellectual equals of a man whom they instinctively respected. He possessed a skill, seldom exhibited by his contemporaries, of combining Christian indoctrination with the development of independently thinking students. And somehow he managed to earn a reputation for being undogmatic by teaching a course that was dedicated to the propagation of Christian dogma. His instruction was animated by a sincere respect for individuals. He carried into the classroom the message of his 1859 baccalaureate address: "Be *yourselves*. Bring out your own individuality. It is your own. . . . Respect that of others . . . appreciate it, and rejoice in its manifestation." [26] The 1845 class notes of one of his students recorded the warning: "One danger in much reading is that of encumbering the mind with thoughts of others, & thus destroying individuality." [27] In the Socratic tendencies of his own teaching he found a method of inspiring students to be individuals, to think as men, to try their mental powers.

"I do not hesitate to say," Horace E. Scudder wrote of his undergraduate experiences, "that the one value which attaches pre-eminently to Williams . . . is the power which belongs to it of inducing independent, vigorous thought." [28] Washington Gladden once remarked that the character of a Williams education was demonstrated by the remarkable number of alumni sitting at editorial desks in the nation's newspaper offices.[29] Undergraduates went so far as to attribute the absence of alumni generosity to the

24. Carter, *Mark Hopkins*, p. 33.
25. *Ibid.*, pp. 325–6.
26. MH, *The Manifoldness of Man: A Baccalaureate Sermon, Delivered at Williamstown, Ms. July 31, 1859* (Boston, T. R. Marvin and Son, 1859), p. 21–2.
27. Allyn S. Kellogg, "Notes on Lectures" (1844–46); MS, WCL.
28. Horace E. Scudder, *Life and Letters of David Coit Scudder, Missionary in Southern India* (New York, Hurd and Houghton, 1864), pp. 67–8.
29. *Williams Review, 2* (1872), 89–91. The editors to whom Gladden referred included William Cullen Bryant of the *New York Post*, Chester P. Dewey of the *Commercial Advertiser*, Samuel I. Prime of the *New York Observer*, and Henry Martin Field of the *Evangelist*.

same cause. "We suspect," wrote an editor of the *Williams Quarterly* in 1867, addressing himself to the subject of the typical Williams alumnus, "that the very excellence of her training, which gave him that independent, self-sufficing character . . . has made him incapable of that all-souled, enthusiastic affection, which men so often blindly feel for institutions that have given them all their knowledge, instead of methods." [30] In some instances the opportunity to think independently proved to be overwhelming. "There is such a vast letting-down of one's own reasoning powers, or rather of one's opinions of these powers, when brought in contact with a man who is possessor of such a mind as Dr. Hopkins," wrote one of his students, "that I, for one, have hardly ventured to think at all, since coming under his instruction, except to follow out his trains of argument and reasoning." [31]

In general, then, although Hopkins managed to conduct his classes in such a way as to inspire individual effort and permit independent thought, he considered the big questions beyond dispute and to their settlement contributed the serenity of a settled mind. Who can miss the tribute to Hopkins the advocate in these nostalgic references to one of his last classes under the president, contained in a letter written by a former student to Hopkins two years after his graduation: "After you had . . . given us somewhat in detail the great principles that underlie all reasoning . . . you laid aside your glasses, passed your hand slowly over your forehead, bowed your head amid the reigning silence for a few seconds, then slowly uttered the words 'But—Nature . . . [is] moral' and the class dismissed." [32]

Mark Hopkins' reputation as a teacher reflected, to a substantial degree, the otherwise almost barren academic offering of Williams College. Until 1853, tutors—young men fresh out of college whose inexperience was a challenge to undergraduate pranksters—supervised most of the instruction of the lower classes. [33] Lectures, metic-

30. *Williams Quarterly, 14* (1867), 197.
31. Charles S. Holt to a member of his family, Oct. 19, 1873; WCL, Misc. MSS, *8*.
32. Alexander Hutchins to MH, Sept. 12, 1859; HP, *4*.
33. In 1859 tutors were first called instructors. In 1868 tutors and instructors disappeared from the Williams payroll, and all instruction was in the hands of professors until 1875, when instructors began to return in force. Professors were somewhat older than instructors and generally had had some kind of postgraduate training, at first in theology and later in professional graduate schools. The first appointment of an associate professor was made in 1869 and of an assistant professor in 1881, but the full-scale development of a system of rank is a 20th-century phenomenon. The introduction of the up-the-ladder, competitive element into fac-

ulous grading of classroom recitations, and memorization characterized much of the formal instruction of upper-class courses. The
caliber of the faculty was never very high. Without fear of con-
tradiction, John Todd, a trustee of the college, declared in 1846,
"The day would be to be deprecated when our colleges should be so
well endowed, that the time of the students must be taken up in
hearing lectures from men living on rich salaries instead of being
occupied in the drilling of the recitation-room." [34]

Todd never had occasion to protest against the existence of a
well-paid faculty at Williams College, although he might have
profited from carefully considering a student attack upon the
trustees which appeared in the *Quarterly* in 1861. Referring to the
trustees, an editor wrote, "Their principal duties are electing in-
ferior graduates to professorships, and squandering the funds." [35]
It is improbable that John Todd would have agreed, but there
could be no doubt that professorships at Williams seemed naturally
to gravitate to her own sons. With the appointment of Gamaliel
Olds of the Class of 1801 as professor of mathematics in 1805, this
early custom of filling professorships was firmly launched. Twenty-
one Williams alumni and only six graduates of other colleges
followed Olds into professorships at Williams before 1872. Able
professors among them frequently abandoned Williamstown when
more lucrative offers appeared from elsewhere.

Professorships sometimes went to the highest bidders. John Tatlock and Thomas E. Clark owed their appointments to friends who
assured the trustees that they would supplement the partial salary
paid by the college.[36] One prospect failed of an appointment in
1859 because his friends did not come to his support.[37] Salaries
were not out of line with those at similar small colleges, but Williams could not compete effectively with a place like Harvard. In
1838, for instance, when the president of Williams was receiving
$1200, Jared Sparks was appointed to the McLean Professorship

ulty life paralleled the similar development in business, which experienced a shift
to the bureaucratic type during the same years.

34. John Todd, *Hints to Undergraduates: An Oration Delivered at the Anni-
versaries of the Literary Societies of Union College. Sept. 21, 1846* (Boston, published by the Societies, 1846), p. 14.

35. *Williams Quarterly, 9* (1861), 61.

36. For Tatlock's arrangements see Joseph Alden to Calvin Durfee, July 20,
1838; WCL, Williams College Autographs, *2*. Also TR, *2*, 196; Aug. 14, 1838. For
Clark's, see T. E. Clark to MH, Apr. 20, 1858; WCL, Misc. MSS, *8*. Also T. E.
Clark to Paul A. Chadbourne, Aug. 24, 1857, and Apr. 28, 1858: WCL, Misc. MSS,
8. See also TR, *2*, 353; Aug. 2, 1858.

37. TR, *2*, 360–1; Apr. 5, 1859. MH to his wife, Apr. 27, 1859; HP, *1*.

of Ancient and Modern History at Harvard, with a salary of
$2,000.[38] In 1860, when professors at Harvard were receiving
$2200, a professor at Williams was being paid $1200.[39] Under
these circumstances, it was probably inevitable that there should
be some relationship between uninspired teaching and the habit
of depending upon Williams graduates to fill professorships.

John Bascom of the Class of 1849 and Arthur Latham Perry of
the Class of 1852 alone among alumni standbys on the faculty
attained the distinction of more than ordinary reputation. Bascom, who left Williams in 1874 to become president of the University of Wisconsin, found his assigned field of instruction, rhetoric,
"partially distasteful," and solved his problem by introducing
English literature and aesthetics into his courses in rhetoric, and
thereby into the curriculum, early in the 1850's.[40] His catholic
interests and somewhat unorthodox religious beliefs, coupled with
a reformer's zeal, led Hopkins to describe him as being "in danger
of that fanaticism . . . by which men sacrifice the finer feelings
and proprieties of life in view of what they call right." [41] Hopkins'
opinion of Bascom was partially colored by the professor's criticisms of Hopkins' Lowell Lectures. In 1862, when Bascom was un-
successfully searching for a magazine that would publish his views,
Hopkins observed, "There will be enough to find fault and it should
not begin here." [42]

Bascom's religious views and Perry's political views, in fact,
were a cause of more than slight concern to the president of the
college. Bascom could be counteracted in part by the overwhelm-
ingly orthodox character of the college itself, although there was
no preventing him from having a student following of his own.
Washington Gladden, the great 19th-century advocate of the social
gospel, and G. Stanley Hall, pioneer American psychologist,
acknowledged an indebtedness to Bascom rather than to Mark
Hopkins.[43]

38. *Dictionary of American Biography, 17,* 433. At Amherst in 1860 professors
were paid $1200, as they were at Williams. See Claude Moore Fuess, *Amherst: The
Story of a New England College* (Boston, Little, Brown, 1935), pp. 183, 210.

39. *University Quarterly, 2* (1860), 167. TR, *2,* 329; Aug. 13, 1855.

40. Bascom, *Things Learned by Living,* p. 58. When Bascom returned to Williams in 1891 as professor of political science, he gave lectures on sociology, thus
introducing a second discipline into the curriculum; in sociology, however, he has
had no successors.

41. MH to Ray Palmer, Dec. 29, 1862; WCL, Hopkins-Palmer MSS.

42. *Ibid.* See also MH to Palmer, Jan. 20, 1863, and Feb. 10, 1863; WCL, Hopkins-Palmer MSS.

43. Washington Gladden, *Recollections* (Boston, Houghton Mifflin, 1909), p. 74.
Hall, *Life and Confessions of a Psychologist,* p. 157.

The Williams Faculty, 1866. *Front row:* Arthur Latham Perry, John Tatlock, and Albert Hopkins; *on porch:* Paul A. Chadbourne, John Bascom, Charles R. Treat, John L. T. Phillips, Mark Hopkins, John G. Davenport, and Franklin Carter.

The college could afford to be embarrassed by this one dissenting voice on doctrinal matters. On the other hand, the voice of Arthur Latham Perry, a fighting champion of free trade, symbolized a very real threat to the stability of American manufacturing —an area of activity which was attracting an increasing share of Williams alumni. Perry's *Political Economy*, published in 1865, became a bible of the free trade movement. At Yale, where President Theodore Dwight Woolsey taught from it, 75 per cent of the Yale senior class were reported, in 1871, to be free traders.[44] James A. Garfield announced in 1870 that the Library of Congress could hardly meet the demands of congressmen for copies of the book.[45] "No other Williams College book has ever had anything like the outward success of this one," Perry proudly reflected in later life, counting up the twenty-two editions and 19,000 sales which his treatise had enjoyed.[46] His reputation as a free trader was further enhanced by barnstorming lecture tours, beginning in 1869, as far west as Detroit and St. Louis; by public debates with Horace Greeley, the arch-protectionist; and by the activities of the American Free Trade League, whose first three presidents were Williams alumni—William Cullen Bryant of the Class of 1813, David Dudley Field of the Class of 1825, and David Ames Wells of the Class of 1847.[47] Eminent as it was, this trio of Williams free traders did not reflect the official thinking of either the college or, unquestionably, most of its alumni.

Mark Hopkins was a determined protectionist, and although he avoided politics as much as possible, he enjoyed a reputation which permitted alumni of the college to assume correctly that he would also be sound on the question of free trade. Nonetheless, Perry's activities, both in the classroom and elsewhere, gave rise to the only serious threat to academic freedom during Hopkins' tenure. After the neighboring press indulged in attacks upon the college —the *Rutland Herald* charging that Williams had become "the

44. *Vidette, 8* (Sept. 16, 1871), 2.
45. *Ibid., 5* (Dec. 10, 1870), 106.
46. For Perry's publishing activities see "Recollections and Diaries," *2,* 582–610. Also, John Bascom, "Arthur Latham Perry," *Collections of the Berkshire Historical and Scientific Society, 3* (1899), 191–206.
47. None of these men studied under Perry. Wells, however, like Perry had been introduced to the virtues of free trade by Perry's predecessor at Williams, Professor Joseph Alden, of whom William Dwight Whitney had observed while he was an undergraduate in 1843: "He has exsplutterated on the tariff till all have wished that the doctrine of free trade had been made the subject of an eleventh commandment, so that the point would not have been disputable." Whitney to D. W. Marsh, Oct. 1, 1843; SML:YU, Whitney MSS. Whitney became a great Sanskrit scholar.

ally and propagandist of free trade" [48]—a committee of the junior
class prevailed upon John Z. Goodrich, a trustee and husband of a
cousin of Hopkins, to counteract Perry's teachings by delivering a
series of protectionist lectures at the college in the spring of 1870.
A majority of the Williams faculty refused to attend the lectures,
and many students resented the insult offered to Professor Perry
by the implication that he was either incompetent or deceitful in his
instruction.[49] That Perry was as convinced of the necessity for free
trade as was Mark Hopkins for temperance there can be no doubt,.
but students testified that he fairly and ably presented, in class, the
protectionist position of Horace Greeley.[50] Perry was appointed
to fill a newly-endowed professorship in political economy in 1870,
but the controversy never died altogether. In 1873 it was reported
that in Cleveland an organization of businessmen had been formed
to discourage young men from entering Williams College. Hopkins
appears to have taken a hands-off position, neither supporting his
objecting alumni nor openly and strongly defending Perry's
academic freedom.[51] He must have been instrumental, however, in
assigning the funds which endowed the professor's chair.

Perry, too, could boast a student following, and although neither
he nor Bascom seriously rivaled Hopkins in popularity or reputation, their following was justly deserved. Among the students who
found Perry more to their liking than Hopkins were James H.
Canfield, later chancellor of the University of Nebraska, and
Samuel Warren Dike, pioneer American sociologist. Other than
Bascom and Perry, however, Williams offered very little challenge
to the eminence accorded Hopkins as a teacher. The ultimate verdict which G. Stanley Hall, psychologist and president of Clark
University, passed upon his Williams education was probably exaggerated by time and embittered by age, but it gave an accurate
impression of the general conditions which prevailed in the Williams classroom. "Professor C. F. Gilson started a course in French
but became paralyzed before we had fairly begun," Hall recalled
of his experiences at Williams in the early 1860's.

The professor of natural history gave a brief course one term
and then was called away, so that we had almost no biology.
The professor of chemistry gave a few dozen demonstrations

48. As quoted in *Vidette, 4* (Nov. 27, 1869), 2.
49. See *Vidette, 4* (Apr. 2, 1870), 2, 6; (May 7, 1870), 4.
50. *Williams Quarterly, 17* (1869), 146; *Vidette, 6* (May 18, 1872), 158.
51. See E. B. Bigelow to MH (Jan. 30, 1869; HP, *4*) for evidence that Hopkins
supported the principle of free discussion in dealing with the Perry controversy.

and was the only man who taught in this way. He, too, left before the close of the course. There was no English literature save the little taught by the professor of rhetoric, who was far more interested in philosophy and economic questions. There was almost no physics, for the professor of natural philosophy was interested chiefly in astronomy.[52]

Above this wasteland towered Mark Hopkins.

The classroom was not everything, however, and as Hopkins had made clear in his inaugural address, it was not even to be considered the most important of the influences which might be brought to bear upon the formation of character. "It is pleasant to see young men study well," he once wrote, "but that is nothing to seeing them inquiring earnestly & practically what God placed them in the world for, & giving themselves up to do his will." [53] Accordingly, more was expected of the example an instructor might set than of the lectures he might give. The relations between faculty and students became, therefore, a subject of more frequent and sincere concern than did the curriculum, the selection of textbooks, or the presentation of lectures.

As early as 1828 a faculty meeting was devoted to a consideration of "the importance of being more familiar with the students." Only Mark's brother Albert seems to have registered any skepticism on that occasion. He observed, "There are certain invariable rules that I have laid down for the regulation of my conduct towards white & black & I don't know as students will form any exception." [54] Intimacy between faculty and students required a kind of artificiality, and it did not always succeed. Nonetheless, the character-forming objective of the college was surely aided when Mark Hopkins umpired a ball game, John Tatlock nursed a sick student, or John Bascom led an excursion to nearby Flora's Glen.

Together with many of the old ways, student-faculty relations suffered in the later years of the Hopkins era. New professors, lacking theological backgrounds and possessing graduate degrees, concerned themselves with scholarship and academic standards and thereby intruded a divisive element into what had been a more carefree relationship. As the character of the student body itself changed, as simple country boys were replaced by sophisticated city boys, the complaint was sometimes heard that the faculty

52. Hall, *Life and Confessions of a Psychologist*, p. 156.
53. MH to AL, Mar. 20, 1852; MHS, MH-AL MSS.
54. Albert Hopkins to MH, Jan. 4, 1828; HL, *3*.

lacked grace and charm.[55] A conscious fostering of faculty-student relationships continued, however, to be one of the official earmarks of the Williams scheme of education. In 1874 the board of trustees passed a resolution in which it respectfully requested "the gentlemen of the Faculty to exercise a fraternal and paternal interest in the students outside of the recitation rooms, and by cultivating personal relations with them, to promote their social and moral welfare." [56]

One further agency of education, in which both the president and his faculty participated, was discipline of conduct. Here, as elsewhere, the appeal was to character. Hopkins' administration inaugurated a new approach to discipline at Williams, one that depended upon student sympathy and respect, rather than law, for its success. Timothy Dwight at Yale and Eliphalet Nott at Union had already attempted to substitute kindness and understanding for punishment in dealing with student offenses against order and decency. Under Hopkins, Williams also abandoned a primary dependence upon law enforcement. Successive editions of the college laws displayed a decreasing dependence upon fines for the maintenance of good conduct; they became less detailed in their references to undergraduate crimes.

A rigorous and overzealous attention to law enforcement, however, had continued during the administration of Hopkins' predecessors, as evidenced by the bitter address which a member of the senior class delivered during the commencement activities of 1835. Smarting under what appears to have been unwarranted punishment, Alexander Hanson Strong, speaking before the faculty and trustees and commencement guests, announced with ill-concealed pleasure that he had decided to refuse his bachelor's degree.[57] The inauguration of Mark Hopkins in the following year had a great deal more to do with changing the method of law enforcement at Williams College than did Strong's commencement address. For Hopkins adhered to the belief that "that college is in the best state in which the least government is necessary." [58] Many years before,

55. *Williams Quarterly, 16* (1868), 55.
56. TR, *3*, 72; June 29, 1874.
57. Alexander H. Strong, *An Oration, Delivered before the Corporation and Faculty of Williams College, at the Adelphic Union Exhibition, July 15, 1835. Together with the Valedictory Address to the Adelphic Union Society* (n.d.), pp. 10–11. In 1855 John J. Ingalls, who later earned a reputation as an orator and as senator from Kansas, treated a commencement audience to a similar speech. Smarting under Hopkins' displeasure at his horn-tooting at a carriage of Pittsfield school girls, Ingalls launched an attack upon the faculty under the title of "Mummy Life."
58. MH, *An Inaugural Discourse, Delivered at Williams College, September 15, 1836,* p. 25.

Mark had written of his early experiences as a schoolmaster:
"When I remarked a scholar doing that which was slightly wrong,
if he did not know that I saw him I usually passed it by because a
punctilious exertion of authority in small matters is sure to destroy
it. A school master should therefore know when to see things and
when not." [59] Such a spirit, under Hopkins' influence, came to
dominate the Williams scene during his presidency.

Reflecting a democratic society in which respect for the individual was deep-seated, he led the college away from the strong discipline of an earlier day. Love and influence replaced fines and
prowling tutors. Offenses against good order were minimized rather
than magnified. Hopkins himself privately dealt with many students whose crimes thereby did not go before the faculty at its
weekly meetings. Although he frequently said that unruly students and problems of discipline were "the most unpleasant in-
gredient" in his office, forgetting perhaps his aversion to money-
raising, he succeeded in becoming a firm but kindly father to his
student body.[60] His comforting response to a student who had just
completed a lengthy and worried confession of being married was:
"Married are you! So am I." [61] On one occasion he is supposed to
have been left flat on his back on a darkened dormitory floor, clutch-
ing in each hand the coat of an unruly student. The two young
men, having been apprehended by Hopkins while creating a town-
disturbing ruckus, successfully bolted from the president's clutches
after assuring themselves of his identity by carefully feeling the
contours of his face, his balding head, and side whiskers. To some
college presidents the experience would have been a blow to executive dignity. For Hopkins, however, the experience was a demonstration of "the cool cunning of these level-headed rogues of whose
future success in life . . . I had not the slightest doubt." [62] Hopkins' approach to discipline strengthened the bond between faculty
and students, avoided a burdensome and unsuccessful attention to
petty misdemeanors, and inculcated in many undergraduates a
sense of independence and sometimes of responsibility.

Major infractions of college regulations, particularly if they
were openly committed, still had to be handled in the traditional
way. And even Hopkins was occasionally confronted by a student
whose sense of independence had been perhaps overdeveloped. Eye-
ing a disheveled student on a train which was carrying them both

59. MH to his brother, Harry Hopkins, Nov. 28 [1822?]; HP, Misc. Vol.
60. MH to AL, Dec. 20, 1847; MHS, MH-AL MSS.
61. John Bascom, "Mark Hopkins," p. 179.
62. *Berkshire Hills, 2* (1902), 809.

back to the Berkshires after a college holiday, Hopkins is reported to have exclaimed, "Been on a drunk!" And the student, it is said, replied with the manliness and independence so desired in a Williams undergraduate: "So've I." [63]

There can be little doubt that kindness and understanding were better calculated than fines and faculty courts to produce the kind of individual whom 19th-century America respected. Aided in execution by the smallness of the college, the evangelical character of the faculty, and the absence of transportation or much incentive to escape periodically from such influences, the Hopkins approach gave evidence of being both workable and rewarding.

As long as an all-pervading Christian influence outweighed the classroom in the Williams scheme of education, official manifestations of intellectual activity are difficult to discover on the Williams campus. The career of the college library is a convincing case in point. Between 1794 (when the first catalogue of the college library was published) and 1861 the number of volumes in the library increased from below 400 to approximately 10,000.[64] An undergraduate who suggested in 1858 that the majority of these books were "coeval with the foundation of the college" was guilty of exaggeration, but he was very close to the truth when he added that "our college library is a full century behind the wants of the present age." [65] Reflecting the evangelical character of the college, catalogues of its library seldom list books of merely secular interest; prejudices against fiction in the college library were not overcome until 1867, when sets of Scott and Dickens were permitted to join classical and religious works.[66]

The use of the library was severely limited. When the college was new, the library was opened one afternoon a week for seniors and juniors, one afternoon for sophomores and freshmen, and then only for the business-like charge and return of books. Not until 1868 were those regulations changed and the policy introduced of

63. *Williams Review, 2* (1872), 145. The story also turned up in the recently discovered diaries of Andrew D. White. See George H. Healey, "Librarian Finds Long-Sought Diaries of University's First President," *Cornell Alumni News, 53* (1951), 311.

64. The series of library catalogues, published irregularly beginning in 1794, generally under the title *Catalogue of Books in the Library of Williams College,* is a useful indicator of official intellectual interest. See also John Larson, "An Evaluation of Literary Societies and the Various Libraries of Williams College 1793–1875," MS course paper, WCL, 1952.

65. *Williams Quarterly, 5* (1858), 232 ff.

66. *Ibid., 14* (1867), 206.

permitting students to consult and read books in the library every day but Sunday.[67] The last orthodox barrier to library use crumbled in 1890, when the trustees authorized the opening of a reading room in the library on Sundays "as an experiment." [68]

The little, untended, and uninviting library of Williams College was as good as Mark Hopkins and his contemporaries needed to fulfill their purposes. They had discovered other, more suitable means with which to pursue the aims of the college. These other ways—the president's course in moral philosophy, a devout faculty, friendly relations between faculty and students, love and influence as a substitute for stringent discipline—aimed at the objective which Hopkins felt had been especially fulfilled in the case of one of his favorite students. Asked by a prospective biographer of James A. Garfield to give an estimate of the Garfield he had known, Hopkins responded, "He . . . did for himself what it is the object of a college to enable every young man to do—he made himself a *man*." [69]

67. *Ibid., 16* (1868), 123.
68. TR, *3,* 355; Oct. 24, 1890.
69. Copy of letter of Hopkins to Edmund Kirke, May 26, 1864; LC, Garfield Papers.

4. *"And a Student on the Other"*

"I KNEW NOTHING about the strength of my attachment [to Williams] till I came to part from it," a young alumnus wrote in a letter to a member of the senior class in 1842. "I love the college grounds, and the college buildings and the streets and the trees and the houses and the church, and the inhabitants and the streams and the fields & the beautiful mountains. . . . I love the faculty and the students and the members of our dear church. . . . That," William Henry Marsh concluded, "is the land . . . that I love best of all." [1] James K. Mills was hardly out of college before he, too, exercised the graduate's privilege of indulging in pleasant reminiscence. "The cigars we have smoked," he wrote to a classmate a month after their graduation in 1851, "are changed into light and fleecy clouds from which memory summons forth the beautiful lightening [*sic*] flashes of jokes and puns & wit." [2]

These young men who had sat on the other end of Mark Hopkins' log were already forgetting how confining the village had once seemed, or how, when they were sick, the country doctor's endless bleedings and blisterings had been almost too much to endure. They were forgetting the disappointment of no letter from home when the stage driver, entering the town at nightfall, galloped his horses through the village, "blowing his horn to call the students to the little post-office." [3] A multitude of happier memories cast a curtain over those homesick evenings when they had stood at their dormitory windows, looking out through the valley toward home. In time, they were to forget the feelings that prompted the observation, "Williamstown is shockingly lonely. . . . I suspect that they keep the girls tied up or that they stay abed all the while, it's so cold." [4] Unless they leafed through the yellowed pages of a diary, they forgot what it had been to be away from home, to be a freshman in a country college. "Oh, my Mother," a freshman confided to his diary on his second day at Williams in 1868, "now do I begin to appreciate your love and care in spending sleepless nights in

1. W. H. Marsh to Addison Ballard, July 5, 1842; WCL, Misc. MSS, *12*.
2. J. K. Mills to E. J. Peck, Sept. 12, 1851; WCL, Peck MSS.
3. Scudder, *Life and Letters of David Coit Scudder*, p. 50.
4. S. C. Armstrong to his family, Dec. 14, 1860, in Edith Armstrong Talbot, *Samuel Chapman Armstrong: A Biographical Study* (New York, Doubleday, Page, 1904), p. 45.

thinking up needful articles for your then unappreciative son to carry." [5]

But if they forgot, they also remembered. Alumni of the 1830's recalled the time of the smallpox epidemic when they scratched themselves with corn cobs to induce an itch and then petitioned the faculty for an immediate adjournment of college.[6] Others looked back to the year in the 1840's when the junior class took to calling its members after United States senators, and the sophomores followed suit by taking their names from members of the House of Lords.[7] At the New York dinners which became a fixture of alumni loyalty later in the century, old men smiled at the remembrance of their good fortune, as New Yorkers in the 1850's, to be dismissed from college two weeks early for the winter vacation so that they might catch the last steamer before the Hudson froze over.[8]

Surely Lyman Calkins of the Class of 1867 must have remembered snowballing in the halls, and Samuel Armstrong could not have forgotten the night when he was elected to the presidency of one of the literary societies and celebrated by treating his "chum" to dinner for the first time.[9] How could they forget the itinerant Jewish peddlers who bought their old clothes at the end of the college year? The breakfasts of woodpecker pot-pie and the dinners of oysters and clams? Moreover, if they forgot the winters, they remembered the summers. "Returning consciousness in the morning is warbled into freshness and life by the tones of a bird chorus," a student wrote in 1861. "A lovely feature of the country is the meadows, on every side, tinged with the purple clover blossoms, white daisies, and yellow buttercups." [10] They remembered the campus characters—Thomas Cox, self-styled "professor of dust and ashes," who for fifty years after 1817 endeared himself to students by simply and good-naturedly serving as a sort of college janitor; Abe Bunter, the remarkably thick-skulled Negro who for a fee would bunt his head goat fashion against a dormitory door;

5. Entry of Sept. 3, 1868, typescript, "Diaries of Marshall J. Hapgood, 1868–69"; WCL. Original MSS are in Wilbur Library, University of Vermont.
6. MH to Harry Hopkins, Dec. 25, 1831; HL, 5. The ruse apparently did not succeed.
7. Thomas Hyde to Mrs. A. H. Farrar, Mar. 25 [1844?]; WCL, Misc. MSS, 15.
8. William D. Porter, "Williams College: The Contrasts of Half a Century," *Reunion of Class of 1850, Williams College, 1900* (n.d.), p. 15.
9. Lyman Calkins to Julia [?], Feb. 8, 1864; MS in possession of Miss Marion Douglas, Westfield, N.J. S. C. Armstrong to Mrs. C. C. Armstrong, Jan. 16, 1862; in "Personal Memories and Letters of General S. C. Armstrong," pp. 58–61.
10. Armstrong to Clara Armstrong, June 1861; *ibid.*, pp. 58–61.

Daniel Pratt, who in the 1860's roamed from college to college
conducting a one-man campaign for the presidency, and another
Pratt named Bill who sawed wood, blacked stoves, and treated
students to nonsense-and-common-sense orations on the slightest
provocation. On some things, to be sure, their memories were
blurred, but on many occasions they summoned a host of remem-
brances like these in support of their love for a college which to
them had been very much more than the strictly official creature
over which Mark Hopkins presided.

A careless observer of American higher education would have
overlooked the college the students themselves had engrafted upon
the official system, which was a very small part of the total educational experience. We are the college, the students said, and year
by year they erected their own set of institutions and adopted their
own customs and established their own values as if to justify their
boast.

Somewhat characteristically of foreign observers, Thomas Colley Grattan, British consul at Boston from 1839 to 1846, mistook
Boston for America and Harvard for American higher education
during his brief sojourn in the United States. His published observations thus hardly succeeded in conveying an accurate impression either of young Americans or of their college experiences:

> Beginning in early youth, children show little or none of the
> mischievous vivacity so common in Europe. . . . The non-
> existence of these manly sports which make the young people
> of Europe so gay . . . is the main cause of that anxious and
> care-worn look which gives the Yankee his proverbially melan-
> choly air. . . . Every man is born middle-aged. The boys are
> sent to college at fourteen. They leave it, with their degrees at
> about seventeen. . . . Their college years offer no occupation
> to give either gracefulness or strength to body or mind. . . .
> They have no breadth, either of shoulders, information, or
> ambition.[11]

Had Grattan looked superficially at Williams he might have
come to many of the same conclusions, for quick study of the college catalogue and a too close attention to official utterances, laws,
and purposes would have led an observer as careless as he to con-

11. Thomas Colley Grattan, *Civilized America* (2d ed. London, Bradbury and
Evans, 1859), *2*, 313–20.

clude that the Williams experience was hardly worth calling an education. What he would have missed was the college of their own invention which American students turned to for breadth of educational experience.

Williams, in company with other American colleges, was largely a creation of its undergraduates because its character depended inescapably upon who its students were and what they did once they arrived in Williamstown. Self-satisfied governing bodies, resting comfortably upon the curricular developments of an earlier century, provided an atmosphere that invited student complaint. Undergraduate energy and ingenuity translated that complaint into an extracurriculum so vast in its scope and time-consuming in its demands that eventually the athletic teams, fraternities, clubs, and newspapers outbid the college itself for student and alumni loyalty. Eventually, too, the college was forced to succumb, enlarging its curriculum and expanding its activities in order to swallow various elements of the extracurriculum. The nature of the student body which fashioned a host of extracurricular interests out of its own energy and in line with its own sense of values underwent a marked change during the administration of Mark Hopkins. Largely because of that change, the extracurriculum grew apace.

Nathaniel Hawthorne, attending the commencement exercises of 1838, jotted into his notebook observations on some of the Williams students he saw there: "Country graduates—rough, brown-featured, schoolmaster looking, half-bumpkin, half-scholar figures, in black ill-cut broadcloth;—their manners quite spoilt by what little of the gentleman there was in them. . . . A rough hewn, heavy set of fellows from the hills and woods in this neighborhood; great, unpolished bumpkins, who had grown up as farmer-boys." [12] Yet a short twenty-five years later Samuel Warren Dike, a farmer's son from rural Connecticut, busily preparing for the commencement exercises of 1863, with difficulty prevailed upon his sister to attend his graduation: she did not want to expose him to the embarrassment which he might feel among his classmates in the presence of a "country sister." [13] Dike's response to his sister's protests was an inelegant "Bosh," a word which the "bricks" and "regular trumps" and "steedy, bleedy boys" among his classmates would have viewed with contempt. By the 1860's

12. *The American Notebooks by Nathaniel Hawthorne,* ed. Randall Stewart (New Haven, Yale University Press, 1932), pp. 47 ff.
13. Samuel W. Dike to "Sis," July 27, 1863; WCL, Misc. MSS, *14.*

country boys and country language, while still possible on the
William.s campus, were no longer setting the tone, as they had at
the commencement of 1838.

Among those who early realized that a change had taken place
was young Samuel Armstrong, son of a New England missionary
to the Hawaiian Islands. "While in college," he wrote to his
brother in 1861, "I wish to be dressed as well as the best. I find it
pleasanter to be received as an equal than to be looked upon as
out of my place. . . . With two thirds of the fellows in college,
style in dress is nothing, and as for them I could dress anyhow,
but the other third care much about fashion and are yet smart
fine and polished fellows—their society gives a man polish." [14] No
clearly-marked path of development led from the Williams of
Hawthorne's "great, unpolished bumpkins" to the Williams of
Armstrong's "smart fine and polished fellows." The change which
their observations suggest was almost imperceptible and, as far as
the college was concerned, both uninvited and uncontrolled.

Mark Hopkins must have noticed, as the years passed, how in-
frequently it became necessary at the opening of the college year
to make the kind of report which he had written in a letter to his
brother Harry in 1832. "Students are coming in, old and new,
fellows that you can tell as far as you can see them, for having come
out of the mountains," he had then written. "There is no use in
grumbling that we don't make gentlemen in colleges. If people
could see the quality of the wool we get I think they would give
us credit for pretty fair cloth." [15] Before long, however, he was
regretting the absence of mountain men. As early as 1846 he
admitted to a certain disappointment with the freshman class
until "three stout full grown men from the Western Reserve"
appeared in Williamstown asking for admission. "One of them
wore a coat of green flannel," he wrote to Amos Lawrence, suggesting that country fashions were already a mark of some uniqueness
on the Williams campus.[16] Hopkins harbored a respect for material success as well as for humble origins, and thus his joy upon
discovering rough-hewn sons of Ohio in his class one morning in
1846 was equaled in 1848 by his pleasure on finding among the
religious students of the college young men "whose family and
standing are equal to any in the country." [17] Both experiences

14. S. C. Armstrong to R. B. Armstrong, April 21, 1861; in "Personal Memories
and Letters of General S. C. Armstrong," pp. 51-2.
15. Sept. 3, 1832; HL, 5.
16. Oct. 19, 1846; MHS, MH-AL MSS.
17. MH to AL, Mar. 3, 1848; MHS, MH-AL MSS.

must have led him to the realization that men of humble origin were less apparent at Williams than they once had been.

Beginning in the 1850's, a rash of articles in student publications revealed the emergence of the concept of the fine gentleman which was being embedded in undergraduate mores. In 1853 an article, in almost unbelievable detail, told how to master the art of conversation and turn that mastery to social advantage.[18] Two years later John J. Ingalls, already equipped with that invective which later made him an asset to the Republican party, catalogued the characteristics of "A Brace of College Characters" whose ascendancy in the Williams social scale he deplored:

> All over the world may be found a class of bifurcate things, by courtesy called *men*, who measure gentility by the length of their coat tails, and whose intelligence . . . ought to be measured by the length of their ears. . . . As the lice and flies infested Egypt . . . these fashion-mongers infest the sacred precincts of the college. [They are characterized by an] attention to whiskers, driveling flirtations, kid gloves . . . the fashionable follies of wealth and dissipation . . . the slang of the turf, the billiard-saloon, and the brothel . . . the drawling languor of a puppyish exquisite.[19]

If Ingalls was right, a new definition of man was being written into the Williams dictionary. Certainly there was little relationship between man as presented in Mark Hopkins' course on moral philosophy and man as described by his future son-in-law at the Class Day exercises of 1862. On that occasion, John H. Denison sounded a great deal more like Oliver Wendell Holmes, the genial advocate of worldly know-how, than like his college president. Although not committing himself to this particular construction of man, young Denison suggested that its adherents among his classmates were many:

> He is neither a sneak, nor a hermit, nor a bigot, nor a dig, nor a bootlick to the Faculty, nor a seeker after the valedictory. He is genial, generous, humane, social. He knows how to behave in company, to get out of a bad scrape and into a good one; can adapt himself to the world, to circumstances, and the ladies. He does not care so much for college rank as for general information; for that which is arbitrary and

18. *Williams Quarterly, 1* (1853), 138–42.
19. John J. Ingalls, "A Brace of College Characters," *Williams Quarterly, 3* (1855), 9–12.

capricious as for that which is broadly and permanently useful. Above all, he is a perfect gentleman.[20]

Lord Chesterfield had said much the same thing with a great deal
more wit and charm in the 18th century, and more recently
Holmes, in America, had become an exponent of the Chesterfieldian
tradition of the fine gentleman. As a prescription for human behavior, however, John Denison's Class Day remarks were a far
cry from the pleas for humility, godliness, stewardship, and
sobriety which characterized the construction that Puritan New
England and official Williams had long placed upon the meaning
of gentleman.

By 1867 nothing seemed to symbolize quite so well what had
happened to the old rugged virtue and unpolished behavior as
the student who refused a chair because " 'he had not got his
sitting down pair on.' " [21] The day had surely come when Hopkins
no longer needed to worry about the uncouthness of Williams undergraduates. Granite had been displaced by marble—some of it
real, some of it synthetic, but all of it polished.

In almost any direction Hopkins could see evidence of the
changing complexion of his student body. Poor boys there were,
but never in such profusion as his predecessors had known. "Many
leave us thro' mere poverty," Ebenezer Fitch had written in 1799,
in explanation of a decline in enrollment.[22] "How shall we provide
for the increasing number of poor & pious youth who have their
eye toward our college?" Edward Dorr Griffin frantically asked
a member of his board of trustees in 1822.[23] As for Hopkins, he
was agitated by a similar concern for poor boys, but the compulsion to worry was less insistent. Enrollments increased steadily
until the Civil War years, from 119 in 1836 to 240 in 1859, although the funds for aiding needy students remained almost
stationary.

In 1836, when a year of tuition, room, and incidental college
charges came to $33, income from endowment available for student
aid amounted to $800. In 1860, with enrollment doubled and the

20. *Williams College, 1862: An Oration, by J. H. Denison, and A Poem, by J. A.
French, Delivered on Class Day, July 11, 1862. Together with a Brief Account of
the Exercises of the Day* (Troy, N.Y., A. W. Scribner, 1862), pp. 6–7. A useful study
is Edwin H. Cady, *The Gentleman in America,* Syracuse, Syracuse University Press,
1949.
21. James H. Canfield, "Editor's Table-Talk," *Williams Quarterly, 15* (1867), 66.
22. Ebenezer Fitch to Mason F. Cogswell, Jan. 13, 1799; WCL, Howe MSS.
23. Edward Dorr Griffin to Alvan Hyde, Jan. 28, 1822; WCL, Misc. MSS, *2.*

college bill up to $51, income for student aid had increased only slightly to $900.[24] A student body of 97 received $783 in direct assistance from the college in 1825; thirty years later an almost equal sum was shared by a student body of 224.[25] Clearly, the proportion of students able to pay their own way was increasing.

Rooming and boarding developments provided another index to the changing character of the student body.[26] Rates at the student boarding clubs, scattered throughout the homes of the village, moved steadily upward during the years of Hopkins' presidency, with no discernible effect upon enrollment before the Civil War. Although college dormitories provided the cheapest rooms in Williamstown—$4.50–$6.00 a year in 1836, $9.00 a year in 1866 —students increasingly moved into more expensive rooming houses in town. As enrollment moved upward, college facilities, which could accommodate between 130 and 140 students after 1842, became less and less adequate, and rather than build another dormitory, the college looked to the town. The percentage of students living in village homes, where the rates ranged from $20 to $50 a year, increased from 18 per cent in 1840 to 47 per cent in 1859. Necessity had at first dictated that students room beyond the confines of the college, but even after an enrollment decline set in during the 1860's, many students chose to pay the higher price of living outside the college. By 1861 the college was no longer able to fill its rooms, and yet 45 per cent of its students lived off the campus. In 1871, when dormitory capacity exceeded the total college enrollment, 40 per cent of the student body lived either in local rooming houses or in fraternity houses.

The trend toward extracollege housing undoubtedly reflected the desire of many students to escape from college order. It reflected as well an official lack of concern, initially for adequate college housing, later for the maintenance of a physical sort of college unity. In 1857, stepping into the breach left by insufficient dormitory space, the fraternities, with the building of a Sigma Phi chapter house, began to assume for themselves a responsibility which the college was apparently willing to forego. The voluntary exodus from the dormitories to rooming houses and fraternities also announced that the Williams student body was being drawn from a wealthier segment of society than it once had been. That the college itself was in some way responsible for the new tend-

24. These figures are found in appropriate numbers of the college catalogue.
25. TR, 2, 60; Sept. 6, 1825.
26. The statistics and information on housing contained in this paragraph have been derived from the college catalogues for the years in question.

encies even Hopkins knew. In 1852, when all college rooms were
filled, he wrote to Amos Lawrence, "The effect will be to raise the
price of rooms in town . . . & drive away poor students." [27]
Ironically, the new housing which the fraternities began to provide in 1857 was exactly the kind which also seemed to invite
poor boys to stay away from Williams.

The college itself began to reflect the change. For one thing,
as early as 1854 an old college custom by which recipients of
official honors informally and simply treated their classmates had
been transformed into the "marshalls' treat," a sometimes rather
elaborate dinner paid for by two elected members of the class.[28]
Significant also is the 1858 report of the editor of the student
magazine that some undergraduates were paying as much as $300
a year for horse hire.[29] The next year an undergraduate writer
complained that poor students could no longer accept appointments to speak at commencement, finding themselves unable to
pay their customary share of the mounting expenses, which included orchestras imported from Boston or New York at a cost of
six to eight hundred dollars.[30] In the 1850's some students were
able to hire Bill Pratt to saw wood for them, a chore which had
once served as a common denominator of student life.[31]

Close observers noticed, too, that the average age of the graduating classes was being lowered, reflecting a corresponding decline in the number of students whose college education was postponed by economic necessity. The average age of the Class of
1810 at graduation was twenty-three years and three months; of
the Class of 1865, twenty-two years and three months; the percentage of very young boys and of very old boys also decreased,
more and more students receiving their diplomas in the twenty-one
to twenty-two age range. In 1835, 25 per cent of the graduates
were in the 21–22 age range; in 1855, 33 per cent; and in 1865,
close to 50 per cent.[32] Here, too, was a reflection of the new
economic and social sources of the Williams student body. As a
student writer suggested in 1872, "Collegiate education . . .
gives . . . a polish and refinement which marks the college-bred

27. July 29, 1852; MHS, MH-AL MSS.
28. See B. H. Hall, *A Collection of College Words and Customs* (Cambridge,
Mass., John Bartlett, 1856), p. 306.
29. TR, *2*, 338; Aug. 4, 1856. *Williams Quarterly, 5* (1858), 378.
30. *Williams Quarterly, 7* (1859), 188. Derick L. Boardman to George S. Boardman, July 3, 1841; WCL, Boardman MSS.
31. Porter, "Williams College," p. 19.
32. Age statistics are based upon biographical information contained in Durfee,
Williams Biographical Annals.

man wherever you find him. . . . The wealthy, with this end in view, send their sons from home with every facility and, as a consequence, they enter and graduate young." [33]

Uncontrolled and uninvited though these changes were, they made a steady advance during the Hopkins administration. Among other things, they underlined the failure of the college to become a neighborhood institution. In the years after 1836 the boys from Williamstown and Pittsfield were overwhelmed by ever larger numbers from New York, Brooklyn, Albany, and Troy. After 1848, New Yorkers increasingly outnumbered boys from Massachusetts.[34] Rural villages which dotted the catalogue of students in 1836 disappeared from the catalogue of 1871: Hancock, Belchertown, Peru, Manchester, Shelburn, Dalton, Schoharie, Stoddard. They were replaced by Philadelphia, Columbus, Cincinnati, Indianapolis, Chicago, Detroit, and St. Louis.

The proliferation of regional colleges elsewhere and the peculiar geographic relationship of Williams to eastern New York conspired to shift the sources of its student body from rural to urban areas, from impoverished farms to the business centers where money in America was being made. This shift not only helped to solve the old college problem of undergraduate manners but also introduced a scale of living and set of values out of character with those to which the college itself was dedicated. Although many young men who went to Williams were well equipped to destroy, or at least undermine, the hold of traditional values, ironically their enrollment at the college was frequently occasioned by the steadfastness with which the college held to the old virtues. Many were the young men whose fathers looked to Mark Hopkins and

33. *Vidette, 6* (June 22, 1872), 181.
34. Comparative enrollment figures for New York and Massachusetts are based upon the college catalogues.

	New York	Mass.	Total College Enrollment
1836	31	43	119
1840	51	59	155
1844	50	59	155
1848	70	54	179
1851	81	61	208
1855	79	69	224
1859	89	76	240
1867	68	53	182
1871	50	20	119

Amherst, on the other hand, depended largely upon Massachusetts for its enrollment. In 1859, 140 of its 242 students were from Massachusetts. *University Quarterly, 1* (1860), 161.

Williams College to administer to whatever ills had overcome
their city-bred sons. Unquestionably what had been in 1836 a
college for poor aspiring clergymen had become, by 1872, an
institution strongly marked by wealth, fashion, city manners, and
all the other requirements of worldly success. At the center of
this transformation, guiding it with their every skill and effort,
were the students.

"They have no breadth, either of shoulders, information, or
ambition," Thomas Colley Grattan, the British consul, had said,
generalizing from too little information on the nature of the
American college student. A close inspection of Williams College,
a more typical manifestation of higher education in the United
States than Harvard or Yale, would have provided him with suitable materials for equally pungent criticism, but not along the
same lines. For the Williams undergraduate and his contemporaries elsewhere, less willing than Grattan to confuse an official
pattern with the real thing, anticipated each of Grattan's complaints by taking matters into their own hands.

If their shoulders were not so broad as Grattan may have wished,
they were nonetheless as broad as time and money would permit. A
sense of worldly ambition and an almost pagan respect for the
human body finally tipped the scales in favor of muscular ambition and introduced organized athletics and intercollegiate competition to the American campus. Until then, however, breadth
of shoulders was the birthright of a Williams undergraduate. A
foreign observer might overlook the statistics which showed that
the boys at country colleges, instead of entering at fourteen, were
more likely to enroll at twenty. Men on the ground were able
enough, on the other hand, to recognize in an advanced entering
age a familiar story—the ambition of a farm boy for learning,
the postponed departure from home until a younger brother could
take his place in the fields, the years devoted to assembling a purse
large enough to make that departure possible. When Williams
undergraduates began to take fewer muscles and fewer years to
college, they more readily subscribed to Grattan's insistence upon
a devotion to playful sports. And then, with a zeal that surpassed
their British contemporaries and left many college presidents
gasping, they broadened their shoulders, some would say, at the
expense of mind and spirit.

A concern for the conscious development of muscle and for the
enjoyment of sport, however, was not attended by any indiffer-

ence to breadth of information or ambition. To Grattan the American college curriculum may justifiably have seemed narrow and stifling. If college students had been satisfied to suffer its confinements, his charge against their ambition and enterprise would have been warranted. He may be excused for not altogether understanding the struggle which was taking place upon American college campuses between the values he—and the students—cherished and the values which the college with diminishing success tried to enforce. He may even be pardoned for looking into the room of an American college student and not finding there the polished, worldly, carefree English gentleman he may have found at Oxford or at Cambridge. His blindness to the pervasiveness and the significance of the extracurriculum was, however, inexcusable.

Convinced that the curriculum by itself was impractical and circumscribing, college students everywhere exhibited characteristic independence and ingenuity by doing something about it.[35] "He finds no sphere within the limits of which he can apply his knowledge to practical purposes as he acquires it" was a characteristic lament for the student's life heard in Williamstown in 1832.[36] "This is an age of utility," wrote another in 1854. "Everything must be reduced to the standard of dollar and cents," he continued, demonstrating that even a study of the ancient languages could lead to financial success.[37] His defense of the classics, however, was unconvincing to one of his fellow students. "The time is gone forever," wrote Edward Isham, "when the languages . . . can be of direct practical utility. . . . The classic tongues are becoming useless. . . . Rules of Prosody will hardly assist . . . in the counting-room." [38] In his happy selection of a metaphor in 1861 another student revealed his American character. "The object of education is first to construct good machinery," he wrote. "Secondly, to gain motive power. It is only through these very wheels and ropes and pullies that we can accomplish anything in the great machine shop." [39]

Despite an inherent interest in the usefulness of what he was doing, the Williams student consciously prepared himself for

35. Thomas Hyde to James Farrar, Oct. 17, 1843; WCL, Misc. MSS, *15*. C. A. Stoddard, "Williams College Improved," *Williams Quarterly, 1* (1853), 64–8. Entry of Apr. 23, 1869; typescript, "Diaries of Marshall J. Hapgood, 1868–69"; WCL.
36. *Adelphi, 1* (1832), 1.
37. *Williams Quarterly, 2* (1854), 118–24.
38. *Ibid., 4* (1856), 179–81.
39. *Ibid., 9* (1861), 48.

more than a machine-shop world. "If the world is a stage, college is its green room; and few appear upon the boards the worse for having been behind the scenes," an undergraduate wrotè in 1865. "It is because the student can here learn men and manners, customs and conventionalities, that makes college the great educator," he concluded.[40] With equal understanding, a classmate added, "Let us hasten to learn that college is not so much the educator as [are] college boys [themselves]." [41]

The education which college boys provided for themselves at Williams during the years of Mark Hopkins' administration was not, however, merely a product of their search for the practical. For them the curriculum was also culturally limited. The extracurriculum which they set down next to the curriculum was therefore generous in the opportunity it gave for the development of those refinements of mind and manner which the college itself neglected. The 19th-century college student, born too soon to experience the gravitation of authority and of action to college administrators, was left free to devise a college to his liking. His ambition, whetted by the poverty of the curriculum and of the college plant, ran rampant at a place like Williams. His energy and his healthy zest for life, held in rein by a sober evangelical orthodoxy, broke through official restraints. The success of what he did and the force of his argument, in time, recommended themselves to the college itself. Until that day, however, he was busy recreating the college to meet his own demands, testing his ingenuity, displaying his independence, developing his sense of responsibility.

The extracurricular jewels of Mark Hopkins' undergraduate days and of the college which he inherited from Edward Dorr Griffin in 1836 were the literary societies, Philologian and Philotechnian, which were coeval in origin with the founding of the college. Few American colleges lacked a pair of these clubs, in which debates and literary exercises and exhibitions compensated for the dearth of literary and political material in the curriculum. As late as 1854 a student at Williams voiced the no longer universal opinion that the literary societies constituted "the most important part of the college course. Without the discipline they impart, the remaining studies are as nothing, and this discipline alone can make a man of influence." [42]

40. *Ibid., 13* (1865), 136–8.
41. *Ibid., 13* (1865), 56–61.
42. *Ibid., 2* (1854), 75 ff.

By 1854, however, the students had found a host of substitutes for the old literary societies. The Adelphic Union, the parent society, the name of which the two societies took when acting together, continued to exhibit their accomplished orators and to invite prominent men to address them. In the 1850's their commencement speakers included Rufus Choate, Ralph Waldo Emerson, Henry Ward Beecher, Edwin P. Whipple, and Wendell Phillips. The subjects which their members chose for orations and disputes continued to reveal an interest in literature and politics which was not satisfied by the curriculum. Student speakers in 1836 discoursed on "Bulwer and Irving," the British and American authors, and on "Gen. William H. Harrison," the unsuccessful Whig candidate for the presidency that year.[43] In the 1850's their meetings were agitated by timely consideration of slavery, social inequality, and solitary confinement as a method of imprisonment. Except in their libraries, however, the vitality which the societies had once known entered upon a steady and permanent decline throughout the Hopkins era.[44]

With the various local organs of evangelical orthodoxy they had symbolized the extracurricular needs of a simple, country college. They had punctuated a dreary college calendar with debates and orations and lectures. They were, however, inadequate to the needs of the fine gentleman to whose station Williams students increasingly aspired. First secret societies, and then organized athletics, captured the student enthusiasm which once had been devoted almost wholly to Philologian and Philotechnian. At the same time that these new institutions were ministering to the social and physical desires of the Williams undergraduate, new and more satisfactory institutions also appeared to appease his thirst for a kind of knowledge which the college neglected. Only in their libraries were the literary societies relatively unchallenged, either by the college or by new student institutions. For in this area they happily provided tools which served the intellect—which the college would serve only incidentally—and tools which met the demands

43. From a program of the 1836 exhibition; WCL, Scrapbook of Adelphic Union Programs.
44. This decline is reflected in frequent criticisms, reports of lowered attendance at meetings, and the fears of old graduates that the college societies were no longer what they once were. See *Williams Quarterly, 8* (1861), 192–6, 212; *9* (1862), 292; *15* (1867), 81–2; *15* (1868), 234; *Vidette, 5* (Mar. 18, 1871), 181, and *6* (Sept. 16, 1871), 2, 3–6. Secret societies, college journalism, and the duties of the curriculum were generally given as reasons for the decline of the literary societies. Similar developments were taking place elsewhere. A Yale student in 1860 attributed their decline in New Haven to class fraternities and other attractions. *University Quarterly, 1* (1860), 120, 124.

of fashion, demands which the student body was ready to answer.

James A. Garfield was able to read the works of Cooper and Dickens in the 1850's because the library of his literary society, not that of the college, welcomed American and English fiction.[45] The Saturday night reading club to which G. Stanley Hall, Francis Lynde Stetson, Hamilton Wright Mabie, and Sanford Dole belonged in the late 1860's fed upon the offerings of the literary societies—Emerson, Carlyle, Coleridge, Wordsworth, and Dante.[46] In 1861 the two literary societies owned over eight thousand books, most of them much more in harmony with student tastes than those to be found among the approximately equal number of books in the college library. Until the decade of the 1860's the student libraries acquired most best-sellers of the day, as well as new and less popular works of fiction by native authors.[47]

In their self-appointed task of garnishing the log the society libraries were aided by the Lyceum of Natural History, which offered a library as one aspect of its earnest pursuit of science. In 1860 a group of students organized a reading room where members were supplied with current periodicals—*Harper's*, the *Atlantic*, and *Leslie's*—and with Boston, Springfield, Troy, New York,

45. Smith, *The Life and Letters of James Abram Garfield, 2,* 97–8.

46. Hall, *Life and Confessions of a Psychologist,* pp. 160–1. Contrary to what Americans have liked to think of boys who spend their Saturday nights in anything so unrobust as a reading club, this group did amazingly well for itself. Hall founded the *American Journal of Psychology* and was the first president of Clark University. Stetson, as personal counsel for the elder J. P. Morgan, handled the legal arrangements which led to the creation of the United States Steel Corporation, and is also credited with first suggesting the use of no par value stock. Mabie was an eminent literary critic and editor of the *Outlook*. Dole, the son of an American missionary to Hawaii, combined a career on the bench with revolutionary activity and became the first governor of the Territory of Hawaii. See appropriate entries in the *Dictionary of American Biography* for biographical sketches.

47. Wyllis E. Wright, librarian of Williams, has tested the literary society catalogues against best-seller lists for the 19th century and has come up with the following statistics:

Years	Number of Generally Recognized Best-Sellers	Number of Best-Sellers Acquired by Literary Societies
1800–09	7	5
1810–19	17	15
1820–29	21	19
1830–39	27	20
1840–49	26	19
1850–59	42	28
1860–69	40	14
1870–79	17	4
1880–99	85	8

and Louisville newspapers.[48] Benefiting from the interest in news created by the Civil War, the reading room eventually placed greater demands upon the time and energy of its student managers than they could afford to spare from either classroom or other phases of the extracurriculum. In 1870 the reading room was abandoned, but the next year the college trustees were confronted with a student petition that they do something to fulfill a need for which the students could no longer adequately provide.[49] In 1867 the senior class began to fill the gaps in the college library with graduation gifts of the works of established authors. The Class of 1867 set the precedent with Thackeray; the Class of 1869 followed with Cooper.[50] In such ways, the Williams undergraduate forced books—the symbols of both fashion and intellect—upon a college whose president once said to one of his professors, "You read books: I don't read any books; in fact I never did read any books." [51]

The undergraduate intellectual and the aspiring gentleman were certainly not new student types at Williams. Aaron Whitney Leland of the Class of 1808 had written and published a student-produced play in which dramatic poetry and carnage were neatly blended. Simeon Howard Calhoun of the Class of 1829 had presided over what must have been a daring kind of dilettante's salon.[52] During the decades of Hopkins' administration the Lelands and the Calhouns multiplied, testifying in part to the shift which was taking place in the sources of the Williams enrollment. The ascendancy of the intellectual and of the gentleman also affirmed the gradual emancipation of mind and behavior from the bonds of religious orthodoxy, and the increasing concern which young men felt for the manners and matters of this world, for the opportunities with which an abundant America enticed them. New extracurricular developments reflected far-reaching intellectual and social changes taking place beyond Williamstown, particularly in the cities where mind and manner won their most significant victories over the old orthodoxy and the old simplicity and where American character was being redefined.

48. *Williams Quarterly, 8* (1860), 64; *9* (1861), 69; *10* (1862), 67; *11* (1863), 140; *11* (1864), 218–19; *13* (1865), 63; *13* (1865), 146; *Vidette, 5* (Nov. 26, 1870), 81.
49. TR, *3, 43;* June 26, 1871. The petition was referred to resident trustees, in whose hands it apparently languished.
50. *Williams Quarterly, 14* (1867), 246; *18* (1869), 45–6.
51. Perry, *Williamstown and Williams College,* p. 504.
52. Aaron Whitney Leland, *The Fatal Error, a Tragedy: Exhibited at Williams College March 25, 1807*, Pittsfield, Mass., Seymour and Smith, 1807. Samuel Irenaeus Prime, *Autobiography and Memorials,* ed. Wendell Prime (New York, Anson D. F. Randolph, 1888), pp. 167–8.

In consciously aping the urban culture which was slowly destroying cherished customs and attitudes, the Williams student fashioned an extracurriculum patterned after a set of characteristic
city institutions—the literary journal, the art museum, the or-
chestra, and the theater. For many years these institutions had
symbolized for the pious the wickedness and the temptations of the
world. At Williams they had been officially banned, on the assumption that they represented a surrender to frivolity and worldliness
inappropriate to sound Christian character, or purposely neglected
on the generally accepted assumption that hard-working men
could not afford to waste time upon them.

John Bascom, it is true, had been able to insinuate English literature into the curriculum under the guise of rhetoric, but the students went beyond him. Literary journals appeared but briefly in
1831 and 1844 and with the arrival of the *Williams Quarterly* in
1853 were permanently established in the extracurriculum. By
1870 the literary life at Williams could boast three competing
journals. All of these undergraduate excursions into belles lettres
revealed an indebtedness to influences which the college in no way
encouraged. A writer for the *Adelphi* in 1831 singled out Thomas
Jefferson, Hugh Henry Brackenridge, Benjamin Franklin, and
James Fenimore Cooper as stars in the American literary firma-
ment, at a time when neither Brackenridge nor Cooper had been
permitted space in the college library.[53] When John A. French used
the columns of the *Quarterly* in 1862 to complain of the absence of
Chaucer in the Williams curriculum, eyebrows were undoubtedly
raised in faculty circles. Yet his criticism was a clear indication of
the kind of problem which secular and urban tendencies were
forcing upon the administrators of orthodox rural colleges:

> When our first parents fell they betook themselves to fig-leaves,
> and it has been a characteristic of their descendants ever since,
> that the lower they fall the more figleaves they put on. . . .
> Give us plain truth in plain words, as old Chaucer gives it in
> his Parson's Tale; for if there is anything we utterly detest,
> it is the mock modesty of an age that in secret does deeds to
> make angels weep, and yet calls a leg, a limb, and clamors for
> an expurgated edition of the good old Anglo Saxon Bible.[54]

The *Quarterly*, while clearly voicing criticism of the college
curriculum, was as well a vehicle for the kind of practical and

53. *Adelphi, 1* (1831), 76–7.
54. John A. French, "Chaucer," *Williams Quarterly, 9* (1862), 239–40.

worldly experience which Williams undergraduates looked upon as excellent preparation for life. The ingenuity and enterprise with which they conducted a series of literary and news journals was likewise displayed in other publishing endeavors. Mark Hopkins owed a debt of gratitude to student initiative and salesmanship for the publication and distribution of many of his sermons and addresses. In 1847 two undergraduates wrote and published the first history of the college.[55] "It was taken up of their own heads entirely, and not seen beforehand by any of us," Hopkins wrote at the time of its publication, adding that he had not had time to read it but supposed it was well done.[56] In 1853, too, the sophomore class undertook the publication of the *College Index*, which assembled between its covers a record of the college year and a guide to student extracurricular life. In 1857 the sophomores passed the *Index* along to the junior class, which changed its name to *Gulielmensian*.[57]

Other urban institutions joined literary and publishing enterprises in the life of extracurricular Williams. Until the early 1850's, music at Williams was under the care of the Handel and Haydn Society, a student choir which provided sacred music at college functions beginning late in the 18th century.[58] In 1829 the trustees prohibited instrumental music at commencement as an unseemly and extravagant expense and in subsequent years did nothing to encourage contemporary secular music.[59] In 1854, however, nine students who had found a teacher outside the college staff presented themselves at a concert in the Mansion House as the Amateur's Philharmonia. Their instrumental and vocal program was drawn from the cheerful and melodic work of Josef Labitzky, Giuseppe Verdi, and Franz Schubert.[60] In 1858 a college singing group was organized as the Mendelssohn Society, and early in the 1860's a rash of class quartets and informal singing and instrumental groups broke out.[61] In their concerts, in Williamstown and as far away as Brooklyn, these groups revealed the

55. David Ames Wells and Samuel H. Davis, *Sketches of Williams College*, Springfield, Mass., H. S. Taylor, 1847.
56. MH to AL, June 15, 1847; MHS, MH-AL MSS.
57. *Williams Quarterly*, *4* (1857), 287.
58. Wells and Davis, p. 68.
59. TR, *2*, 103; Sept. 1, 1829.
60. Program, "Soirée of the Amateur's Philharmonia of Williams College"; WCL, Scrapbook.
61. *Williams Quarterly, 6* (1858), 36–40; *6* (1859), 381; 7 (1859), 190; 7 (1860), 287; *8* (1861), 213; *9* (1861), 69; *10* (1862), 68; *12* (1864), 141; *12* (1865), 288–93, 302–3; *17* (1870), 292–3. *Vidette, 4* (Oct. 9, 1869), 2.

new respect which Williams undergraduates held for music, both
instrumental and vocal, and for trained masculine voices.

The outbreak of music at Williams in the 1850's, including the
undergraduate publication of the first college song book in 1859,
revealed the willingness of the Williams undergraduate to be
merry with his voice, to shake off the shrouds which orthodoxy
had wrapped around cheerful music.[62] Welcoming the example
which had been set in American cities after 1848 by German singing groups in the wake of the new immigrations, the Williams undergraduate succeeded in erecting another monument to his growing sense of respect for polished attainment and secular learning.
A similar career was experienced at Williams by those other ancient
symbols of temptation and of sin—those other ornaments of urban
culture: art and the theater. In 1860 a drama group of fourteen
undergraduates organized themselves into a Thalian Association.
Within two years, having changed its name to the Thespian Club,
it was joined by other informal groups which met to read plays
and present amateur performances. In 1872 the sophomore class
presented "Sampson Agonistes, or Virtue Rewarded." The tendency toward satire was irresistible, and by 1882 it was necessary
for the trustees to announce that it was not desirable for students
to give minstrel shows.[63]

No student enterprise was more ambitious than the Williams
Art Association, an organization—apparently the first of its kind
in American colleges—which in 1858 took as its purpose the advancement of art at Williams. Under the leadership of a group of
students influenced by the work of John Ruskin, who was cultivating a revival of art interest in England, the Art Association
endeavored to live up to the demands of one of its founders who
wrote in the *Quarterly* in 1858, "What we want is a good collection
of paintings which shall furnish food for thought, and give lessons
in refinement." [64] Before its collections were turned over to the col-

62. *Songs of Williams,* ed. Washington Gladden, New York, Baker and Godwin,
1859.

63. *Williams Quarterly, 7* (1860), 287; *9* (1862), 294; *19* (1872), 86. TR, *3,* 189,
July 1, 1882.

64. *Williams Quarterly, 5* (1858), 332–3. The early undergraduate leaders of this
group included Horace E. Scudder—who achieved a notable career as editor for
Houghton, Mifflin and Co. and the *Atlantic Monthly*—and S. G. W. Benjamin, son
of an American missionary to Constantinople, who even before entering Williams
had sent acceptable drawings of the Crimean War to the *London Illustrated News.*
Benjamin later became a successful marine painter and author and was the first
United States minister to Persia. The career of the Williams Art Association may
be followed in the *Williams Quarterly, 5* (1858), 381; *6* (1858), 95; *6* (1858), 188–9;
6 (1859), 283; *7* (1859), 65–74, 96; *7* (1859), 167–71; *7* (1860), 251–3, 287; *8* (1860),

lege in 1870, the association succeeded in assembling engravings of the work of Landseer, Raphael, Turner, Delaroche, Murillo, Church, and Faed, and in laying the foundations of a modest art library. It exhibited the work of its own members, including a "Street Scene in Constantinople" and an undergraduate's design for a new college gymnasium. The problems of operating an art gallery—some original works were also on exhibition—proved to be too much for the students to manage by themselves, and when their genuine Murillo turned out to be a fraud, they abandoned the cause.

While it lasted, however, the Association helped to overcome the fears which Washington Gladden had expressed in extending the *Quarterly's* welcome to the Art Association and the Mendelssohn Society in 1858. "There is great danger that back here, with only mountains and bears for our companions," he wrote, "we shall acquire such a ravenous love for nature that we shall neither be fit for refined society, nor capable of enjoying . . . the 'pleasures of taste.' " Its work fitted neatly into the new extracurricular pattern. As a *Quarterly* editor remarked in 1861, the Williams Art Association was providing an experience which was necessary if undergraduates expected to associate with cultivated people.[65] As for the college, the answer to a question posed by a student in 1870 was a long time coming: "When is Williams College to have a Professorship of the Fine Arts?" [66] Richard Austin Rice was appointed to a professorship of art and history of civilization at Williams College in 1903.

Foreigners and natives surveying the American scene have been impressed by the capacity and penchant of Americans for organization. No other people, it has seemed, has joined so many clubs or organized for so many purposes. Explanations for this phenomenon, although not so plentiful as its manifestations, have nonetheless been suggestive: loneliness, enforced either by the desolateness of frontier life or the unfriendliness of cities, spawned the fraternal orders and the service clubs; a necessity for order and dispatch, required by the challenge of an unexploited continent, led to American achievements in corporate organization;

65; *8* (1861), 209; *9* (1861), 69; *9* (1862), 292; *10* (1862), 67; *11* (1863), 65; *11* (1864), 218; *11* (1864), 285; *12* (1865), 301–2; *13* (1865), 63; *14* (1867), 249; *16* (1869), 268. See also *Vidette, 4* (June 18, 1870), 2.

   65. *Williams Quarterly, 6* (1858), 188; *9* (1861), 141.

   66. *Vidette, 4* (Feb. 5, 1870), 4.

the prestige which adhered to the law and to lawyers as a consequence of ample experience in constitution making was transferred to everyday life: everywhere there was a respected or aspiring lawyer who knew parliamentary procedure and could write a constitution; the democratic right of every American to be heard found a convenient and fruitful resting place in organized causes. All of these explanations help to account for the ease and the readiness with which Williams undergraduates turned to one organizational form or another to express their desires and their scale of values.

By 1826 the sophomore class had taken possession of the Fourth of July, turning its celebration over to the student Anti-slavery Society, the first in Massachusetts.[67] The next year the day was shared with an undergraduate Temperance Society, and as late as 1854 the sophomores functioned as the self-appointed caretakers of patriotism and antislavery sentiment on the Williams campus.[68]

Beginning in 1857, annual birthday parties for Ephraim Williams—sponsored and eventually endowed by Nathan Jackson, a benefactor who understood students well—became a tribute to their capacity for turning a simple idea into an elaborate occasion. To the supper which Jackson contributed they added mirthful toasts and speeches, including a grateful speech in 1860 on "the lady that wouldn't have Colonel Williams!"

Class suppers and a multitude of other class functions were characteristic student enterprises. Creating a bond among classmates, providing a central authority for carrying out the majority will, the formal class organization became an institution to which students readily attached themselves. The sophomores' "Burial of Euclid"—a custom apparently imported from Yale early in the history of Williams—offered an escape from college routine by way of an elaborate ceremonial in which a hole was bored through a battered copy of Euclid in order that the students might at last see through the problems of geometry, and the book was finally cremated on a funeral pyre in order that light might at last be thrown upon the subject.[69] The appearance of class caps in 1845, the custom of wearing badges of mourning for deceased classmates,

67. See Leverett W. Spring, *A History of Williams College* (Boston, Houghton Mifflin, 1917), pp. 139–40; and Alice Dana Adams, *The Neglected Period of Antislavery in America (1808–1831)* (Boston, Ginn, 1908), pp. 140–1. Programs for the celebrations, 1829–43, may be found in WCL. Two early products of the society's activities are William Pitt Palmer, *Poem, Spoken July 4, 1828, before the Antislavery Society of Williams College*, Williamstown, Ridley Bannister, 1828; and Giles B. Kellogg, *An Oration Delivered July 4, 1829, before the Anti-slavery Society of Williams College*, Williamstown, Ridley Bannister, 1829.

68. *Williams Quarterly, 2* (1854), 93.

69. Hall, *College Words and Customs*, pp. 41–6.

the introduction in 1859 of a Freshman Wake at which farewells were sung and drunk to the freshman year, the adoption of Class Day by the seniors in 1861—these were the studied directions which class activity took during the Hopkins years.[70]

Class spirit was frequently diverted into damaging college rows and into acrimonious pamphlets attacking members of other classes.[71] Eventually class spirit was greatly dissipated by the growth of college spirit, benefiting from the development of intercollegiate athletic competition, and by the ascendancy of those smaller pockets of loyalty, the fraternities. For many years, however, the class and the class meeting and the campaign for class political office remained at the center of undergraduate experience. Washington Gladden wrote, in the *Quarterly* of 1859, "Class attachments are peculiarly strong. . . . It is one of the great animating forces of college life, and serves an important purpose, both in stimulating to labor and in restraining from transgression." [72] Two years later another student writer referred to the class meeting as "the safety-valve of college life." [73] Entries in the minute book of the Class of 1856 verify the accuracy of these student observations:

June 5, 1854   The class treasurer was authorized to receive as compensation 5 per cent of all money paid into the treasury.

June 13, 1854   It was voted to take action "tonight" against William Mosby McLain, the freshman "who threw the egg into the Sophomore recitation room."

June 15, 1854   A committee was appointed to ask Mark Hopkins if the West College hydrant could be repaired "so as to supply water."

June 20, 1854   A committee was appointed to suggest a coat of arms for the class.

June 22, 1854   A letter was read from Horace Greeley, explaining the origin of false reports on the

70. *Williams Monthly Miscellany, 1* (1845), 464. *Williams Quarterly, 1* (1854), 288; *7* (1860), 288; *8* (1860), 137, 144; *12* (1864), 142; *15* (1868), 308–9.

71. See especially *The Sophomore*, Boston, Boston Tract Society, 1871. This pamphlet, published by the Class of 1873, attacks the Classes of 1872 and 1874.

72. Washington Gladden, "College Life in America," *Williams Quarterly, 6* (1859), 197.

73. *Williams Quarterly, 8* (1861), 225–32.

conduct of Williams students on Mountain Day, recently printed in the *Tribune*.

July 17, 1854   Janitorial care of the sophomore recitation room was awarded to the lowest bidding member of the class, who won the post with a bid of $44.00.

July 20, 1854   A committee was appointed to confer with the faculty on the elimination of the biennial examinations on subjects studied during freshman and sophomore years.

October 3, 1855   An invitation from the senior class of Amherst College to attend the christening of a mountain near Shelburne Falls was accepted.

May 30, 1856   An engraver and artist were commissioned to produce a portrait of Mark Hopkins, for the sum of eighty dollars plus one half of the traveling expenses of the artist.[74]

The reaction of the subject of that portrait to this obvious expenditure of time and energy upon the extracurriculum was a mixture of skepticism and approval. As student initiative and enterprise introduced some new custom or spawned some new institution, he greeted the changes which they implied with reservation. Good and evil, he felt, attended every innovation. He could not stem the tide that flooded the campus with symbols of an outside world which increasingly pressed closer upon the college. He could maintain the old faith, the old curriculum, the old virtues, however, and hope that they might counter the worldly evil which accompanied almost every innovation. To the suggestion of Edward Hitchcock, president of Amherst, that the undergraduate bodies of both colleges sponsor a joint literary journal, he responded in 1848: "I have no faith in college periodicals." [75] On the other hand, in 1863 he admitted that "when young men have their own organization, write their own papers, carry on their own discussions . . . their knowledge becomes incorporated into them,

74. "Journal of the Class of 1856"; MS, WCL.
75. Edward Hitchcock to MH, July 12, 1848; WCL, Misc. MSS, *10*. MH to Edward Hitchcock, July 25, 1848; typescript, Amherst College Library.

it becomes practical." [76] The extracurriculum, after all, was a perfect complement to his own frequently expressed belief that it was the responsibility of Williams College to turn out independent and self-disciplined young men.

The students went further with their extracurriculum, both in distance and coverage, than he would have wished. For although the fraternities, the athletic teams, the literary journals, and the class meetings were in a sense merely a reflection of an American tendency to organize almost anything, they also were an explicit pronouncement upon the official concept of education which prevailed at Williams College. Every organization which the students developed, every new custom which they introduced, helped them immeasurably in adjusting to the confining atmosphere of Williamstown and preparing for the world they eagerly anticipated. Every extracurricular activity measured their skill, their ambition, their ingenuity, their enterprise, their values. The extracurriculum, however, was preeminently a monument to the dissatisfaction which succeeding generations of students felt for "the log" that stretched between them and Mark Hopkins.

76. MH, *Fruit in Old Age: A Discourse, Commemorative of Nathan Jackson, Delivered by Request of the Students, in the Chapel of Williams College. May 17, 1863* (Boston, T. R. Marvin, 1862), p. 9.

Part Two: GOD

5. Albert Hopkins and the Nurture of Piety

"CHUM, GOD IS HERE!" With these momentous words a Williams undergraduate in 1825 welcomed his roommate back to Williamstown and into the vale of tears, agony, and delight that betokened a revival of evangelical Protestantism.[1] Similar news greeted other Williams students during the 19th century, as long as Congregational orthodoxy characterized the religious life of the college. Until May 1872, when Mark's brother, Professor Albert Hopkins, died, any student might have written with authority, as one had written twenty years before, that "the President and his brother are deeply interested in the religious welfare of the institution and their influence is great in giving a religious tone to it."[2] By then, however, evangelical Protestantism and its characteristic revivalism was coming to the end of its long dominion. Its place would be taken by a Protestantism less dependent upon emotionalism for its appeal.

In an age as tinged with romanticism as had been pre-Civil War America, emotional intensity had been an especially appropriate means of strengthening and inspiring religious experience. By 1872, however, Protestantism was beginning to come to grips with new realities—industrialism, urbanism, science, biblical scholarship—realities that were to be faced with a kind of sober and unemotional faith which had not characterized much of the old religion. All denominations of American Protestantism had not been equally dependent upon the emotions, nor had emotional extravagance been everywhere acceptable, even in the camp of evangelical orthodoxy. Observers of religious life in America during the first half of the 19th century noticed that a Congregational revival was likely to be more quiet than a Methodist revival; that the exhortations of a Presbyterian minister were quiet or intense, depending upon whether the minister tended a flock in an eastern city or on the western frontier; that the Episcopalians preferred ritual and contemplation as methods of promoting Christianity. At Williams, where Congregational influence had prevailed since its

1. Albert Hopkins, "Revivals of Religion in Williams College," *Quarterly Journal of the American Education Society, 8* (1844), 463.
2. Henry M. Grout to his family, Oct. 5, 1850; in *Williams Alumni Review, 19* (1926), 58.

founding, the college for many years adhered to an evangelical orthodoxy in harmony with eastern Congregational practice. This orthodoxy contributed immeasurably toward maintaining an atmosphere of religious dedication at Williams.

Yet Albert Hopkins knew that the millennium had not arrived at the college, and he was not in the habit of expecting that it would.[3] Referring to the role of religion in the history of Williams, he once remarked, "If its influence has been of a mixed character this is no more than we must be compelled to allow of all human institutions." [4] When he wrote a history of revivals at Williams, the story he told was flavored by the stirring struggle of religion to find a welcome in the college community. It was a story of dedicated fervor, spurned and triumphant, neglected and encouraged, attacked and consecrated. It was a story, always, of a small body of men—never a majority—who had recognized their unworthiness and found, in conversion, a new hope and new purpose. "We cannot *compel* men to prefer the cool outward air of a summer's morning and the odor of a flower bed to a pent up room filled with the fumes of tobacco," he once said.[5] For Albert Hopkins, therefore, the road to conversion did not lie in compulsion. The only road was surrender.

Preparing the way for surrender, in every instance, was Albert himself, whose determination to be a Christian, on evangelical orthodox terms, was so great that an 1832 entry in his journal admitted: "Betrayed into some levity this evening." [6] His brother Mark was quite right when he suggested in 1851 that almost everything that had been done in the way of religion at Williams in recent years had been the work of Albert.[7] When he died he was something of an anachronism on the Williams campus. Be that as it may, he embodied the romance, the ideals, the techniques, the ambitions—but also the shortcomings—of evangelical piety.

As Albert Hopkins was painfully aware, piety at Williams suffered a particular handicap that was not characteristic of most

3. Two short sketches of Albert Hopkins by a colleague are John Bascom, "Albert Hopkins," *Bibliotheca Sacra and Theological Eclectic, 32* (1875), 350–62; and "Prof. Albert Hopkins," *Collections of the Berkshire Historical Society, 1* (1892), 39–52.

4. Albert Hopkins, "Revivals of Religion in Williams College," p. 473.

5. *Ibid.,* 469.

6. Diary entry of Feb. 23, 1832; cited in Albert C. Sewall, *Life of Prof. Albert Hopkins* (New York, Anson D. F. Randolph, 1879), p. 46. Efforts to locate the original MS of this diary, from which Sewall drew for his biography, have been unsuccessful.

7. MH to AL, July 30, 1851; MHS, MH-AL MSS.

early American colleges. Williams, founded by a soldier for the purely secular purpose of giving the sons of his soldiers a basic elementary education, never became in the true sense a church college. Chartered by the Commonwealth during a period of profound religious indifference, Williams was not required to make room upon its board of trustees for clergymen. Higher learning and religion, however, were so completely coupled in the New England mind that Williams, of course, made no effort to resist the traditional connection. Yet of its original board of twelve, only four were ministers, and of the twenty-nine trustees appointed during the Hopkins administration but ten were clergymen. At Princeton and Yale, on the other hand, church influences were predominant until the 20th century. Required clerical representation on the governing board of Harvard was not repealed until 1851, and on that of Amherst not until 1916.[8]

Divorced as it was from any official connection with the church, Williams discovered during the period of agitation for removal to the Connecticut Valley that its lay friends were less ready to abandon the college than were the clergy. The three minority members of the board who protested against the petitions for removal were laymen; the Society of Alumni, organized in 1821, was lay in inspiration. On the other hand, the agents on the board who pressed for removal were clergymen.[9] The clergy's position was not madness. The Connecticut Valley was a more strategic location in which to establish a bastion against Unitarian influences emanating from Harvard.

Madness or not, however, the clergy placed the college, upon the accession of Edward Dorr Griffin in 1821, in less debt to the church than were many other American colleges. Griffin went ahead and restored the college, giving it six effective revivals of religion and thus enhancing its reputation for Christian influence. But the work he did was largely a personal triumph, aided significantly by Albert Hopkins of the Class of 1825, the young professor of natural philosophy who in 1827 had returned to Williams as a tutor fresh from his profession of religious belief the year before.

Albert Hopkins took up his tutorial duties during the closing

8. See Thomas J. Wertenbaker, *Princeton 1746-1896* (Princeton, Princeton University Press, 1946), pp. 375 ff.; George Wilson Pierson, *Yale College: An Educational History 1871-1921* (New Haven, Yale University Press, 1952), p. 61; Samuel Eliot Morison, *Three Centuries of Harvard 1636-1936* (Cambridge, Mass., Harvard University Press, 1946), p. 289; and Fuess, *Amherst: The Story of a New England College*, p. 341.

9. See above, p. 9. Perry, *Williamstown and Williams College*, pp. 399-401. Timothy Woodbridge, *The Autobiography of a Blind Minister* (Boston, John P. Jewett, 1856), pp. 158-9.

years of an extended period of evangelical revivalism which is known as the Second Great Awakening, second in time to the 18th-century evangelical revivalism of Jonathan Edwards and his contemporaries. This awakening of religious life, which ran roughly from 1795 to 1830, was inspired by a pressing need to combat the indifference and infidelity which had permeated American society during the years of the Revolution and the early federal period. At Williams, as elsewhere, the awakening did not go unchallenged. In 1805 infidels planned an attack upon Algernon Sidney Bailey of the Class of 1806, a young man who, as an agent of evangelicalism, had become a "terror to the wicked, both in town and college." [10] Throughout the revival of 1812 "a knot of young men . . . warded off their convictions by drinking secretly, and by card-playing." [11] Even Albert Hopkins, then a student, wrote home during the early years of Griffin's administration, "It is in fact rather hard to get up every morning before sun-rise and go clear over to that west college, in the cold, to hear prayers—which do not warm any body very much." [12] But the work was done, sometimes as the result of powerful sermons or careful prayer, sometimes by the simple instrument of conversation with the president. "My dear," Griffin once shouted up the stairs to his wife, upon being informed by young Samuel Prime that he suspected that he was about to undergo the experience of conversion, "Prime . . . is anxious about the salvation of his soul, pray for him." [13] To the perpetuation and intensification of such work as this Albert Hopkins dedicated himself during his long tenure at Williams. For forty-two years he aimed at guaranteeing to every class at least one inspiring religious revival during its four years in Williamstown, and he seldom failed.

In his work Albert Hopkins drew heavily for support upon his brother Mark, whose sermons, weekly religious meetings, and instruction to the senior class exposed the student body to sound influence. As he moved through the lectures on moral philosophy, the president approached each spring the question of choice, at which time he made abundantly clear to every senior that within his own power lay the opportunity to choose God or reject Him. The penalty of rejection was heavy; the benefit of choosing was salvation. As Mark wrote to his mother in 1838:

10. Albert Hopkins, "Revivals of Religion in Williams College," 344–5.
11. *Ibid.*, 461.
12. Albert Hopkins to Harry Hopkins, undated [1825?]; HL, *2*.
13. Samuel Irenaeus Prime, *Autobiography and Memorials,* ed. Wendell Prime (New York, Anson D. F. Randolph, 1888), p. 165.

I consider religion in its essential and saving act to be a plain and practical matter. . . . We feel our need of pardon and salvation. . . . We make Christ the object of trust. . . . We believe that he is able to bestow the blessing and that he will do it if we submit implicitly to his directions. It is that combined but not uncommon act of trust and submission that constitutes . . . faith.[14]

Because religion was for him both practical and necessary, Mark Hopkins looked with favor upon each new outpouring of religious enthusiasm in the college. "We rejoice greatly to see young men devoting themselves understandingly to the service of their God and Savior from gratitude and love," he wrote during a revival in 1847.[15] He understood the challenge which confronted religion in a community of growing boys and admitted that "there are few places where it is more difficult to get & retain a pervading religious influence than in a college. . . . If this cannot be done in our colleges, I should feel very little interest in having them sustained. What is education if it does not lead the mind to its true good? How much better to be a ploughboy & a Christian, than be a vicious, sensual, conceited collegian!" [16]

To turn ploughboys into Christians he exerted as much energy as was possible for a college president whose duties knew no boundary. His responsibilities encompassed relations with town, faculty, and trustees; problems of discipline, finance, and recruitment. He carried as heavy a teaching load as any of his professors. Yet he found time to invite students into his home, where he discussed with them the condition of their souls. Young David Scudder, who died a missionary in India, wrote to his parents in 1852 that such a conversation had convinced him that he was ready to profess his faith.[17] When the college was blessed with a revival, the president made it a point not to leave Williamstown, that he might be on hand to contribute a measure of support through sermons, prayers, and conversations with his students.[18]

Because his own faith had never been shaken since his own conversion during a revival in 1826, Mark Hopkins performed the essential service of providing the college with unassailable Christian leadership. "He never pursues novelties," Calvin Durfee said of him in 1871, and since this was so, he realized the ambition of his

14. Sept. 29, 1838; MHS, Hopkins Family MSS.
15. MH to AL, Mar. 25, 1847; MHS, MH-AL MSS.
16. MH to AL, July 30, 1851; MHS, MH-AL MSS.
17. Scudder, *Life and Letters of David Coit Scudder*, p. 37.
18. MH to AL, Mar. 27, 1848; MHS, MH-AL MSS.

inaugural address to make Williams a "safe" college.[19] Because he
was neither a social reformer nor a theologian, he was seldom embroiled in the kind of secular or religious controversy which com-
forted the unfaithful and indifferent. Indeed, he cared so little for
theology as such that the clear exposition of simple truths which
characterized his preaching gave the college something of a nonsectarian character. While others disputed upon the proper modes
of baptism, he concluded that "it has always seemed to me so far
secondary that I have found it difficult to understand the importance attached to it." In "the renewing of the Holy Ghost," he
said, "the quantity of water is not important." [20] When he engaged
in theological controversy, as he did with President James McCosh
of Princeton in 1863 over the question of ultimate moral authority,
he was uncomfortable and out of character.

Of that last generation of college presidents whose special concern was the soul, not the mind, of youth, he performed his job
with steadfast, if cautious, application. His steady and calm hand
made the ambitions of his brother Albert realizable, for the climate
necessary to religious conversion was a climate undisturbed by intense argument and violent disagreement. It had been no accident
that the revivalism of Fitch was cut short by the administration of
Zephaniah Swift Moore, who kept the college and the community so
embroiled in worldly turmoil that no revival occurred during his
tenure at Williams. Mark Hopkins did not become a leader in the
antislavery movement, nor did he ruffle the quiet of Williamstown
with the demands of any of the more spectacular reform movements
which characterized the first half of the 19th century. By giving
to the college a conservative character, in some ways he may have
made Williams a less exciting place than was Oberlin under Charles
Grandison Finney or Michigan under Henry Tappan. Nevertheless, the young men at Williams who between 1838 and 1858 participated in the eight major revivals of religion during his administration found the kind of excitement for which the college and Mark
Hopkins had been building.

For the creative and guiding hand in the religious life of the
college, however, the pious turned from the president to the
younger brother Albert, who charged the atmosphere with an
evangelism as electric as a summer storm. Possessed with a curiosity
about the world of nature, Albert Hopkins had early given promise

19. Durfee, *Williams Biographical Annals*, p. 32.
20. MH to William W. Hayden, Feb. 25, 1876; HP, *2*.

of becoming a scientist of some importance. In 1834 he became the first Williams professor to visit Europe, and while there he purchased instruments which went into the completion in 1838 of the first permanent astronomical observatory in the United States. He inspired and led, in 1835, an undergraduate expedition to Nova Scotia—the first scientific expedition of its sort in the history of American education. By 1855, however, his students in astronomy and natural philosophy were protesting against his inadequacies as a teacher.[21]

His Williams contemporaries supposed—as did Helen Hunt Jackson when she made him, in the character of Parson Dorrance, the hero of her novel *Mercy Philbrick's Choice*—that his career as a scientist was wrecked by his marriage in 1841 to Louisa Payson, daughter of an eminent Maine tractarian.[22] After the birth of their son Edward in 1843 Louisa never regained her health, her illness bordering on insanity. The uncomplaining care which Albert gave to his wife warranted the letter which Samuel Armstrong wrote to his mother from the Hopkins parlor in January 1862, where he sat as one of the watchers beside the coffin of Louisa Hopkins. "Her husband has been a tireless devoted nurse by night and day," he observed. He "entered upon a life of servitude to her and quietly laid aside all that men value. . . . This has made him very austere in appearance, and he is not lovable in respect to his looks—his eye is the most eagle-like I ever saw." [23]

The care which Louisa required certainly impinged upon his time, but it would be a misreading of the man to picture his life as a tragedy in which promise went to seed. It is doubtful whether Albert Hopkins ever intended that science should be, for him, anything but a hobby. Writing to his mother in 1838, he confessed, "I have no doubt that science is useful, but still the time is so near when knowledge shall vanish away, that I become sometimes almost discouraged at the idea of tasking my energies and occupying my time about it." [24] Albert Hopkins surrendered to the Creator, not to creation. Although the agony and disappointment which at-

---

21. Perry, "Recollections and Diaries," *1*, 153–4.

22. Helen Hunt Jackson, *Mercy Philbrick's Choice*, Boston, Roberts Brothers, 1876.

23. Samuel C. Armstrong to Mrs. C. C. Armstrong, Jan. 26, 1862; in "Personal Memories and Letters of General S. C. Armstrong."

24. Nov. 16, 1838, as given in Sewall, *Life of Prof. Albert Hopkins*, p. 165. See Sewall, pp. 124 ff., for evidence that Hopkins was apparently under the impression that the Second Coming was imminent. William Miller, founder of the Adventist sect, began preaching the Second Coming in 1833. There is no evidence that Hopkins, although under the influence of Millennialism, fell under Miller's sway.

tended his marriage to Louisa Payson may have stayed his development as a scientist, they did not challenge his belief. Indeed, they
served only to strengthen him in the conviction which he had recorded in his journal upon becoming a professor at Williams in
1829: "The past year I have been called upon to enter public life.
In doing this I was enabled to dedicate myself privately to God." [25]
If science suffered, his dedication to God never did.

When Louisa was away from Williamstown, seeking relief in
some more congenial climate, he boarded with students, exchanging,
by his fiat, verses of scripture with them at breakfast.[26] If he suspected a student who was frequently absent from prayers of
malingering, he would visit him in his room to make sure. Convinced
once that he was confronted with a case of feigned illness, he
promptly remarked to the student, "A great deal of sickness in
college, but *very few deaths!*" [27] While at prayers, if he heard the
shouting of students in the streets, he was moved to tears, "re-
membering how long we had been praying for them." [28] Seeing an
as yet unconvinced student leave a religious meeting, he walked up
quietly behind him, tapped him on the shoulder, and softly said,
"Come with us, and we will do you good." [29] He took a nature walk
with some students through the Berkshires one summer, placing
them in neighboring pulpits on Sundays, holding meetings of a
religious character wherever the people were willing.[30] His mind
was full of plans for the religious life of the college and the community.

In 1856 he proposed the establishment of a missionary seminary
in connection with the college; in 1864, two years after the death of
Louisa and shortly after the loss of his only son in the Civil War,
he and a group of students projected a missionary colonization of
northern South America; in 1866 he built a chapel for the poor in
the almost barbaric hilly backwash of Williamstown.[31] Among small
groups of Williams students he never lost his hold, a hold that
he developed through careful and constant application to the nurture of the religious exercises of the college—the noonday prayer

25. Sewall, *Life of Prof. Albert Hopkins*, p. 28.
26. *Ibid.*, p. 115.
27. *Ibid.*, p. 116.
28. *Ibid.*, p. 59.
29. *Ibid.*, p. 134.
30. Albert Hopkins to Edwin Dwight, Apr. 28, 1840; WCL, Williams College Autographs, 2.
31. Sewall, *Life of Prof. Albert Hopkins*, pp. 144-6, 218.

meetings, the annual day of fasting and prayer for colleges, and the impromptu prayer meetings occasioned by a suspicion that an awakening was imminent. Of his influence over the pious, Arthur Latham Perry wrote: "He could hold them, if he chose, still standing after the parting hymn had been sung, by a look, or dismiss them by the same." [32] Such was the power of this pious man, whose sharp eye and physical strength and flowing white beard gave him the appearance of an Old Testament prophet.

Compulsory morning and evening prayers were imported to Williams from Yale when the college was founded, and they remained a characteristic of the college until long after Mark Hopkins had retired from the presidency. Despite its enduring quality, however, compulsion was more a symbol of collegiate respectability than it was an instrument of conversion. Albert Hopkins was among the first to design new and more effective instruments for capturing the indifferent and the infidel.

As late as 1872 a student's compulsory religious exercises equaled his "literary" exercises, but the devout never thought of looking at the faces of the young men at morning prayers to discover whether there were any new religious experiences on campus. Instead, they looked to the noonday chapel service—a voluntary meeting of pious and hopeful students which Hopkins introduced into the life of American education—and to the quickening of spirits which invariably characterized the day set aside each February as a concert of prayer for the colleges, a custom which was originated by a Williams senior during a revival in 1812 and which became a tradition in the colleges and seminaries of 19th-century America.

For Albert Hopkins the noonday meeting was the inspiration of necessity. Disturbed by the mutable character of evangelical religion, which had experienced heights of great achievement as well as depths of disrepute, he searched for an instrument that would give to the religious life of the college a sense of stability and permanence, a stimulus toward constant application that would replace a dependence upon the unpredictable or the accidental—a student's death, a great sermon—to provoke religious enthusiasm. Intrigued by a promise in the writings of his father-in-law, the late Edward Payson, of a time when every day would be like Sunday, he set to work antedating the future by organizing the

32. Perry, "Recollections and Diaries," *2*, 626.

first daily noon prayer meeting one pleasant June day during a college revival in 1832.[33] The meeting, it was thought, "would furnish a strong antidote against a tendency. . . . to fall in with the tide of worldliness." Albert called the meeting "a dam at mid-day," and with it for almost forty years he sought to steady and hold back the currents which threatened Christianity.[34]

The meetings became, at Williams, a test of the intensity of religious sentiment on the campus. "The prayer meetings at noon are now very interesting," a student wrote in his diary in 1850, adding, "Prof. Hopkins is much engaged for a revival." [35] In 1851 Mark wrote to Amos Lawrence that the college was in the midst of a revival, which had first manifested itself at one of Albert's noon prayer meetings.[36] When Albert wrote an account of revivals at Williams, he used the meetings as a sort of barometer, finding in the attendance records which he kept in his journal the evidence that permitted him to move from year to year, judging their religious character as good, bad, or indifferent. The meetings never involved a majority of the college; in the very best of religious times perhaps seventy students—the professing and the hopeful— would crowd into the junior recitation room for a half hour of devotion, central to which was the recitation of a biblical text by each man present—and correction by the leader when the rendition was faulty.[37] As long as the meetings continued, the flame of fervor did not burn out.

Once each year the flame was fanned to a glowing brightness upon the occasion of the annual concert of prayer for colleges, when classes did not meet and the attention of the young men was respectfully directed toward the salvation of their souls. On the eve of the day in 1840, for instance, Albert preached a sermon in which he melodramatically stopped midway and then broke out, "Where are the men to whom I am preaching? They are in yonder rooms; they are not here. But they will hear my sermon tonight." [38] They heard, and by morning the college was in the throes of a

33. Asa Cummings, *A Memoir of the Rev. Edward Payson, D.D., Late Pastor of the Second Church in Portland,* Boston, Crocker and Brewster, 1830.

34. The circumstances are recorded in Albert Hopkins, "Revivals of Religion in Williams College," *Quarterly Journal of the American Education Society, 13* (1841), 466–7; and in his "Religious History of the College from 1836–1860," in Durfee, *A History of Williams College,* pp. 339–41.

35. Entry of Oct. 29, 1850, in Perry, "Recollections and Diaries," *1,* 294.

36. Apr. 14, 1851; MHS, MH-AL MSS.

37. Perry, *Williamstown and Williams College,* pp. 557–8. Durfee, *A History of Williams College,* pp. 314–15.

38. Sewall, *Life of Prof. Albert Hopkins,* pp. 126–7.

revival. There were eight outpourings of religious fervor at Williams between 1838 and 1858, and it was not a coincidence that they appeared on the horizon or received a powerful impetus at the time of the annual concert of prayer for colleges.[39]

Sometimes the flames could not be fanned and the coals sent off nothing but smoke, but the moral reflexes of the pious were conditioned to expect a renewal of enthusiasm at the end of each February and beginning of each March. In 1852 a pious undergraduate recorded in his diary on the day after the day of prayer, "The spirit of God seems to be in our midst." When this same student returned as a member of the faculty, he recorded on the occasion of the day of prayer in 1854, "A very solemn day"; in 1856, "We hope and believe that God is very nigh us"; in 1857, "Much solemnity rests upon the college today." [40] These were all disappointing years for conversions, but the sense of expectation and the interest manifest in this particular diary in the late winter and early spring of each year is a demonstration of the function which the annual concert of prayer was expected to fulfill: the minds of the pious were forcefully directed toward the great work that was yet to be done, and the minds of the impenitent were exposed to a college holiday in which the faithful prayed for them.

The manifestations of the revivals touched off by the day of prayer at Williams did not change, although their frequency and results did. In March 1840 public confession of guilt and sinfulness was so great that Mark Hopkins wrote to his mother that "we have the greatest reason to bless God that he has visited a place so dreadfully wicked. . . . Young men of irreproachable character and high standing in the community came out with disclosures that no one could have expected." [41] In 1848 James T. Ford of the freshman class underwent a profound experience and called upon the president of the college in order to tell him about it.

He said [Mark wrote to his mother] he had long been trying to make his heart better so that God could accept him, but all at once he saw that he could never succeed in that, but that if God could accept him in Christ just as he was, then indeed he should be saved, and God would have all the glory, and he thought he was able to go just as he was and cast himself upon

39. The revival years were 1838, 1840, 1842, 1847, 1848, 1851, 1853, 1858—as ascertained from Albert Hopkins' histories.

40. Perry, "Recollections and Diaries," 2 (1852), 397–8; 2 (1854), 490; 2 (1856), 563; 2 (1857), 572.

41. Mar. 27, 1840; MHS, Hopkins Family MSS.

the Savior, and he believed that he was accepted. Then he had peace.[42]

In 1853 David Coit Scudder walked into his college room, "threw himself on the floor, and began to weep and moan and roll about, seemingly in great agony. . . . It was that night," his roommate supposed, "that the struggle was over." As with many other young men, the struggle was not over, and the next year, in a letter to his family, young Scudder wrote: "Circumstances conspire to render me perfectly miserable; a very agreeable condition, I assure you. . . . Today I have almost wished to die." [43]

Evangelical revivalism at Williams spent itself in the morbidness of a youngster like David Scudder and in the discovery of a freshman like James Ford. But it found its greatest encouragement in Albert Hopkins who, when the moment was propitious, was capable of a sermon almost every night in addition to appropriate exhortations at the noonday prayer meetings. Yet, evangelism was not nurtured at Williams without a struggle—a struggle which it lost. The formation of a college church in 1834 was a welcome addition to the apparatus of Christian revivalism—as the admissions to the church during revival years would indicate.[44] But the year before the founding of "The Church in Williams College" there appeared in Williamstown a new and terrible heresy—Greek letter fraternities, little groups of men whose activities neatly symbolized the conflict being waged on the Williams campus between the proponents of evangelical orthodoxy and young men who would fashion their lives according to a different outlook.

42. Mar. 2, 1848; MHS, Hopkins Family MSS.
43. Scudder, *Life and Letters of David Coit Scudder*, pp. 33, 56.
44. See "Record of the Church in Williams College [1834–83]," MSS, Admissions office, Williams College.

6. The New Heresy: Greek Letter Fraternities

No ONE has ever furnished any evidence to prove the story that fraternities were introduced at Williams College in 1833 by accident. As it is told in the histories of Kappa Alpha, a group of boys went over the hill to Schenectady one fine fall day in search of a Phi Beta Kappa charter and came back to town swinging Kappa Alpha keys at their waists.[1] President Edward Dorr Griffin is supposed to have given them a warm welcome, so delighted was this Yale Phi Beta Kappa of the class of 1790 by the resemblance between a Kappa Alpha key and a Phi Beta Kappa key. The story is at least believable, and although not everyone was so gracious in his welcome as was President Griffin, the fraternity movement had been launched at Williams College.

The most congenial soil for the founding and proliferation of the Greek letter fraternity was surely a place like Williamstown, a small, remote village on the frontier. From parent chapters at Union and Hamilton, the Greek letter fraternity was introduced into most of the colleges of New England and New York by 1840. Between the founding at Union College of Kappa Alpha in 1825 and Theta Delta Chi in 1847, four other national fraternities were born there: Sigma Phi, Delta Phi, Chi Psi, and Psi Upsilon. Founded in the country, they moved into the cities, where frequently the demand for new chapters came from graduate members in pursuit of still higher learning.

Alpha Delta Phi, founded at Hamilton in 1832, sponsored within a decade the first fraternity chapters at Amherst, Bowdoin, Brown, Columbia, Harvard, Yale, and Western Reserve and Miami in Ohio. Beta Theta Pi, founded at Miami in 1839, introduced the Greek letter society into Michigan, Princeton, Wabash, Washington and Jefferson, and Centre College of Kentucky before 1850. Local fraternities appeared at the University of Vermont, Wesleyan, and Dartmouth between 1837 and 1842.[2] Few American colleges were left untouched by this movement which so ably characterized the enterprise and initiative of the 19th-century college undergraduate. It was organized by students, it was spread by

1. *Kappa Alpha Record* (Clinton, Mass., Colonial Press, 1941), p. 101.
2. For fraternity statistics see *Baird's Manual: American College Fraternities*, ed. Alvan E. Duerr, Menasha, Wisc., George Banta, 1940.

students. Before they knew what had happened, most college presidents found that their undergraduates had ushered into the American college community a social system which they had neither invited nor encouraged. In 1845 the president of Amherst was asking of the president of Williams, "Would it be desirable to have these societies cease in our colleges?" [3]

If it is demonstrable that the Greek fraternity movement was spawned on the frontier, it is not equally easy to document a ready explanation. By 1895 fraternity officials, seeking roots for their hoary traditions, were writing, as one Delta Kappa Epsilon historian did: "The reason for its existence seems to have been an endeavor on the part of the undergraduates to supplement the rather rigid mechanical college curriculum with other training, designed to give them ease and fluency in the art of expression." [4] There is not a particle of truth in this explanation. Rival literary societies were an integral part of every college long before fraternities were founded—at Williams, Philologian and Philotechnian; at Union, Philomathian and Adelphic; at Yale, Linonia and Brothers in Unity; at Dartmouth, Socials and Fraters.[5] Their membership records and the minutes of their meetings are testimony of the ample degree to which the literary societies provided for the extracurricular literary and disputative needs of the student.[6]

At Williams and elsewhere the literary societies declined in the decades after the introduction of fraternities. They declined, however, not so much because the fraternities robbed them of their purpose as because the fraternities created a higher level of loyalty and intruded new political complications into their elections. Fraternities had their literary exercises, but literary exercises merely amounted to something to do, once a fraternity was founded.

The Greek letter fraternity was intended to fill an emotional rather than a curricular vacuum. One fraternity chronicler who worked in the archives of Kappa Alpha concluded that "the atmosphere of Phi Beta Kappa, strictly academic, stimulated in the imagination the dream of new and more intimate relationships. . . . *The yearning of the unsatisfied was for fellowship of kindred*

3. Edward Hitchcock to MH, Dec. 9, 1845; Amherst College Library MSS.

4. *The Plans and Exterior of Society Hall at Williams College for Delta Kappa Epsilon* (1895), p. 5.

5. See Frederick C. Waite, *Western Reserve University: The Hudson Era* (Cleveland, Western Reserve University Press, 1943), pp. 228–30, for a discussion of these and other college literary societies.

6. See MS Records of Philologian and Philotechnian in WCL.

souls." [7] Another decided that Kappa Alpha "owed its origin mainly to that desire for a circle of intimate friends, so natural to those transferred from home relations." [8] The preamble to the constitution of Sigma Phi declared the society's purposes to be "amusement, the cultivation of social policy," and—apparently for good measure—"the direction in all respects whatever of all matters and concerns pertaining to the Western Continent." [9] Of the founders of Alpha Delta Phi, a fraternity historian has written, "They felt the need of warmer nutriment for their *souls* than that furnished by the drilled dry lessons of the class-room"; they postulated a "society of a higher nature and more comprehensive and higher principle" than the literary societies, a society where man's "moral, social, and intellectual" being would be nourished.[10] In the archives of one Williams fraternity there exists a memorandum by a member of the Class of 1836 setting forth the criteria to be followed in selecting members; the final test, it is suggested, is provided by the question: "Would you want your sister to marry him?" The spirit, and therefore the purpose, of the fraternity movement may merely be implicit in these fragmentary statements, but it is obvious: among the barbarians, we are the Greeks.

Greek letter fraternities were intended to bring together the most urbane young men on the campus into small groups that would fill the vacuum left by removal from the family and the home community. The fraternity was something to which to belong, as exclusive as the family, as dependable as the home. Writing to a fraternity brother in 1850, a Williams undergraduate exclaimed, "There is nothing on earth for which I cherish a more ardent affection than the Zeta Psi. I recognize everyone who bears our badge as a brother & a member of *the same family.*" [11]

At times the demands of these new Greek families challenged the firmness of even blood relationships. And so another member of Zeta Psi, writing of his younger brother, revealed the anguish of a young man who had discovered that he had two families: "I think Tony was not made for a society man & he had best remain a neutral. I can't tell you how many times my feelings were wounded

7. Fisher Howe, "In the Beginning," *Kappa Alpha Record*, p. 17.
8. *A Biographical Record of the Kappa Alpha Society in Williams College, Williamstown, Mass., from Its Foundation to the Present Time, 1833–1881* (New York, Kappa Alpha Society, 1881), p. 7.
9. Elias Lyman, VI, "The Alpha of Vermont, 1845–1945," *Sigma Phi Flame* (Oct. 1947), p. 5.
10. *The Alpha Delta Phi: 1832–1882,* ed. Talcott Williams (Boston, Alpha Delta Phi, 1882), pp. 3–4.
11. Samuel B. Sumner to Ezra J. Peck, July 3, 1850; WCL, Peck MSS.

by remarks which would have been insults if offered by gentlemen
or those who had the least delicacy of soul, in my presence, on
Tony's peculiarities of appearance & disposition." [12] Reporting to
a recent alumnus on the fortunes of Sigma Phi, an undergraduate
thrilled in 1845: "Bailey is our pride. He is a noble looking fellow; with a tall fine form, splendid forehead, and curling hair." [13]
As William Dwight Whitney put it, more concretely, when writing
of an undergraduate contemporary in 1842, "Davis . . . is a perfect gentleman, and no one could say that he could not get into
any society that he chose to join." These new collegiate homes, it
was obvious, were intended to accommodate gentlemen of the
world.[14]

Fraternities may in time have grown beyond their purposes, but
it was not pretense which caused them to adopt, as slogans, variations on the idealistic theme of "friendship, love, and truth." These
were values which had been nurtured in the American home and
which American family life had maintained for two centuries.
Moreover, the early 19th-century families which young men left
when they went to college were in themselves strong social organizations—patriarchal, large, communal, and often socially self-
sufficient. There was, however, more than a longing for mother, father, brother, and sister in the fraternity movement. Not many
homes in the United States in the 1830's placed so high a premium
upon the Greek alphabet, secrecy, and mystic hocus-pocus. That
the fraternity was intended to domesticate the frontier college
community there can be no doubt, but there was something more.
There was also escape.

It was escape from the monotony, dreariness, and unpleasantness
of the collegiate regimen which began with prayers before dawn
and ended with prayers after dark; escape from the long winters
and ingrown college world, from the dormitory with its lack of
privacy. Fraternities institutionalized various escapes—drinking,
smoking, card playing, singing, and seducing—but they did not
introduce these diversions, which long antedated their founding.
By channeling traditional means of escape into a brotherhood of
devoted men, the fraternity gave new meaning to a cigar, a drink,
a girl, a song, and in time it was not really possible to distinguish
purpose from manifestation.

12. Henry Axtell to Ezra J. Peck, Dec. 10, 1851; WCL, Peck MSS.
13. Freeman J. Bumstead to William Dwight Whitney, Oct. 2, 1845; SML:YU,
Whitney MSS.
14. William Dwight Whitney to Dwight W. Marsh, Oct. 14, 1842; SML:YU, Whitney MSS.

Members of Sigma Phi, *ca.* 1866, sitting on the porch of their chapter house, the first building in America erected as a fraternity house, 1857.

The avenue of escape provided by the fraternities, however, was
constructed of something more than a willing acquiescence in
worldly pleasure. It was constructed, as their songs and symbols
readily declared, of fairylands, of fountains, Greek temples, ladies
with harps, bearded patriarchs, and angels; of knights and ostrich
plumes, of gardens full of calla lilies, ivy, laurel, and oak; of innocent maidens, cornucopias, burning pyres, and crusaders in mailed
armor.[15] It was, indeed, constructed of anything that was beyond
reality, beyond the reality of the rural frontier which helped to
provoke this determined return to the romance of Greece. Founded
during the years of the Greek Revolution, by young men who knew
Greek certainly as well as modern college students know English,
the fraternity movement owes many of its trappings, if not its inspiration, to Greece. To the trappings of Greece were added those
of Freemasonry. Aided by the disclosure of the practices and
terminology of Freemasonry, a disclosure produced by the anti-
masonic movement which captured eastern politics in the years
after 1826, the fraternities incorporated much of the masonic spirit
into their movement. The ritual of Beta Theta Pi is patterned on
Freemasonry, and it is no accident that a Kappa Alpha and a
masonic chapter house are still both known as lodges.[16]

The movement found a cure for loneliness in exclusiveness, for
monotony in romanticism. It was consciously selective, consciously
scornful of equality, at the very time that Andrew Jackson was
becoming a spokesman for equality of opportunity. It substituted
for the always open society of Christian believers the closed society
of "kindred souls." At a time when Freemasonry was being attacked as irreligious and contrary to democratic promise, the fraternity movement freely partook of its ritual, its terminology,
and its spirit. In the process it provoked a virile opposition which
recognized from the very beginning that the democracy of the
country college was being seriously threatened by its own offspring.

Although there was loneliness and drabness in Williamstown,
there was enough of piety and romantic liberalism to challenge the
pretensions of the Greek societies. At Williams, liberalism found its
defenders in a group of young men who immediately organized

15. See the frontispieces to the following fraternity catalogues: *Catalogue of Beta
Theta Pi*, New York, 1911; *The Delta Upsilon Quinquennial Catalogue*, New York,
1891; *Fourth Decennial Catalogue of the Chi Psi Fraternity*, New York, 1883;
Catalogue of the Sigma Phi, New York, 1915.
16. Waite, *Western Reserve University*, p. 258.

themseIves into a nonexclusive antisecret fraternity. And piety did what it could.

As early as 1824 the specter of secrecy and exclusiveness had cast its shadow in Williamstown. That year Mark Hopkins, then a member of the senior class, wrote in a letter home, "The masons are to celebrate St. John's Day on Friday. . . . I suppose we shall have a holiday as half the students are masons." [17] The masonic lodge, however, as well as a local college fraternity which appeared at this time, fell to the intensity of the town and college religious revival of 1825. When the revival was over, secrets had been bared, memberships had been recanted, and Christian fellowship had won the day.[18] Not until 1833, with the arrival of Kappa Alpha and the birth of a local fraternity which the next year became Sigma Phi, were secret societies again to ruffle the college scene. The 1825 victory of evangelical religion over fraternal secrecy was its last.

Albert Hopkins, occupied in 1841 in writing a history of evangelism at Williams, was forced to admit that he could not do the job without introducing the subject of secret societies. Hopkins had gone to Europe in search of scientific apparatus in 1834. On his return that fall he noticed a new atmosphere at the college. "I could scarcely compare College to anything but a bee-hive," he wrote. "Little collections were gathered about . . . engaged in earnest disputation and apparently angry conversation. . . . Certain societies termed secret had been introduced during my absence, and it was ill feeling growing out of this circumstance which gave rise to the excitement." He continued:

> Some, it appeared, had been elected members of these associations, others not. Some Christians had been elected, others not. Distinctions were thus created, which gave rise to jealousies, and hard feelings sprang up both between those who were professedly Christians and those who were not. . . . Animosities sprung up between the secret societies themselves. . . . Alienation of feeling grew up so bitter . . . that individuals of the same class, and some of them professors of religion, were not on speaking terms with one another. Under such circumstances there was no room to urge the apostolic exhortation, "let brotherly love continue." Nor was it possible to bring about any thing like concentrated religious effort.[19]

17. MH to Harry Hopkins, June 10, 1825; HL, 3.
18. Albert Hopkins, "Revivals of Religion in Williams College," p. 471.
19. Ibid., 471-2.

As his narrative continued, he described how in 1840 the efforts of the religious spirits of the college to maintain a revival broke down. As the revival reached its pitch, at an evening meeting attended by almost every member of college and characterized by confessions of lying, stealing, card-playing, drinking, and keeping liquor in college rooms, "it was made evident that there was a dark corner not yet entered."

Hiding in the dark corner were the Greek letter societies. "Equally with other things contrary to the spirit of the gospel, it was thought that these should be confessed to. . . . But alas! all that we could do, and probably all that prudence allowed, was to hush the tendency to restlessness, which became manifest when a system seemed likely to be endangered, in which the feelings of the individuals had become so deeply enlisted." [20] Seven years after the arrival of Kappa Alpha the fraternity system at Williams was sufficiently entrenched to thwart, on the eve of its success, a religious revival which had revealed great promise. Fraternities did not cause religious intensity to disappear from Williams, but they weakened the fabric in which orthodoxy hoped to capture disciples. From 1833 on, the fraternity would symbolize and nurture disunity in the Christian community. It would provide, too, as one student recorded in his diary in 1851, a new ritual—the fraternity initiation—which carried an appeal that could overwhelm an orthodox ritual of long standing, the hour of quiet prayer in which roommates converted drab college rooms into centers of divine worship. "As Henry and I were at prayer this evening," Arthur Latham Perry wrote, "George Moore rapped at the door, and when we admitted him, he said that Crapo and Gilman from Yale had come for the Purpose of initiation." By midnight, the first initiation of Alpha Delta Phi at Williams was completed, and the two boys who had left their prayers to arrange the preliminaries were charter members. [21]

From another direction, in November 1834, a frontal attack upon the fraternities was undertaken by a group of thirty students who took a determined stand against exclusiveness and secrecy. The constitution of the Social Fraternity, which they formed, proclaimed that its members, "feeling a deep interest in the peace and prosperity of the Institution to which we belong, and believing that all combinations and societies not founded upon liberal principles, are calculated to destroy the harmony of College," did thereby

20. *Ibid.*, 470–2.
21. Perry, "Recollections and Diaries," *2*, 346; entry of July 1, 1851.

form themselves into a "society, for the purpose of counteracting the evil tendency of associations of which we disapprove, and for the purpose of literary, mutual, and social improvement." [22] In its 1838 Constitution the new fraternity announced: "We would invest no class of our fellow students with factitious advantages, but would place all upon an equal footing in running the race of honorable distinction." [23]

Known variously during its history as the Social Fraternity, the Anti-Secret Society, the Equitable Fraternity, Oudens, and finally Delta Upsilon, the new fraternity showed, in its passing reference to "social improvement," a tendency to ape the enemy. Until 1842, visitors at its open meetings were freely invited to join, but thereafter new members had to be specifically proposed. After much debate, the society on July 16, 1850, adopted resolutions which effectively restricted membership and helped to pave the way toward the confusion of purpose that led to its temporary collapse in 1862. [24] In its early years, however, the mother chapter of Delta Upsilon fought valiantly for democratic values. Although it had remarkable initial success, the Social Fraternity was unequal to the task of coping with the very situation which had inspired the Greek letter societies. Its lack of secrecy, its early open-door membership policy, did not answer the need which the secret societies so capably fulfilled. Its early success can be attributed in part to widespread hostility to the principle of secrecy, but as the fraternities grew in numbers and membership, and the Social Fraternity itself increasingly took on certain attributes of its rivals, it lost its hold on the antifraternity group.

The weakening of the antifraternity organization's popularity and purpose is evident in membership statistics. In the classes from 1838 to 1848 members of the antifraternity society outnumbered secret society members; beginning with the class of 1849, the Social Fraternity moved behind the secret societies in total membership, and the next year it moved into a permanent third place, being surpassed by the neutrals. [25] That the antifraternity society ap-

22. *Catalogue of the Social Fraternity, Williams College, October, 1836* (Northampton, Mass., 1836), p. 7.

23. *Catalogue of the Social Fraternity, Williams College, November, 1838* (n.d.), pp. 9–10.

24. William F. Galpin, *Delta Upsilon: One Hundred Years, 1834–1934* (New York, Delta Upsilon Fraternity, 1934), pp. 9–12. This volume is by all odds the best of fraternity histories, marked by a candidness and historical skill that seldom characterize fraternity writing.

25. Statistics and information on membership, here and elsewhere in this chapter,

THE NEW HERESY: FRATERNITIES   109

pealed, in the beginning, to the especially pious Williams undergraduate there can be little doubt. Between 1833 and 1872 Williams College produced 543 alumni who became ordained clergymen: 131 came from the 1,031 secret society men, 212 from the
894 neutrals, and 201 from the 503 members of the society of antifraternity students. After the antifraternity organization took a
turn toward exclusion in 1850, its contribution to the clerical ranks
fell behind that of the neutrals.[26] As long as the antifraternity
society withstood the tendency to become just another fraternity, it
apparently provided a congenial atmosphere for the more pious
Williams undergraduate. In 1844, in fact, the membership of the
undergraduate theological society was drawn entirely from the
antifraternity society, until a sophomore member was pledged
by Sigma Phi.[27] Albert Hopkins' prediction in 1834 that the
"dissocial element, embodied in a regular organization, would be
likely to . . . become . . . a perpetual source of gangrene" is
manifest in these statistics.[28] It cannot be accident that caused the
Greek letter societies, which comprised 42 per cent of the student
body of the classes between 1836 and 1872, to produce only 24
per cent of the ordained clergymen. From its very beginnings, then,
the fraternity system at Williams was a divisive force of serious
consequence. In time, class spirit, college spirit, the literary
societies, and open social intercourse were to feel the same cutting
edge which had been first felt by orthodoxy and piety.

Soon after the Kappa Alpha initiation in the fall of 1836, a
Williams sophomore hurried off a letter to a boyhood friend, con-
fiding, "It is ridiculous." [29] At the commencement meeting of the

have been based upon a study of fraternity and college catalogues. The following
have been especially useful: *Catalogue of the Alpha Delta Phi 1832–1928*, New
York, the Fraternity, 1928; *Catalogue of Beta Theta Pi*, New York, the Fraternity,
1911; *Fourth Decennial Catalogue of the Chi Psi Fraternity*, New York, the Fraternity, 1883; *Delta Kappa Epsilon*, 1874; *Catalogue of Members of the Lambda
Chapter, Fraternity of Delta Psi*, 1903; *The Delta Upsilon Quinquennial Catalogue*,
Boston, the Fraternity, 1891; *Kappa Alpha Record: 1825–1940*, Clinton, Mass.,
1941; and *Catalogue of Sigma Phi*, New York, the Fraternity, 1915.
26. It was possible to determine the clerical and nonclerical membership of the
various social groups by reference to fraternity catalogues and to the *General Catalogues* of the College, which, through the edition of 1920, printed the names of all
clergymen in italics.
27. William Dwight Whitney to Dwight W. Marsh, Oct. 28, 1844; SML:YU,
Whitney MSS.
28. Albert Hopkins, "Revivals of Religion," 472.
29. William W. Mitchell to Henry L. Dawes, Nov. 6, 1836; WCL, Misc. MSS, *12*.

college alumni in 1880 David Dudley Field declared that if he
were a trustee of Williams he would tear up the fraternity system
by its roots.[30] In the forty-four years between this bemused observation of an undergraduate and the irate charges of the then
grand old man of the Williams alumni body, there were few quiet
moments on the fraternity front. In 1838, two years after becoming
president of Williams, Mark Hopkins suggested to President Heman Humphrey of Amherst that simultaneous action by eastern
college authorities might destroy the fraternity system before it
was too late.[31] In 1846 he wrote to Edward Hitchcock, Humphrey's
successor at Amherst, "The influences . . . have been evil. . . .
They create class and factions, and put men socially in regard to
each other into an artificial and false position. . . . The alienation
of feeling and want of cordiality thus created are not favorable to
a right moral and religious state." [32] In 1855 a college debate on the
subject of secret societies was organized (James A. Garfield of the
Class of 1856 spent his vacation in New York libraries building
his case against them) but was canceled when the secret societies
withdrew from the agreement.[33] In 1861 the *Quarterly* devoted
most of an issue to articles on the fraternity question. In July 1868
the board of trustees received a student petition asking that the
fraternities be abolished.[34] In September, on the first Sunday of the
new college year, Professor John Bascom delivered a biting sermon on secret societies.[35]

Opposition to fraternities, however, was clearly unproductive.
Six new chapters of national fraternities migrated to the Williams
campus before the Civil War. Among them was Delta Psi, whose
founder, Williams' most generous benefactor in the 19th century,
had gone to Williams from Columbia in 1853 for the express purpose of establishing the chapter.[36] Membership in fraternities
mounted steadily until beginning with the Class of 1850 secret
society membership began frequently to encompass more than
50 per cent of any class, and beginning with the Class of 1866

30. *Springfield Republican*, July 7, 1880; cited in Leverett W. Spring, *A History
of Williams College* (Boston, Houghton, Mifflin, 1917), p. 289.

31. Heman Humphrey to MH, July 30, 1838, in which Humphrey agreed with
Hopkins; WCL, Misc. MSS, *13*.

32. MH to Edward Hitchcock, Aug. 8, 1846; photostat, Amherst College Library.

33. Smith, *The Life and Letters of James Abram Garfield, 1*, 91. See also John
H. Goodhue, '62, "Secrecy—a Word in Reply," *Williams Quarterly, 9* (1861), 49–58.

34. TR, *3*, 2; July 27, 1868.

35. John Bascom, *Secret Societies in College*, Pittsfield, Mass., Berkshire Eagle,
1868; sermon delivered Sept. 6, 1868.

36. *Obituary Record of the Alumni of Williams College 1898–99*, pp. 116–23.

it was an abnormal situation if fewer than 50 per cent of a class belonged to secret societies.[37]

Fraternities not only challenged deeply held religious values— their membership campaigns disrupted college order. Albert Hopkins wrote of one "electioneering campaign" which, by the end of the fall term of 1841, had inspired undergraduates to walk the streets with clubs "either for purposes of attack or of self-defense."[38] "The main thing of the day has been a talk with Bates," a student wrote in his diary. "He has finally concluded to join our Society."[39] A recently graduated alumnus urged his fraternity chapter at Williams in 1850 to "Strike! & keep striking! Heaven & earth must be moved to get that Niles."[40] Had those who objected to the time-consuming nature of fraternity electioneering read these words written by a Williams undergraduate in 1850, their worst fears would have been confirmed: "I intend to make the advancement of the Zeta Psi fraternity the first object of my labor. For the next year everything else shall be but instrument for the accomplishment of this great object."[41]

Not only did the fraternities electioneer; so did their prospects. "Whitehead is here," a student wrote in 1852, and "has been bootlicking the KA's considerably."[42] For the benefit of new freshmen, fraternity members described the loneliness of college life without fraternity membership; they played the home-away-from-home theme for what it was worth; they pointed out how fraternity membership served as an antidote for the dissocializing influence of too much study; they claimed for their brotherhoods an important role in the cultivation of manners and of social refinement; they pointed out what a group of jolly good fellows they really were.[43] The refinements which electioneering encouraged are suggested by a

37. At Amherst not until 1880 did half the student body belong to fraternities, nor was it until 1874 that Alpha Delta Phi became the first Amherst fraternity to own its own chapter house. At Williams, fraternities maintained a 50 per cent hold on the student body in the 1860's. Sigma Phi built its own chapter house, the first to do so in the United States, in 1857, and Kappa Alpha bought a house in 1864. At Amherst, on the other hand, prospective clergymen were turned out with regularity longer and more profusely. See Thomas Le Duc, *Piety and Intellect at Amherst College 1865–1912* (New York, Columbia University Press, 1946), pp. 119–27; and Fuess, *Amherst: The Story of a New England College,* p. 138.

38. Albert Hopkins, "Revivals of Religion," 473.

39. Perry, "Recollections and Diaries," *1,* 275; entry for Aug. 7, 1850.

40. Samuel B. Sumner to Ezra J. Peck, Sept. 16, 1850; WCL, Peck MSS.

41. Thomas Gilfillan to Ezra J. Peck, Aug. 26, 1850; WCL, Peck MSS.

42. Anthony D. Axtell to Ezra J. Peck, July 9, 1852; WCL, Peck MSS.

43. Frank Porter Woodbury, "College Societies, Secret and Anti-secret," *Williams Quarterly, 8* (1861), 288.

student who wrote in 1852: "I don't think that KA . . . stands
very well. . . . They got 'sold' on one fellow. They supposed
that he did not belong to any Society. He is from Hamilton Coll.
and one of the [Kaps] proposed to sleep with him one night, by
way of electioneering. He told him, he did not think he liked to sleep
with *him*, for he was a Sigma Phi." [44]

In addition to siphoning off energy and talents from more traditional outlets, the fraternity system introduced a new element into
the political life of the college. Combinations were created to dominate class and literary society elections, and frequently the various
college elections were fought between two rival camps—each composed of several of the secret societies, and one of them sometimes
making room for the antifraternity society or even the neutrals. [45]

By 1865 fraternity politics were so successful in keeping merit
out of the prize rhetorical contests that the faculty could think of
no solution other than to take the election of speakers away from
the classes and make up the speaking slate themselves. In 1859
Philotechnian seriously floundered as each of its quarterly elections
became a fraternity battleground. [46] In 1866 the annual Class Day
celebrations were colored by disharmony: the unsuccessful fraternity combination refused to participate in the exercises. [47] In
1870, in fact, Class Day was entirely omitted because the differences
between the two combinations could not be resolved. [48] In the same
year the five existing fraternities and neutrals were so embroiled
in a struggle for extracurricular prestige that three rather similar
publications (*Quarterly, Vidette,* and *Review*) were being showered
upon the college community simultaneously.

Early critics of Williams fraternities were as much disturbed by
their impact upon individualism as by their disruption of the college community. Basing his conclusions upon a study of Delta
Kappa Epsilon membership between 1855 and 1872, a friendly
DKE historian decided that "individualism [was] ever in conflict

44. Anthony D. Axtell to Ezra J. Peck, Sept. 28, 1852; WCL, Peck MSS.
45. One such was a Chi Psi-Socii coalition against Sigma Phi in 1843 (William
Dwight Whitney to Dwight W. Marsh, March 16, 1843; SML:YU, Whitney MSS).
See also "College Elections," *Williams Quarterly,* 7 (1859), 144–6; William Swan,
"College Influences," *Williams Quarterly, 10* (1862), 75. In 1844, as the result of
dissatisfaction with the outcome of elections in the two literary societies, some
fraternity men founded a third literary society, Clionian, which, however, did not
survive the year. William Dwight Whitney to D. W. Marsh, Jan. 19, 1844, and
Oct. 28, 1844; SML:YU, Whitney MSS.
46. "Coalitions," *Williams Quarterly,* 7 (1860), 246.
47. *Williams Quarterly, 13* (1866), 276; *14* (1866), 55.
48. *Ibid., 17* (1870), 290.

with brotherhood." [49] Franklin Carter, president of Williams between 1881 and 1901, proposed during his senior year in 1862 that
fraternities be abolished, arguing that it was difficult enough to
resist the tendency toward conformity in a small college. Fraternities, he suggested, provided institutions where a student was "too
apt to surrender his total individuality." [50] Professor Bascom, who
as a student at Williams had been an early member of Beta Theta
Pi, complained in his 1868 sermon, "Secret organizations . . .
foreclose the truly private question of friendship, stepping in to
settle it on common and general grounds, not on its rightful, individual ones." [51]

It was further charged that fraternities were snobbish and un-
democratic. In 1852 college gossip reported that Sigma Phi was
intending to close its Hobart chapter "as there is danger of its
becoming too plebeian." [52] Among Bascom's complaints was his
objection to the creation of "artificial, vexatious, and often times
unjust distinctions and barriers in a community otherwise homogeneous and democratic." [53] His complaint was but an echo of a
similar charge that went back as far as the 1834 antecedents of
Delta Upsilon. Yet the critics themselves did not altogether understand what the fraternity movement actually involved. Who could
expect them to see that it proposed the substitution of worldly
prowess for spiritual grace as a measure of prestige; the substitution of social status for Christian status; the substitution of attitudes and skills necessary for success in this world, for those considered appropriate for success in the next? [54]

Nothing better epitomizes the degree to which the critics missed
the meaning of fraternities than some of John Bascom's remarks
in his Sunday chapel sermon of 1868. "You would," he said,
"doubtless, be ashamed to confess how much you are influenced by
these bits of metal; how greatly you covet them." [55] There is no
reason, however, to believe that the student who ended his letter of
1850 with a "greet all the brethren with a holy kiss" would have

49. Eli H. Botsford, *Epsilon Chapter of Delta Kappa Epsilon* (Williamstown,
1938), p. 30.
50. Franklin Carter, "Independence in College," *Williams Quarterly*, 9 (1862),
149.
51. Bascom, *Secret Societies in College*, p. 7.
52. Charles C. Whitney to Ezra J. Peck, Feb. 17, 1853; WCL, Peck MSS.
53. Bascom, *Secret Societies in College*, p. 9.
54. See Le Duc, *Piety and Intellect at Amherst College*, p. 123, for similar conclusions on fraternities at Amherst.
55. Bascom, *Secret Societies in College*, p. 8.

been at all ashamed to admit that for him his fraternity pin had meaning.[56] For, although the fraternity movement, with its mystic ties, was an escape from reality, it was also more concrete and more worldly than its symbolism suggested. Had Bascom understood the wellsprings of an analysis of the antifraternity society which appeared in the *Quarterly* in 1861, he might have been alarmed, but he would not have made so much of secrecy and "bits of metal." Reviewing the history of the antifraternity society at Williams, Augustus Brown, a senior member of Kappa Alpha, had concluded:

> The members are chosen not because they possess in any marked degree those qualities which will render them desirable companions; but simply because they are supposed to "practice strict morality" and their opinions upon a single subject happen to be considered correct. . . . A motley set of good, bad and indifferent young men are thrown together, having no interest in or congeniality with each other. . . . They neglect the cultivation of those finer feelings and affections which fit men for society.[57]

Not only were these remarks Brown's case against the antifraternity society; by inference they were also the defense upon which the fraternity movement itself was willing to rest. In essence the movement was institutionalizing new prestige values, the attributes of a successful man of the world, of *this* world, at the expense of those various signs of grace—humility, equality, and, notwithstanding Brown's criterion, morality—which it had long been the purpose of the college to foster. Neither secrecy nor mysticism made the fraternity movement so powerfully antireligious, as Albert Hopkins thought. The fall from grace was facilitated by the recognition which the fraternity movement gave to secular values, to good friendship, good looks, good clothes, good family, and good income.

Among those who did not thoroughly understand the fraternity movement was Mark Hopkins. At first glance, it seems as if he did. For he likened it to other "associations . . . formed on a basis for the most part purely selfish," and, while convinced that they endangered "the best interests and hopes of the country," he was forced to admit that they were "characteristic of the present age." He regarded "the general spirit of secret societies as opposed to

56. Charles H. Thomson to Ezra J. Peck, Oct. 1850; WCL, Peck MSS.
57. Augustus C. Brown, "Anti-secret Societies," *Williams Quarterly*, 8 (1861), 282.

that of our Republican institutions and of Christianity." [58] Yet
even Hopkins, in answer to an inquiry from President Hitchcock
of Amherst in 1846, found some good in the fraternity movement.
"I ought to add," he wrote in response, "that I have reason to suppose that one object of some of the Societies here is the cultivation
of manners, and so far they have improved." [59] The fraternities
not only cultivated manners, as Mark Hopkins supposed, but they
also rewarded those who possessed them with invitations to join the
magic circle. This very concern with manners, which Hopkins as
well as many other critics greeted with approval, helps tremen-
dously in explaining the appeal of the movement as well as its
significance. For in the end polished manners are necessary for
success in this world, not the next.

James A. Garfield was neither the first nor the last to complain
of Williams that "the absence of females from table and society
takes away a very wholesome restraint and leaves roughness in
its stead," but as a critic of the secret societies, he overlooked their
role in overcoming the coarseness which he found so unpalatable.[60]
Another young man at Williams did not. Samuel Chapman Armstrong, who belonged to no fraternity, in 1862 wrote to his sister
in Hawaii, comparing the fortunes of a fellow student from Hawaii
with his own at Williams:

> He hasn't got rid of his coarseness & vulgarity. . . . He has
> been too poor to cut a very good figure, has lived in a wretched
> room & been little benefitted by the rough ways of students. I
> have been more fortunate, board in a club of capital fellows,
> all classmates. . . . The fellows are many of them from N.Y.
> City, are all genteel, dress well and exhibit polite manners;
> their society, I value a great deal for its refining influence; &
> I need it because my manners at the island became very poor &
> rough by my never mingling at all in good society.[61]

58. *Opinions of Distinguished Men, on the Influence of Secret Societies* (n.d.),
p. 4. Distributed by the antifraternity group to parents of incoming freshmen, according to *Williams Quarterly*, 8 (1861), 279, this pamphlet also contains adverse
opinions on fraternities by Albert Hopkins, President Jeremiah Day of Yale,
President Edward Everett of Harvard, and Daniel Webster. The copy used was
in the collected collegeana of W. T. R. Marvin, '54, WCL, suggesting that it was
distributed some time between 1850 and 1854.

59. MH to Edward Hitchcock, Aug. 8, 1846; photostat, Amherst College Library
MSS.

60. Smith, *The Life and Letters of James Abram Garfield, 1*, 75; from a letter
to C. E. Fuller, July 30, 1854.

61. Samuel Chapman Armstrong to Ellen Armstrong, Sept. 22, 1862; WCL, Armstrong MSS.

Who were these "capital fellows" whose manners the son of a New
England missionary to Hawaii found so inspiring? There were
seventeen of them, all members of secret societies; four of them
were editors of the *Quarterly*, one was president of the glee club;
two were Class Day marshals and therefore wealthy boys, for this
honor entailed providing the senior class with an all-night dinner.
None belonged to the Shakespeare Club, the Thespian Club, or the
Mozart Quintette Club, and only two belonged to the Lyceum of
Natural History.[62] There could have been no better preparation
for success in the second half of the 19th century than to have
mingled daily with these young men who not only epitomized new
success patterns but had institutionalized them in the secret society
movement.

Williams owed more than a new set of prestige values to the fraternities. It was indebted, as well, for a good number of its students.
Fraternity men, it may be supposed, were sometimes as important
as the reputation of Mark Hopkins in the recruitment of new students. In 1850 a Williams junior wrote from Northampton to a
classmate, looking forward to the next electioneering campaign,
"There are a number going to college from here. I shall endeavor
to induce some good ones to enter Williams. If not this year next
year will do nearly as well as we shall want men every year." [63] The
college was indebted to the fraternities for expanding social horizons that finally encompassed the faculty itself: in 1869 Kappa
Alpha and Sigma Phi opened their doors on Class Day to students,
families, and faculty.[64] In providing a common meeting ground for
men of all four college classes the fraternities helped to eliminate
much that was disruptive and narrowing in traditional class rival-
ries. And there can be little doubt that the intercollegiate ties which
the fraternity movement promoted facilitated a greater inter-
change of information and ideas between colleges than had hitherto
been possible.

In 1868 secret societies were first mentioned in the minutes of
the board of trustees. The student petition of that year asking that
the societies be abolished was referred to a committee with instruc-
tions to report at the next meeting, and there the matter rested.
That the petition died is not surprising. Sometime before 1845
the board had overruled Mark Hopkins in his desire to abolish the

---

62. *Williams Quarterly, 9* (1862), 294, gives a list of the members of Armstrong's
eating club. The *Gulielmensian* (Boston, 1862) gives their undergraduate records.
63. Thomas Gilfillan to Ezra J. Peck, Aug. 26, 1850; WCL, Peck MSS.
64. *Williams Quarterly, 18* (1869), 45.

fraternities; after 1845 Hopkins felt that they were too deeply
rooted to be attacked successfully.[65] Every trustee who was elected
to the board during the presidency of Mark Hopkins and who was
a member of a class graduating after the arrival of Kappa Alpha
in 1833 was a fraternity member. Hopkins' oldest son, Henry, of
the Class of 1858, was a neutral while at Williams; his brothers
Archibald, '62, Amos, '63, and Mark, '71, were all members of
Delta Psi, as was their cousin Edward, '64, only son of Albert Hopkins. That the college took no action against the fraternities, and
that the Hopkins boys themselves became members, does not mean
that orthodoxy ever gave up its preference for a brotherhood of
professing Christians. It could not, however, argue very persua-
sively against the attributes and values of worldly success.

65. In his letter to President Hitchcock of Amherst in 1845, Hopkins wrote:
"At an early period I was in favor of taking strong measures . . . but was overruled." Although Hopkins accepted the fraternities, he was still worrying about
them in 1856. Arthur Latham Perry recorded in his diary, Jan. 24, 1856: "Long
conversation with Dr. Hopkins this morning on Secret Societies, and on our duty
to look after the young men, especially those going astray." "Recollections and
Diaries," 2, 562.

7. The Decline of Evangelical Orthodoxy

ALTHOUGH a growing fraternity movement clearly spelled trouble for the career of evangelical piety at Williams, religious revivals during the Hopkins administration were successful in stemming the tide of the world at least eight times. This achievement, which depended so much on the labor and love of Albert Hopkins, reflected the continuing strength of a Protestantism which was rooted in emotion and moral asceticism. In time, however, orthodox Protestantism itself moved away from the stress which Albert Hopkins had placed upon the importance of religious experience based on a sense of sin and a redeeming reconciliation with God through Christ. And even during the years of his own great work at Williams, he was exposed to countless reminders of what appeared to be the increasing hopelessness of his mission.

During the period from 1836 through 1858, for instance, the years of great evangelical revivals were so scattered that, on the average, a revival occurred once in about three years. Twice, in 1843–46 and 1854–57, the ground was altogether parched for a period of four consecutive years. Statistics indicate that in 1831 and 1855 less than half of the student body had experienced conversion. Even so, the ratio of religiously dedicated young men at Williams was generally higher than elsewhere. In 1831 Williams boasted proportionately more professing Christians than Yale, Harvard, Princeton, and Amherst. In 1855 it similarly outranked Bowdoin, Middlebury, Brown, Yale, and Union, although both Amherst and Wesleyan surpassed it.[1] If these statistics suggest a hard core of resistance to conversion in all colleges, as well as Williams, they also warrant the supposition that the indifferent and the unwilling knew what they were doing when they persisted in being boys.

Evangelical Christianity asked its converts to stop behaving like boys—there can be no doubt about that. Periods of religious fervor, therefore, were salutary as far as the discipline of the college was concerned, even though the mood was difficult to maintain and as

1. In 1831, 54 undergraduates of a student body of 115 were reported to be professing Christians; in 1855, 110 of 224. See *Quarterly Journal of the American Education Society, 3* (1831), 294, and a printed leaflet entitled "Religious Condition of Colleges," distributed by the Society of Inquiry of Amherst College, dated Feb. 17, 1855.

difficult to make attractive. In 1841 Albert Hopkins indulged his imagination long enough to envision the horrors of a college without "effectual religious restraints," remarking that "in such a state of things, the ingenuity of the young, their scheming and planning powers, instead of being exercised on . . . expansive and ennobling objects . . . are employed in conceiving various kinds of mischief and in practicing low and malicious annoyances." [2]

When, therefore, emotional evangelical Protestantism of the sort which flourished at Williams could gain the adherence of a sufficiently large number of students—among whom might be a major culprit or so—peace and quiet filled the college halls and lawns and the faculty punishment book collected dust. In 1812 a revival disrupted an outburst of infidelity that had manifested itself in a drunken mock celebration of the Lord's supper, and the leading undergraduate deist was so won over that he later became a Congregational clergyman. In 1845, when Mark Hopkins observed a general good order and heard faculty reports of "unusual attention to study," he decided—although prematurely—that possibly a revival was in the air.[3] During the revival of 1848 he admitted to Amos Lawrence that an outburst of religious enthusiasm naturally meant "increased labor and responsibility," but there was, he added, a compensation. "College government at such times is nothing—we have no trouble." [4]

The reverse of the coin was equally clear: when there were no revivals, there was trouble. The Williams student appeared to be at least as ready to prove his depravity as he was ready to confess it. In March 1802 the college was in a state of insurrection for ten days in protest against an examination schedule. In 1808 a student riot left the college so depleted of faculty that Ebenezer Fitch called a four-week recess.[5] An unbounded sense of playfulness rather than major rioting, however, was more characteristic of the Williams student. Fighting with water pails in the dormitories, filling the college halls with logs and stones and bricks and ashes, breaking freshman windows, scattering chicken feathers on town porches, locking faculty members out of classrooms—these were some of the manifestations of undergraduate playfulness which college authorities hoped evangelical religion might prevent. The result of Albert Hopkins' pious suggestion to the Class of 1845—

2. Albert Hopkins, "Revivals of Religion in Williams College," pp. 348-9.
3. MH to AL, Mar. 11, 1845; MHS, MH-AL MSS.
4. MH to AL, Mar. 3, 1848; MHS, MH-AL MSS.
5. For an account of these two rebellions see Wells and Davis, *Sketches of Williams College*, pp. 19-22.

that it report to Professor Tatlock for extracurricular instruction
in an unfamiliar branch of mathematics in order that its members
might more gainfully employ their afternoons—is evidence of both
his concern for student behavior and the spirit of the undergraduates. After one afternoon of following Hopkins' suggestion, a
member of the class reported, "We . . . finally turned our backs
on the whole affair [and] found it necessary to take some refresh-
ments & accordingly adjourned to Ma'am Nichols' & finished a few
bottles of beer." [6]

Evangelical Protestantism was, on the whole, no more successful
in stemming the tide of worldliness than it was in taking the play
out of youth. Even Albert Hopkins, in his early years at Williams,
contained himself within the confines of the other world only with
difficulty. An 1836 entry in his journal confessed: "See the ocean
of worldly thoughts like a high dam kept in only by a thin paste.
I am walking under it. See that it will make a break upon me unless
I run into Christ." [7] Among those who experienced similar difficulties was a young tutor who dreamed one night that he was "walking on through green fields pleasantly and prosperously, when all
at once a snake darted out from the grass and twined himself about
my body. I instantly drew the moral," he concluded. "Earthly
pleasures are mixed with pain." [8] Perhaps they were—and it was
a function of evangelical orthodoxy to prove it—but hosts of undergraduates, just the same, were willing partners in the pursuit
of worldly pleasure.

The first set of college laws had established a code of moral conduct, with appropriate fines for surrender to earthly pleasures.[9]
For frequenting a house of ill fame for the purpose of "expensive
entertainment" the fine was six shillings; the fine for fornication
was ten—until 1805, when expulsion seemed more fitting; for wearing "woman's apparel" the punishment was "public admonition,
suspension, or rustication." Whether these fines were more suitable
to Yale, from which they were imported, than they were to Williams, it is not possible to say. Early disciplinary records have not
survived, and even if they had, the euphemisms for recording violations against the code would probably have made them useless. Even

6. William Dwight Whitney to Elizabeth Whitney, June 2, 1844; SML:YU, Whitney MSS.
7. Entry of June 3, 1836; in Sewall, *Life of Prof. Albert Hopkins,* p. 152.
8. Entry of Apr. 28, 1854; in Perry, "Recollections and Diaries," *2,* 497.
9. *The Laws of Williams College,* Stockbridge, Mass., Loring Andrews, 1795.

the records which have survived are not especially revealing. What, for instance, was the "outrageous conduct" which led to the expulsion of a Williams junior in 1869? [10] What was a student doing one night in 1837 when he was fined "for sleeping out of his room"? [11] No one knows.

However elusive to the historian, sex was never altogether subdued in Williamstown. This was hardly an innocent letter which a former student wrote from Troy to a member of the senior class in 1832: "How are the fair sex? Bad times you must have in the city of Williams these cold winter nights. I have not [been] to visit the Chic—since I went with you." [12] As early as the 1830's an early version of the 20th-century pin-up girl was being nailed to student walls.[13] "I feel the want of the company of some female very sensibly," a student wailed in 1843.[14] A member of the Class of 1848, who refused to deny the want, imported a prostitute into Williamstown, for which, in addition to "having also been very irregular in his studies," he was expelled in 1845. (Within a month he was entered at Princeton.) [15] In 1863 a freshman was dismissed for a commencement week speech in which he mentioned two local prostitutes by name, expressing his regret that he and his associates "could not embrace them any more," one of them having just died in the service of a Williams man.[16] (The speaker was graduated from Yale in 1867.) The same year Mark Hopkins received a letter from an undergraduate member of the Theological Society, charging that "some of the young men who are first and loudest in their professions in our social meetings are, to my knowledge, and to the knowledge of the whole college, fornicators—drunken and profane." [17]

Whether this letter particularly worried Hopkins is not a matter of record, nor is there sufficient evidence to judge properly whether there really was during his administration sufficient deviation from Christian morality in matters of sex to warrant alarm. One fact,

10. Faculty Records, Feb. 17, 1869; Williams College, Admissions office, MSS.
11. Faculty Records, 1837; Williams College, Admissions office, MSS.
12. Thomas ——— to Nathan T. Rossiter, Nov. 15, 1832; WCL, Misc. MSS, 9.
13. *Williams Quarterly, 1* (1853), 94.
14. William Dwight Whitney to Dwight W. Marsh, Mar. 16, 1843; SML:YU, Whitney MSS.
15. Faculty Records; July 9, 1845. Horatio N. Brinsmade to MH, Aug. 11, 1845; WCL, Misc. MSS, *1.*
16. *New York Daily Transcript,* Sept. 14, 1863. E. B. Jennings to MH, Aug. 1, 1864; WCL, Misc. MSS, *10.*
17. "A Brother in the Church" to MH, Oct. 31, 1863; WCL, Misc. MSS, *10.*

however, is very certain. He did worry about the prevalence of a particular undergraduate outlet for carnal pleasure—masturbation.[18] For several years after 1838, his attention having been drawn to cases of undergraduates who "were on the borders of ruin," he lectured to the college on its evils and distributed among the students copies of Samuel Woodward's *Hints for the Young in Relation to the Health of Body and Mind*, a handbook on the subject, its consequences, and its sinfulness.[19] In 1843 or 1844, satisfied that he and Woodward had subjected the students of Williams College to right views on the matter, Hopkins abandoned his lectures and the distribution of the book. In 1846, however, certain that he could not "let it rest thus much longer," he welcomed a letter from Amos Lawrence enclosing a new manual that might prove as useful as had Woodward in the past. With the help of the new manual, he enlisted all the techniques of scare, including the threat of insanity, in an effort to root out an activity that ran counter to Christian precept.

College officials were more ready to record violations of the laws against drinking and students were more ready to write letters about intoxication than either were about fornication. Indeed, both the incidence and the discovery of intemperance were probably higher. Samuel Austin Talcott of the Class of 1806 may be the only Williams man who ever delivered a drunken valedictory at commencement, but he had many imitators on less formal occasions.[20] Before the temperance movement, a product of the Second Great Awakening, became an adjunct of evangelical orthodoxy, drinking was not the worst of self-indulgences at Williams. In fact, an occasional drink was permissible. When Albert Hopkins was an undergraduate, he wrote to his brother Harry about a game of ball in which "we had three or four bottles on the carpet, and some of the fellows got pretty well on towards the West Indies before we got through."[21]

Liquor received its first serious setback at Williams in 1823, when the faculty forbade alcoholic treats by successful appointees to commencement honors, "except wine by permission of the

18. See AL to MH, June 22, 1846, and Hopkins' response, June 29, 1846; MHS, MH-AL MSS.
19. Samuel Bayard Woodward, *Hints for the Young in Relation to the Health of Body and Mind,* Boston, William D. Ticknor, 1838.
20. Keyes Danforth, *Boyhood Reminiscences* (New York, Gazlay Brothers, 1895), pp. 112–13.
21. Mar. 1823; HL, 2.

faculty." [22] This restriction was inspired by an especially drunken treat which terminated with the burning of the college privy.[23] The temperance movement took firmer hold, however, and by 1828, two years after the founding of the American Temperance Society (Justin Edwards, valedictorian of the Class of 1810, was its first secretary), there were two undergraduate temperance societies—one that favored total abstinence and one that permitted the drinking of wine.[24] By 1830 the movement had completely engulfed Williamstown. The trustees authorized the faculty "to forbid students to board at any house where they have reason to believe wine or spirits are furnished or sold to them." [25] The "new and delightful theme," as Mary Hopkins wrote to her mother-in-law, so captured the community that on February 24, 1833, her husband delivered two temperance lectures.[26] Beginning in 1845 every student was required to sign a pledge promising that he would "neither drink intoxicating drinks, nor supply it to others, nor have any agency in introducing it into the college." [27]

But temperance speakers and the laws which their work inspired could not kill drink. The student who was warned in 1836 for drinking wine in his room was one of a goodly company. Infractions of the laws against drinking went before the faculty every year, until in 1849 five men were expelled for drinking in their rooms, among them the son of Secretary of War William L. Marcy.[28] In the 1850's, cases of discipline involving the use of liquor waned, while infractions of the law against leaving town without permission increased, suggesting that the Williams undergraduate realized that worldly pleasure could be found beyond the confines of Williamstown. In 1858 a group of students operated an undercover liquor agency, perhaps the earliest of agencies that aimed at fulfilling undergraduate needs.[29] Just the same, one freshman of the 1850's, when told that a classmate had been drunk the night

22. TR, *2*, 32–3; Sept. 2, 1823.
23. Recounted in a letter from Albert Hopkins to Harry Hopkins, Aug. 7, 1823; HL, *2*.
24. Albert Hopkins to Harry Hopkins, Nov. 15, 1828; HL, *4*.
25. TR, *2*, 109; Aug. 31, 1830.
26. Mary Hubbell Hopkins to Mary Curtis Hopkins, Feb. 24, 1833; HL, *5*.
27. TR, *2*, 249; Aug. 19, 1845.
28. MH to AL, Apr. 2, 1849; MHS, MH-AL MSS. Expulsion apparently did young Edmund Marcy no good. According to Arthur Latham Perry, four years later he was hanged from the yard-arm of a naval vessel for mutiny. *Williamstown and Williams College*, p. 615.
29. *Williams Quarterly*, *5* (1858), 378.

before, is supposed to have exclaimed in response: "Drunk! A fellow in college, and in our class drunk! Why, I did not know that any one in college ever was drunk." [30]

Albert Hopkins never succeeded in enlisting half of the student body in his army of model boys. Nor did he succeed in convincing most Williams men that, all in all, it was a pretty awful world they lived in. "They are telling us what a marvelous thing it is that a man can now be in Vienna, London, New York, and Chicago, all in the short month of February," Albert declared in the early 1840's. "Well, what if he can? Whether that be a blessing to either the man or the world depends altogether on what sort of a man he is. If he is a bad man the stiller he keeps the better." [31]

The Williams boys were too confident about America's future, too eager to exploit and to create its abundance, too imbued with a sense of freedom—of mind and of action—to take seriously Albert Hopkins' strictures upon railroads and steamships. The bottomless pit, against which evangelical Protestantism warned, yawned before them, but they fell in more often than they crossed it. James Richards of the Class of 1809, who died while serving as a missionary in Ceylon, was representative of the early Williams, but by 1833 the college was turning out, in a man like Horace Clark, a product that was to be more typical of the ensuing decades. The son of a Presbyterian minister, Clark was admitted to the New York bar in 1837, married a daughter of Cornelius Vanderbilt in 1848, was elected to the United States House of Representatives in 1856, and in time was president or vice-president of a number of Vanderbilt railroads. Not every Williams man achieved the success of Horace Clark, but more of them aimed in his direction than ever took the path of James Richards.

The career of Clark is symbolic of a major problem which confronted evangelical piety at Williams as well as elsewhere. The last great religious outpouring at Williams—and one of the last in the country as a whole—occurred in 1858, when the pious took advantage of the temporary loss of confidence in materialism provoked by the panic of 1857 to win the worldly to orthodoxy. The panic was temporary, and so was the renewal of evangelical enthusiasm. In a country that was possessed of so great a material promise it was not possible to be disillusioned about the future for

30. Scudder, *Life and Letters of David Coit Scudder*, pp. 25–6.
31. Addison Ballard, "Remarks at Semi-centennial of the Class of '42, Williams, June 21, 1892"; in typescript "Memorabilia," pp. 17–18; WCL.

long. As for Clark, he spent the years 1857 and 1858 buying up railroad stocks.[32]

After 1858, wherever they looked, Albert Hopkins and men of similar persuasion were confronted with increasing evidence that the hold of evangelical orthodoxy on the Williams undergraduate was visibly weakening. Positive and apparent decline could hardly be blamed upon the weather, although for many years a cardinal tactic of evangelicalism had called for concentrating its artillery in the last weeks of winter, when, it was thought, the impenitent would welcome escape. The seasons of the year being what they are, however, weather was both a partner and an enemy of conversion. The orthodox, for instance, were quick to attribute a relaxation in religious activity, in the spring and summer months, to the fact that balmy days, with their invitation to outdoor activity, put stronger weapons in the hands of the indifferent.[33] When the usual undergraduate riots and scrapes failed to appear in the early spring of 1832, Mark Hopkins remarked, "The winter has been so cold, perhaps they have not got thawed out yet."[34] Naturally, orthodoxy aimed at capturing the impenitent before they did thaw out, and, as it happened in 1832, they did.

But the history of weather in Williamstown indicates that there is no reason to suppose that as the century grew older the winters grew warmer—in 1861 Samuel Warren Dike of the Class of 1863 froze his nose going from prayers to supper—or that spring and summer were never unpleasantly cold.[35] On May 29, 1861, Samuel Chapman Armstrong wrote to his sister, "To-day I feel disgusted. When it was winter people said that a beautiful spring-time would soon come, so I tried to endure the cold days and be cheerful. . . . But here it is almost June and we are wearing our winter clothing and sit by the fire. . . . We see the sun now and then from week to week and everybody runs to see it when they get a chance."[36] The pious, seeking an explanation for increasing manifestations of indifference, were obliged to look elsewhere than to the weather.

32. See *Dictionary of American Biography*, *4*, 132–3, for a short sketch of Clark.

33. See, for instance, Albert Hopkins in Durfee, *A History of Williams College*, p. 233.

34. MH to Harry Hopkins, Mar. 16, 1832; HL, *5*. For other references to the spring as a harbinger of trouble see these letters of Mark Hopkins: to Harvey Rice, Nov. 18, 1825[?], HL, *2;* to Harry Hopkins, May 15, 1833, HL, *5;* to Amos Lawrence, May 8, 1845, MHS, MH-AL MSS.

35. Samuel Warren Dike to his sister, Feb. 17, 1861; WCL, Dike MSS. See Willis I. Milham, *Meteorology in Williams College* (Williamstown, 1936), pp. 10–11, for weather records.

36. In "Personal Memories and Letters of General S. C. Armstrong," pp. 56–56*b*.

Compulsory morning and evening prayers had never been a test of the religious spirit of the college, but mounting disrespect and demands that they be abolished gave evidence of a new problem of serious concern to the orthodox. Deliberate absenteeism, augmented by feigned illness, was but one indication that the prestige of required religious attendance was reaching a new low at Williams in the 1850's and 1860's. At the chapel itself indifference and disrespect were apparent in the incidence of unwashed, uncombed, half-dressed undergraduates and in the sullen reception which frequently met visiting preachers. Students whiled away the time by ogling feminine visitors, writing obscene doggerel on the fly-leaves of hymnals, or testing their powers of expectoration with tobacco juice in the chapel aisle.[37] Beginning in 1858, a revival year, the *Quarterly* ran editorials recommending the abolition of compulsory prayers.[38] An editor in 1864 observed, "We recollect not a few times, when the 'Amen' seemed the most appropriate and beautiful part of the service." [39]

When they looked from the chapel to the undergraduate societies that claimed the extracurricular attention of the pious, Albert Hopkins and his friends found no cause for comfort. Offspring of the Second Great Awakening, the Theological Society, founded in 1805, and the "Society of Williams College for inquiry into the state of missions, and the duty of young men to engage in them," founded in 1818, had joined forces in 1849 as a means of shoring up their weakening underpinnings. As the Mills Theological Society, the new organization continued to serve the function of its predecessors which, as their names suggested, had concerned themselves with problems of the ministry and of foreign missions. The theologians had built their meetings around disputes on such matters as whether Episcopalians could be pious and whether Christians should take one another into courts of law. Members of the Society of Inquiry had entertained themselves with accounts of their own religious experiences and had listened to lectures from visiting missionaries.

Although membership in the organization created by their union in 1849 reflected a sizable increase, attendance never remotely paralleled the membership, even falling as low as seven at one of the

37. See Charles [?] to his sister, May 7, 1851 [1857?]; WCL, Misc. MSS, 8. *Williams Quarterly, 11* (1864), 280–1; *13* (1865), 37–8; *15* (1868), 233. *Vidette, 2* (Nov. 7, 1868), 5. *Williams Quarterly, 17* (1869), 53. *Vidette, 4* (Oct. 9, 1869), 4; *4* (Nov. 6, 1869), 4.
38. *Williams Quarterly, 6* (1858), 91.
39. *Ibid.* (1864), 209.

last meetings in 1873, the year when the society voted itself out of business. At a meeting on November 5, 1873, the society passed a resolution stating, "We, the members of the Mills Theological Society, believe that in the Providence of God the time has come when this organization is of no avail in the accomplishment of the purpose for which it was founded." [40]

Some comfort was to be derived from the statistics of Williams men who were clergymen or who intended to be, but the comfort was as hollow as knowing that a unit of the Y.M.C.A. was ready to pick up the pieces of the Mills Theological Society. Statistics demonstrated that in 1827, 27 per cent of the alumni of Williams College were clergymen, that in 1856 the percentage had increased to 30, and in 1869 to 31.[41] But by refusing to consider as an alumnus any man who did not receive a diploma, the statisticians and necrologists of the college succeeded in hiding the grim evidence that for the number of students passing through its walls, it was actually getting fewer clergymen in return. Twenty-eight per cent of the members of the classes of 1836 through 1845 became clergymen; 22 per cent of the members of the classes of 1846 through 1865, and only 13 per cent of the members of the classes from 1866 to 1872. By 1891 the decline in clergymen among the alumni was so apparent that the trustees abolished the practice of conducting an alumni prayer meeting on the Sunday evening of commencement week.[42] When the Classes of 1867, 1868, and 1871 recorded their probable careers for the benefit of their class historians, law stood first in the Class of 1867, business in the Class of 1868, and law in the Class of 1871.[43] Evangelical Protestantism could look for consolation neither to the alumni nor to the undergraduates. Everywhere businessmen, lawyers, and doctors were surpassing the clergy among the sons of Williams.

Even the faculty exhibited the same tendency toward a relaxation of evangelical interest. The faculty stalwarts of the early years of the Hopkins administration were as well equipped as their president to exert a sound Christian influence. No fewer than seven

40. A similar development was taking place on other college campuses, as is pointed out in C. Howard Hopkins, *History of the Y.M.C.A. in North America* (New York, Association Press, 1951), pp. 271–308.

41. *Quarterly Journal of the American Education Society, 2* (1827), 26. *American Journal of Education and College Review, 1* (1856), 581. *Williams Quarterly, 16* (1869), 212. These statistics were derived from general catalogues of the college which listed only graduates.

42. TR, *3*, 361; May 22, 1891.

43. *Williams Quarterly, 14* (1867), 250–1. *Vidette, 2* (July 4, 1868), 6. *Williams Quarterly, 18* (1871), 171–2.

professors with long tenure were products of theological seminaries; most of the others were active parishioners or lay preachers. Beginning with the appointment of Thomas E. Clark to the professorship of chemistry in 1858, a new element was introduced into the faculty. Clark was the first professionally trained professor in the history of the college, having received a Doctor's degree from Göttingen in 1856. He was followed by Franklin Carter in 1864, who spent the year before he took up his professorial reins at Williams studying in Germany and Paris; and in 1868, by Charles F. Gilson, who had studied at Heidelberg; William R. Dimmock, who had had graduate training in law at Harvard; and A. W. Wright, whose postgraduate career had included study at Yale, Heidelberg, and Berlin.[44] Even before the arrival of these men, whose careers in graduate study revealed a shift in emphasis from teaching as a calling in the work of God to teaching as a profession, the trustees had inserted an intimation of a slackening in faculty piety in a new edition of the college laws in 1863. The faculty, the trustees reminded, were to consider it their duty, as well as that of the students, to attend the religious exercises of the college.

The signposts of decline were manifold. As disturbing as anything to the pious was the popular reception which greeted Ralph Waldo Emerson on his visits to the campus in 1854 and 1865: Emerson, who had strayed so far from the fold of orthodoxy that he was wayward even in his Unitarianism, was in every sense a campus idol in 1865. The college itself relaxed its laws on religious attendance.[45] In 1857 the time of morning prayers was changed from sunrise to after breakfast, and in 1867 evening prayers were omitted on Wednesdays and Saturdays in order not to take the spirit of the playing field into the chapel.[46] A change took place in the personnel of college fund-raising committees; in 1825 a six-man committee appointed by the trustees to raise money was composed entirely of clerics; in a similar drive of 1868 the committee was composed of bankers, lawyers, and businessmen. And in 1868

44. When President Theodore Dwight Woolsey of Yale wrote a letter of recommendation for Wright to Mark Hopkins on Jan. 20, 1868, he added: "There is one drawback. He was supposed when we elected him tutor to be skeptical. . . . I regard him as . . . probably a Christian in difficulty. I have no doubt he would teach chemistry better than it is taught here." WCL, Misc. MSS, _10_. Wright returned to Yale in 1872.

45. TR, _2_, 459; July 29, 1867.

46. In 1857 Harvard and Brown eliminated evening prayers; Yale followed suit in 1859, but at Amherst and Wesleyan, as at Williams, abolition was restricted to Wednesday and Saturday evenings.

the most telling blow of all was struck. The barometer of piety was destroyed: the noonday chapel service was discontinued.[47]

The explanations for the decline of evangelical piety at Williams College are many. Basic to them all is the simple fact that orthodoxy demanded too much. "The Christian faith is not naturally so fascinating to the young," a student wrote in 1871, "that its teachers can afford to make it still less so." [48] The evidence is overwhelming that the teachers, of whom Albert Hopkins was an able representative, tried so hard to take the fascination out of living in this world that piety itself foundered on the rocks of worldliness. Even Samuel Chapman Armstrong, himself a pious youth and son of a missionary, found cause for complaint. He informed members of the Theological Society in 1861 that it was "all humbug" that they should be willing to go out and labor among the heathen without decent financial support that would provide the necessary comforts.[49] When, in 1863, the trustees substituted a pledge promising the avoidance of intemperance for the old total abstinence pledge of 1845, the *Quarterly* promptly announced that "no discredit attaches itself, in College, to a disregard of these pledges. . . . The old pledge was regarded by the majority of the students as a joke upon the Freshmen." [50] In 1865 the complaint was voiced that "it is as unjust as it is foolish to condemn dancing because aristocrats and savages choose to dance in a state of partial or complete nudity." [51] In 1869 *Vidette* subscribed to the attractions of this world by publishing an article entitled "Beyond the River," a report on Mount Holyoke Seminary for the elucidation of Williams undergraduates.[52]

What the majority of students *did* is as important as what they said. In the career of the fraternities at Williams the failure of orthodoxy to make itself heard in protest against secular values and ambitions is of course most clearly demonstrated. It is significant, too, that when the Mills Theological Society held its last meeting in 1873, it turned its records over to a new, and apparently

47. Perry, *Williamstown and Williams College*, p. 556. *Vidette, 2* (Sept. 26, 1868), 6. Perry gives the date as 1867, but the *Vidette* item speaks of "poorly attended" noon meetings as late as Sept. 1868.
48. *Vidette, 6* (Oct. 28, 1871), 37.
49. To Ellen Armstrong, Feb. 17, 1861; WCL, Armstrong MSS.
50. *Williams Quarterly, 11* (1863), 118.
51. *Ibid., 12* (1865), 244.
52. *Vidette, 4* (Oct. 23, 1869), 6.

more appropriate, agency of Christian influence, the undergraduate Y.M.C.A., in which the concern was not only the religious life of its members, but the social, physical, and intellectual as well. The victory of *this* world over the next showed itself as well in a new respect for learning at Williams and in the homes from which the Williams undergraduate came. The letters which Moses Hallock, the Plainfield cleric and schoolmaster, wrote to his sons William and Gerard between 1816 and 1819 were quite clear in their insistence that Godliness rather than scholarship was to be pursued. "The knowledge, not of books, but of the true God, through Jesus Christ, saves the soul. Your mother and I . . . feel interested in your scholarship and in your character; but we forget these, to think of your immortal part," he wrote them in 1816.[53] "I mean to be a good scholar," young Arthur Latham Perry wrote in 1850, "but I hope I shall remember that scholarship is nothing, that all worldly good is nothing compared with heavenly good." [54]

By 1867, however, worldly good was a compelling attraction, and scholarship was of considerable assistance, although certainly not essential in its attainment. A new kind of letter was being written to their sons at Williams by fathers who had carved out careers for themselves in a nation where hard work was rewarded by material success. "You do not *devote* yourselves to study," Edward G. Whelen wrote to his son Russell, a Williams sophomore, in 1867. "Your social indulgence interferes constantly with your *study*. . . . I studied French, whilst doing a large business on the railroad station, on the steamboat—waiting five minutes anywhere —a book was in my hand." When Edward Whelen touched upon the subject that had been uppermost in the parental concern of Moses Hallock, he reminded his son that attendance at compulsory chapel would not seem such a hardship "if you had walked down year after year in a driving snow storm to open a store, and make a fire for *no* pay, & then back to breakfast." [55]

Paralleling a father's hope that a Williams education might prove a material asset, of course, was the development of new fields of practical learning—symbolized by the Sheffield Scientific School at Yale and the Lawrence Scientific School at Harvard. In other fields as well American scholarship began to show the influence of work which had been exciting scholars in German universities for

53. Letter of Mar. 19, 1816, in Cyrus Yale, *Life of the Rev. Jeremiah Hallock, of Canton, Conn. to Which is Added a Sketch of the Life of The Rev. Moses Hallock, of Plainfield, Mass.* (New York, American Tract Society, 1866), pp. 341-2.

54. Entry of Apr. 26, 1850, in Perry, "Recollections and Diaries," *1*, 225.

55. Sept. 21, 1867; HP, *5*.

a long time. German scholarship began to penetrate the American college at Harvard in the early decades of the 19th century; in the later years of the Hopkins era, when Williams appointed a new professor to the faculty, it found itself more and more participating in the new-found interest in sound learning, scholarship, scientific experiment, and graduate training. The old-time professor, for whom a chair at a college was an evangelical opportunity, was ill-equipped to compete intellectually with the products of the German universities or the new American graduate schools. When the college finally did capitulate outright to learning, as it did with seven new appointments in 1881 and 1882, the divorce between learning and evangelical piety was readily apparent. "My expectations in regard to the new professors are not fully met, in the religious way," the new president of Williams, Franklin Carter, complained in 1882. "In the scholarly way they are perfectly met. . . . but [we] want more efficient Christian help. . . . There is danger from the secular tendencies of [the] new men." [56]

Evangelical orthodoxy did not go down to defeat, however, without a battle. Albert Hopkins shifted his center of interest, after the demise of the noon chapel service, to the impenitent hill folk on the outskirts of Williamstown. In 1866 piety displayed an official confidence in the future when the trustees subscribed $5,000 to the erection of a new building for the Congregational Church in Williamstown, and in 1867 it built itself a monument commemorating the men of the haystack.[57] In 1869 the board of trustees expressed a favorable opinion upon the desirability of having at least seven clergymen among its seventeen members.[58] In 1870 the faculty bowed to the demands of Episcopal students that they be permitted to attend their own denominational services on Sundays, but required that written permission be granted by their parents.[59] In 1871, after Arthur Latham Perry, in chapel, began to read out of a Unitarian translation of the Bible which he preferred to the King James version, the trustees reinstated the King James version.[60]

Efforts were made to soften the tenor of compulsory chapel: the

56. Franklin Carter to Charles W. Huntington, in a series of letters urging Huntington to join the Williams faculty: Mar. 31, Apr. 10, Apr. 29, 1882; WCL, Misc. MSS, 6.

57. TR, 2, 439; Mar. 22, 1866. *Williams Quarterly, 14* (1867), 246.

58. TR, 3, 20; June 21, 1869.

59. Faculty Records, Feb. 1870.

60. TR, 3, 40; June 26, 1871. Perry, "Recollections and Diaries," 2, 636–45. See also MH to Charles Stoddard, Dec. 13, 1870, and Charles Stoddard to members of the board of trustees, Dec. 15, 1870: WCL, Joseph White Papers.

evangelical invocation was omitted, the service was shortened, a
student choir was added, the penalty for excessive absences was
eased.[61] Yet the hope that something might be gained by attention
to the superficial mechanics of the college religious exercises was
unwarranted: "Religion cannot be forced," a student observed in
1868.[62] The hope was as unwarranted as the new fears of Mark
Hopkins were ominous. As he neared the end of his presidency,
Hopkins decried the flood of naturalism that was taking hold of
the minds of young men, depriving them of a regard for the
presence of God as well as "any deep sense of sin." And he asked
his friend Ray Palmer "whether it is true all over the country that
when a man gets rich he goes into the Episcopal Church, and if
so whether this is necessary." [63]

The flood of naturalism of which Hopkins complained and the
siphoning off of materially successful Congregationalists into the
ranks of the Episcopalians continued unabated in the decades which
followed, but really the day of evangelicalism was at an end when
Mark Hopkins turned over the presidency of the college to Paul
Chadbourne in 1872. The college which he passed on was a college
with an athletic program instead of organized nature walks, a
Theological Society which within a year was to become a college
unit of the Y.M.C.A., an increasingly professional rather than a
dedicated faculty, a college with more fraternity meetings than
prayer meetings. Evangelical orthodoxy had had its day. Its
sobriety and self-denial ran counter to the optimism and buoyancy
of American youth. Its restraints ran counter to an American sense
of freedom, and its moral code challenged the attributes of worldly
success. Given the choice between the attractions of this world and
the asceticism necessary to prepare for the next, young Americans
at Williams, as elsewhere, chose the open prairie, the stock exchange, the legislative chamber. In overwhelming numbers they
agreed with an observation which a troubled Albert Hopkins had
written in his journal in 1831: "Have been able to compare living
religiously to nothing but swimming with a millstone around my
neck." [64]

61. *Williams Quarterly,* 7 (1859), 189; 8 (1860), 136. Faculty Records, Dec. 15,
1869.

62. *Vidette, 2* (Nov. 7, 1868), 5.

63. MH to Ray Palmer, Jan. 29, 1872, and Jan. 29, 1873; WCL, Hopkins-Palmer
MSS.

64. Entry in his journal for May 13, 1831; cited in Sewall, *Life of Prof. Albert
Hopkins,* p. 38.

Part Three: NATURE

8. Nature Is Sublime: The Official View

FOR YEARS, the Berkshire hills, despite their natural beauties, were a cross which Williams, in its relations with the outside world, bore with embarrassment. But within the college itself an abundance of nature, for which a symbol was found in Mount Greylock, was turned into an asset. Although they proceeded in different directions, college officials and undergraduates both found inspiration in the surrounding countryside and on the towering hills. To counterbalance a science curriculum which almost literally satisfied its purposes by pointing to the nearby mountains as evidence of divine creation, Williams students created and sustained a vital extracurricular Lyceum of Natural History. As a substitute for the mountain climbing which the college encouraged as a means of communion with God, they introduced a program of athletics and gymnastics. In the official scheme of things man, nature, and God were divinely related—and it was the function of the college to so demonstrate. In the ways of youth, however, nature and man were put to other uses, in which the satisfaction of a desire for excitement, the thrill and rewards of competition, the prestige of physical attractiveness, and the quest for practical scientific knowledge intruded themselves.

Henry David Thoreau, who sometimes talked as if *he* had discovered nature, visited Williamstown in 1844 and was inspired by a visit to Greylock to remark, "It would be no small advantage if every college were thus located at the base of a mountain." To the hermit of Walden the location of Williams College was "as good at least as one well-endowed professorship." [1] Although the college was hardly interested in subscribing to the notions of Thoreau or his Concord friends, the professorship of natural history, introduced in 1833, was not supported by any endowment at all until 1912. To compensate for this situation, in which a man like Thoreau might well find cause for satisfaction, the Williams undergraduate went to work with the kind of robust energy which prompted Thoreau's good friend, Ralph Waldo Emerson, to say, upon being exposed to the same scenery in 1865, "For the mountains, I don't quite like the proximity of a college and its noisy

1. Henry David Thoreau, *A Week on the Concord and Merrimack Rivers* (Boston, Houghton, Mifflin, 1894), p. 244.

students." [2] Thoreau and Emerson had disagreed before, and more profoundly, but on this occasion they were both placing a higher value upon the mountains than the students of Williams College were inclined to do. For in 1839 the students would have much preferred a well-endowed professorship in natural science to Greylock, and in 1865 they were probably as noisy as Emerson suggested because they had given up mountain climbing for baseball. They never forgot the mountains, but the meaning and the uses to which they were put surely changed.

In his inaugural address of 1836 Mark Hopkins postulated a number of traditional and universally acceptable contributions which were incumbent upon a college to provide in the formation of character in young men. To these contributions he added "fine scenery," suggesting perhaps that he and his listeners were influenced by a rural orientation, but, more important, raising to the level of books and professors the role of scenery in the formation of character.[3] Hopkins' high regard for scenery owed its inspiration, in large measure, to his awareness that natural scientists had historically tended to divorce their findings from religion. In company with other men of faith, the president of Williams met the fresh assaults of science in the 19th century not only by tying the mountains to the Gospel but by attempting altogether to capture them from wayward geologists and botanists. He reminded the students of the theological seminary at Andover in 1837 that whether geologists knew it or not, they were only laying bare a physical order which corresponded to a moral order that had been struck off by God many centuries before.[4]

To the scenery of Williamstown, therefore, Hopkins quite naturally assigned the task of demonstrating to his students the links which welded the moral and the physical into one. He called upon the same scenery which led Nathaniel Hawthorne to decide that "the students ought to be day dreamers, all of them,—when cloudland is one and the same thing with the substantial earth." [5]

2. *Journals of Ralph Waldo Emerson,* ed. Edward Waldo Emerson and Waldo Emerson Forbes (10 vols. Boston, Houghton, Mifflin, 1909–14), *10,* 118.

3. MH, *An Inaugural Discourse, Delivered at Williams College. September 15, 1836,* p. 6.

4. MH, *An Address, Delivered before the Porter Rhetorical Society of the Theological Seminary, at Its Anniversary. Sept. 5, 1837* (Andover, Gould and Newman, 1837), pp. 7, 10–11, 56.

5. Entry of Aug. 22, 1838, in *The American Notebooks by Nathaniel Hawthorne,* ed. Stewart, p. 54.

But Mark Hopkins was not interested in making day dreamers. The scenery was the same as Hawthorne's, but the thoughts which he hoped it would inspire among his undergraduates were the same as those of James McCosh, the Scottish philosopher who became president of Princeton. Said McCosh of his first impression of Williamstown and its encircling hills, "It struck me as a spot in which the Last Judgment might be held." [6]

Addressing themselves to the subject of nature with equal vigor and similar purpose, the stalwarts of Mark Hopkins' faculty participated in the challenge which their president regularly hurled at natural science. And, with him, they arrived at the same answers. When his brother Albert, far in advance of other American college professors, erected an observatory in Williamstown in 1838, "the leading idea . . . which lay at [its] foundation, was," in his words, *"that nature is to be studied rather than books."* [7] Why, Albert made explicitly clear in the address which he delivered at the dedication of the observatory. In their worship of the practical, he declared, men were losing sight of the moral. Education itself was being subverted by a prevailing notion that it was intended to whet the intellect, sharpen mental powers, and prepare "for action, action, action." [8] To counteract these influences, he confessed, he had decided that what Williams College needed most was an astronomical observatory, where the students could elevate their thoughts "toward that fathomless fountain and author of being, who has constituted matter and all its accidents as lively emblems of the immaterial kingdom." [9]

Fifteen years later the same message was being delivered to the students of Williams College by John Bascom. Subscribing to the position which had been taken by the brothers Hopkins, he went, however, beyond the assertion which was becoming a platitude on the Williams campus, that nature was "an expression of the great-

6. Quoted in M. A. DeWolfe Howe, *Classic Shades* (Boston, Little, Brown, 1928), p. 84.
7. Undated newspaper clipping from the [Boston?] *Courier*, entitled "Correspondence to the Courier," under the name of Albert Hopkins, Mar. 21, 1841; WCL, Scrapbook.
8. Albert Hopkins, *An Address Delivered at the Opening of the Observatory of Williams College. June 12, 1838* (Pittsfield, Phinehas Allen and Son, 1838), p. 6. Willis I. Milham, in his *Early American Observatories: Which Was the First Astronomical Observatory in America?* (Williamstown, 1938), concludes that Williams can lay claim to erecting the first substantial observatory in the United States; an earlier observatory which did not survive was erected at the University of North Carolina in 1831.
9. *Ibid.,* p. 19.

ness and goodness of God." [10] In addition, he constructed a theory of aesthetics upon the form, color, motion, and sound which nature manifested in the surrounding hills. Touched with a bit of mysticism, Bascom's views, in the end, were the old ones. Let man look to the mountains for the wonders that have been performed by God.

During the Hopkins administration the curriculum in the natural and physical sciences served the same purposes as the nearby mountains. The study of science at Williams received its original impulse from two early graduates of the college, Amos Eaton of the Class of 1799 and Chester Dewey of the Class of 1806. Dewey, who spent a week or ten days in 1812 learning enough chemistry from Benjamin Silliman at Yale to give a course at Williams, imparted a contagious enthusiasm to his students, from 1810 to 1827, in the many fields which came under his care—mathematics, astronomy, physics, botany, mineralogy, and geology. And the steam generated by Eaton's lectures on botany and geology before the students and faculty in 1817 sufficed to carry the college well past the Hopkins administration. Dewey and Eaton, it is true, did not introduce science into the Williams curriculum: from 1793 until after 1872 one term of chemistry was a constant in the study of the junior year. Eaton's visit of 1817, however, awoke the college to its physical environment and introduced, although certainly by the back door, botany and geology into the curriculum. The pattern set by his lectures was occasionally enlarged upon during the ensuing decades, but in general the student at Williams in 1872 was learning little more about his physical environment, in the classroom, than he had during the pioneering days of Amos Eaton and Chester Dewey.[11]

Eaton, fresh from study under Benjamin Silliman and Eli Ives at Yale, literally overwhelmed the college during his residence in Williamstown in 1817. Although not employed by the college— students and faculty paid for the lectures by subscription—he found a ready audience for his daily discourses on botany and mineralogy. Every member of the two upper classes, all but four students of the two lower classes, and the entire faculty, with the exception of President Moore, participated in this great exposure

10. John Bascom, *Address, Delivered before the Horticultural and Landscape Gardening Association, of Williams College* (North Adams, Greylock Sentinel Press, 1853), p. 13.

11. Appropriate numbers of the college catalogues and the early editions of the college laws are the source for establishing the date of arrival of the various disciplines into the curriculum.

to the world of science.[12] The college revealed its official approval by excusing twelve men a day from classes that they might roam the hills in search of minerals, plants, and other specimens of natural history. His students, whom Eaton described as "a noble spirited class," urged upon him the preparation of a botanical manual that proved to be immensely popular, to which they contributed descriptive material as well as the entire cost of publication.[13] "Some of them will be excellent naturalists," he predicted, singling out William A. Hallock as "the best." [14] Hallock, instead, became the first secretary of the American Tract Society, but in his audience were the Williams professor of natural history Chester Dewey, who in 1819 contributed a "Sketch of the Mineralogy and Geology of the Vicinity of Williams College" to the first volume of Benjamin Silliman's *American Journal of Science;* Ebenezer Emmons of the Class of 1818, a member of the Williams faculty from 1828 to 1859, whose work as the state geologist of both New York and North Carolina placed him among the pioneers of American geology; and Moses Ashley Curtis of the Class of 1827, coming under Eaton's influence during a later course of lectures at Williams, who pioneered in the study of southern lichens.

Whatever the enthusiasm provoked by Eaton's visit may have suggested to the officials of Williams College, the curriculum, which might have found more room for science had the college been willing or able, remained almost inflexible. Dewey, however, took up the task of delivering yearly nonrequired lectures in botany and mineralogy patterned upon Eaton's performance of 1817, and was followed by John Torrey in 1827 and by Emmons in 1828. Natural philosophy, from which modern physics stemmed, had been in the curriculum since the college was founded, invariably covering two terms of work in the junior year. Astronomy entered the junior course of study in 1830 and remained there beyond

12. Carl S. Hoar, "Biology at Williams," *Williams Alumni Review, 17* (1925), 332.

13. Published in Albany in 1817 under the title *A Manual of Botany for the Northern States,* Eaton's book described the publishers as being "the members of the Botanical Class in Williams' College (Mass.)." Eaton is reported to have said that he could find no established publisher willing to take the risk, although a thousand copies were sold within six months and a second edition was necessary in 1818. This pioneering botanical manual is a tribute to the enterprise of the 19th-century American undergraduate. For Eaton's remarks on his indebtedness to the Williams students who published his manual, see Alden B. Whipple, "The Early Botany of Berkshire," *Collections of the Berkshire Historical and Scientific Society* (Pittsfield, 1892), *1,* 17.

14. Quoted in Ethel M. McAllister, *Amos Eaton: Scientist and Educator* (Philadelphia, University of Pennsylvania Press, 1941), p. 173.

1872, fluctuating from one to two terms and finally being offered, beginning in 1869, to juniors and seniors for a term each. Botany did not enter the required course work of a Williams undergraduate until 1845, when a term was required of all juniors; after being temporarily transferred to the sophomore year between 1858 and 1861, botany came to rest in the sophomore year in 1868, when the sophomores and seniors were also, for the first time, introduced to a term of zoology. Mineralogy made its appearance as a one-term sophomore course in 1852, to which was added, in 1861, a term of geology for juniors.

The introduction of subjects previously offered as noncredit lectures into the body of the program of study itself and the extension of scientific subjects down into the sophomore year and up into the senior year revealed a recognition of the importance of natural science. It would be a mistake, therefore, to describe the Williams curriculum as altogether inflexible. Its growth, however, was hardly consonant with the enthusiasm of 1817.

The uneven growth of science at Williams reflected, of course, the embryonic nature of the studies involved and the unavailability of suitable texts. The introduction of mineralogy into the curriculum in 1842, for instance, was made possible by the publication of James Dwight Dana's *System of Mineralogy* in 1837. Tardiness in the development of science reflected as well the financial embarrassments of the college. Chemistry at Williams between 1835 and 1852 owed its support to the independent income of Professor Edward Lasell, who accepted a token salary each year of two hundred dollars and returned much of it in books and apparatus which the college was unable to buy.[15] Yet the stage of development of the sciences and the financial difficulties of the college do not altogether explain why no branch of science shared in the endowments which were established at the college during the 1850's.

These endowments—professorships in Greek, Latin, theology, and rhetoric, to the exclusion of science—reveal the official attitude. Williams College taught as much science as it felt was necessary to serve its purposes. Inasmuch as it proposed primarily to develop Christian character, it saw no more necessity for turning the curriculum upside down in the interest of natural science than it would have seen for abolishing compulsory chapel in the interest of free thought. Young men went to Williams College to have their sights

15. MH to AL, Feb. 19, 1852; MHS, MH-AL MSS.

raised, to have their minds focused upon noble purposes, and Williams would teach exactly as much science as was necessary to meet that particular demand.

When the first scientific endowment did come to Williams, in 1865, it went to the chair of astronomy held by Albert Hopkins, who was boring his students with a paucity of astronomy and an overabundance of evangelical piety. Paul Ansel Chadbourne, who between 1853 and 1867 taught botany, geology, and chemistry, at one time or another, demonstrated the uses to which natural science was put in the Williams classroom. In 1860, speaking before a group at the Smithsonian Institution in Washington, he said little that had not been said by Mark Hopkins over thirty years before. In this year after the publication of Darwin's *Origin of Species* he confidently announced that every stratum of rock betrayed a new creation, that the adaptations in nature were so brilliant and diverse as to preclude the operation of any agent but God. The importance of natural history, he concluded, did not lie in the practical uses to which it might be put in the quest for money, but instead in the reassuring answer that it provided to the question: "If He cared for the fishes of the Silurian seas, will He not care for us?" [16]

Because man was a creature of God, he, too, was fitted into the scheme by which the college combined Bible and nature in furthering its official purposes. Guiding his students through the maze of senior year, Mark Hopkins concluded that man was "the priest of nature, standing at its head . . . alone recognizing the Creator." [17] As the priest of nature, the Williams undergraduate was carefully instructed in the use of the body which God had given him. In his freshman year he read from a little book which, among other things, guided him toward proper exercise, cautioning him, "before adopting any exercise, to consider whether it is in harmony with the mode of action assigned by the Creator to the parts which are to perform it." The author's advice to the young man who would properly develop his muscles, his perceptive faculties, and his moral and intellectual sentiments, was to get out

16. Paul A. Chadbourne, *Lectures on Natural History: Its Relations to Intellect, Taste, Wealth, and Religion* (New York, A. S. Barnes and Burr, 1860), esp. pp. 137–54.

17. MH, *An Outline Study of Man; or, the Body and Mind in One System* (New York, Scribner, Armstrong, 1873), p. 300. See also *The Bible and Pantheism: A Baccalaureate Sermon, Delivered at Williamstown, Ms. July 29, 1866*, Boston, T. R. Marvin and Son, 1866; and *Liberality—Its Limits: A Baccalaureate Sermon, Delivered at Williamstown, Mass. July 28, 1867*, Boston, T. R. Marvin and Son, 1867.

of the classroom and "look at the works of God." [18] These sentiments so coincided with the official position of the college, it is no wonder that once introduced into the curriculum this little book survived for over thirty years.

The college, as a matter of fact, had anticipated such advice some years before when, in 1835, Albert Hopkins sponsored an organization on the Williams campus explicitly designed to get Williams men out of the classroom and the dormitory. To the Horticultural and Landscape Gardening Association he assigned these many functions: the gratification of scientific curiosity, the development of muscle and the cure of dyspepsia, the encouragement of model behavior, the beautification of the college grounds, and, above all, communication with God. Probably no organization could have served these many purposes better than did the Association, whose members, under Hopkins' direction, tended a college garden, planted the elms and maples which, in time, became an asset to the entire community, and constructed an artificial trout pond which was known as Christmas Lake.[19]

To what degree the Association fulfilled the purposes which Albert Hopkins assigned to it is impossible to determine. For many years, certainly, the college depended upon it for what little work was done in caring for the college grounds.[20] Albert himself testified that in the arsenal of orthodoxy the Association performed a useful work, turning boisterous boys into quiet gardeners and the unfaithful into believers. As for its role in the development of health, "the effect has been most happy," Mark Hopkins reported.[21]

The Horticultural and Landscape Gardening Association was not called upon to do its work alone. Having delivered a catalogue of undergraduate sins which ranged from eating too many raisins to sitting up late at night, Mark Hopkins at his inauguration declared, "Let them saw their own wood, let botany and mineralogy lead them over the hills." [22] And to make certain, college holidays were developed which institutionalized the ramblings that had been

18. Andrew Combe, *The Principles of Physiology Applied to the Preservation of Health, and to the Improvement of Physical and Mental Education* (New York, Harper and Brothers, 1834), p. 146. This book was adopted in 1844 and was used at least through 1872.

19. See Albert Hopkins' remarks on the Association in Durfee, *A History of Williams College*, pp. 313–14. Also, Wells and Davis, *Sketches of Williams College*, p. 68. TR, *2*, 176; Aug. 17, 1836.

20. MH to AL, June 4, 1847; MHS, MH-AL MSS.

21. MH, *An Address, Delivered before the Society of Alumni of Williams College at the Celebration of the Semi-centennial Anniversary*, p. 28.

22. MH, *An Inaugural Discourse*, p. 10

inspired by Amos Eaton, and the wood-sawing which was every student's labor. Chip Day, in the spring, suggested that winter was over, the last log sawed, and the time at hand to clean up from the college yards the chips where they had fallen. In the summer was Mountain Day, an invitation to climb to the top of Mount Greylock, there to speculate upon His wondrous ways. And on irregular occasions there was a Botany Day or a Mineral Day, when the undergraduates, instead of attending classes, were sent off into the woods and fields in search of nature.

For the robust and practical-minded Williams undergraduate, nature, in its official version, did not turn out to be as attractive as it was to the president and faculty. The Williams students did not object to college holidays, but many of them lost interest in the kind which the college granted. They did not fail to appreciate Mount Greylock, but they left to an earlier generation the communion with God which was possible once its summit was reached. They enjoyed the prospect of an avenue of trees as much as anyone, but many students found, on their terms, better uses to which to put their time. Nature, conceived by the college as an instrument of religious orthodoxy, a landscape gardening club, and a curriculum with a modicum of natural science, became, in the hands of the students, something much more worldly.

The young ladies of Williamstown so well understood the meaning which nature held for the Williams undergraduate that they held a strawberry festival in the summer of 1855, the proceeds of which were divided between the student gymnasium and the student Lyceum of Natural History. In their act of generosity they symbolized the directions which nature, under more youthful auspices, was to take in the decades to come. Man was the priest of nature, Mark Hopkins had said. The Williams undergraduate did not necessarily disagree, but he operated upon the assumption that the man of solid form and muscle, who knew something about disgorging the earth of its ores and robbing the forests of its timber, was more than priest. He was high priest. And that is what the Williams student would be, if he could.

9. *Nature Is Practical: The Lyceum of Natural History*

No DEVELOPMENT during the Hopkins era was more indicative of a mounting conflict between tradition and innovation, the past and the future, than was the career of the Lyceum of Natural History. The college took science quite as seriously as did the students, but what each found in it revealed a difference so profound that the conflict between official and undergraduate views turned into a struggle of tremendous consequence.

Founded in 1835 by eight students who fixed as its object "the study of natural sciences, and the prosecution of antiquarian researches," the Lyceum could trace its history as far back as an undergraduate Mineralogical Society, a short-lived product of Amos Eaton's 1817 lectures. The Lyceum's immediate predecessor, the Linnaean Society, was active at least as late as 1828, for its members included Moses Ashley Curtis of the Class of 1827 and John Darby of the Class of 1831, eminent contributors to the pursuit of botanical studies in the South. In 1835, however, the Lyceum itself was something new.[1]

When it was organized that year in the spring, the Lyceum must have given the appearance of being little more than what every new extracurricular activity suggested—a forthright criticism of the college curriculum. Its founders, indeed, inserted into the preamble of its constitution the very explicit assertion that "the proportion of time allotted" to the study of natural history by the college was "inadequate to its importance."[2] In preparing itself to remedy so lamentable a situation, the Lyceum could not escape the influences which permeated the environment in which it hoped to take hold. It immediately bowed to the recent arrival of the first secret society at Williams by swearing its own members to secrecy and contriving for itself the Greek-letter designation Phi Beta Theta. Its nod of compliance with the official view of nature held by the college was as freely given: for its motto it chose "Nature, the book of God."

The power of these external influences, however, did not pre-

---

1. "Records of the Lyceum of Natural History"; MS, WCL. Perry, *Williamstown and Williams College*, p. 291; and "Science and Scientists at Williams," mimeographed, ed. Arthur H. Buffinton (Williamstown, 1933), p. 12.
2. "Records of the Lyceum of Natural History," *1;* Apr. 2, 1835.

dominate. Nor did they last. What had been Phi Beta Theta in April became the Lyceum of Natural History in October; within two years the secrecy pledge, hardly conducive to the free pursuit of science, was expunged from the constitution. As for the motto, it was not wholly ignored. It could not be, as long as Albert Hopkins, made an honorary member in 1835, maintained his life-long interest in the affairs of the society.

Hopkins, who led the members in a scientific expedition through Berkshire County in 1840 and set them to conducting prayer meetings in the evenings, found support among the members. The undergraduate secretary of the society, reviewing the work of various committees which were busy classifying the flora and fauna of Williamstown in 1841, complimented the members for availing themselves of an opportunity to see in nature's works "signs of consummate wisdom in the hand that moulded their delicate forms and brought them into being." [3] And in 1855, when the Lyceum erected its own museum building, over an archway an inscription declared: "Lo! these are parts of His ways." Even so, the motto and the inscription were like most of their kind—appropriate, non-controversial, and incapable of expressing in their entirety the purposes and functions of the society. The same secretary, for example, who saw in nature "signs of consummate wisdom," also decided that the members were proving that the Lyceum was "an association of gentlemen truly jealous for the promotion of science —and ardently in love with her for her own sake." [4] Albert Hopkins might write of the society's expedition to Nova Scotia in 1835 that he hoped exposure to nature had made its members "better," but Ebenezer Emmons, who also made the trip, concluded a report on the expedition for Silliman's *American Journal of Science* questioning, upon the basis of his observations, generally accepted views of Creation. [5] As for the archway in the society's museum building, its pious inscription told so little that its student architects perched over the front door a great bronze cast of an American eagle. [6]

3. *Ibid.*, June 19, 1841.

4. *Ibid.*, May 1, 1841.

5. Albert Hopkins, "Scientific Expedition of Students of Williams College from Boston along the Eastern Coast to St. John's, N.B. and Halifax and Windsor, N.S.," pp. 36–7; typescript, WCL, copied from the *American Traveller* of Nov. 13, 17, 20, 1835. Ebenezer Emmons, "Notice of a Scientific Expedition," *American Journal of Science, 30* (1836), 353–4.

6. William B. Rogers, *Address before the Lyceum of Natural History of Williams College. August 14, 1855* (Boston, T. R. Marvin and Son, 1855), includes, pp. 30–4, an account of the exercises at which the new building was dedicated.

The eagle said more than did the inscription. Instead of a lesson, it conveyed the spirit of adventuresome young men, of practical bent and curious mind, whose ingenuity and self-assertion were creating the life of which the eagle screamed. Neither the eagle nor the Lyceum, to be sure, were patriotic gestures, but they were manifestations of a national spirit in which the young men of Williams College freely joined. Even if, as is probable, most of its members did not lose sight of God, the Lyceum was an instrument of many purposes in which "Nature, the book of God," became, as well, an encyclopedia of practical knowledge and a tale of wonder and adventure.

The encyclopedia which the Lyceum found in nature received an early reading when, in 1835, the members heard an undergraduate paper on the subject of flying machines.[7] Thirty-five years later, when their collections were enlarged by a student contribution of dye-stuffs used in the manufacture of cotton cloth, the young naturalists of Williams College still revealed an abiding interest in the practical application of science to life.[8] They brought the outside world into Williamstown with an avidness which combined the theoretical and the practical so well that in the course of the Hopkins administration their attention was drawn to the usefulness of spiders in the manufacture of raw silk, the culture and manufacture of cotton, the principles of artesian wells, and the mechanical operations of nest building. America's abundance of natural resources, whose exploitive possibilities were a discovery of the first half of the 19th century, were reported upon at society meetings by students who described coal beds, whale fisheries, oil wells, and iron ores. Visiting lecturers were brought into meetings to discourse upon architecture and—on the heels of the discoveries of 1849—upon the techniques of gold mining.[9] If the formal curriculum of the liberal arts college could not be made practical, the members of the Lyceum were ready to make sure that a liberal education somehow could be.

There is no indication that the organizing of a botany class in 1836 by the Lyceum, the laying of foundations for a science library in 1839, publishing a catalogue of its specimens in 1852, raising money and constructing a building of its own in 1855, and hiring

7. "Records of the Lyceum of Natural History," *1;* Nov. 7, 1835.
8. *Ibid., 2;* Jan. 26, 1870.
9. *Ibid., passim.*

an assistant of Louis Agassiz to aid in the classification of fishes in 1863 made the college feel in any way remiss.[10] On the contrary, that the college felt itself absolved of all responsibility for the Lyceum once it had provided a room, however inadequate, for its meetings is readily apparent from the desperation which drove the Lyceum in 1854 to raise the necessary funds and erect a building commensurate with its needs. When Amos Lawrence gave some books on natural history to the Lyceum in 1847, Mark Hopkins wrote him that "the Society has been struggling along under embarrassment, and it will encourage them." [11] But the embarrassment under which the society suffered was not engendered by a lack of interest or of numbers. Hopkins himself had told Lawrence that "all who have a taste for [natural science] join." [12] At its founding in 1835 the society limited its membership to thirty, but in 1841 the constitutional provision was raised to thirty-five, and in 1846, in order to satisfy student interest, the ceiling was lifted altogether, paving the way for a membership that ranged between forty and fifty during the next twenty-five years.[13] Hopkins' assumption that all undergraduates of scientific bent found their way into the Lyceum was apparently accurate. Every Williams alumnus of the Hopkins period whose subsequent career in natural science rendered him worthy of inclusion in the *Dictionary of American Biography* was a member of the Lyceum while at Williams, beginning with William Henry Edwards of the Class of 1842, a pioneer American entomologist, and ending with Francis H. Snow of the Class of 1862, who has been described as "the pioneer naturalist of Kansas." [14] The embarrassment of the Lyceum was neither of numbers nor of interest but of the funds necessary to support its ambitions. With characteristic self-application, the members overcame this embarrassment in the 1850's.

Jackson Hall, named for Nathan Jackson, the donor-relative of the undergraduate president of the Lyceum who had the good sense to send his uncle a circular describing the wants of the society,

10. *Ibid.*, June 4, 1836; Feb. 16, 1839; Mar. 3, 1852. *Williams Quarterly, 11* (1863), 140.

11. Nov. 16, 1847; MHS, MH-AL MSS.

12. Sept. 28, 1847; MHS, MH-AL MSS.

13. "Records of the Lyceum of Natural History," *1;* Mar. 6, 1841; Apr. 8, 1846; and *passim.*

14. The others: James Orton, '55, explorer and collector; Henry A. Ward, '55, naturalist and collector; Robert Emmet McMath, '57, civil engineer and expert on river hydraulics; Samuel H. Scudder, '57, entomologist; Richard H. Ward, '58, microscopist; John T. Gulick, '59, student of the evolution of Hawaiian snails.

was the first student-conceived and erected building devoted to natural history on an American campus.[15] It suggested the degree to which the American college undergraduate refused to be thwarted by lack of official encouragement.[16] "A silent rebuke to the College for doing so little," bewailed Paul A. Chadbourne, professor of natural history, in 1858.[17]

While rebukes, silent and otherwise, descended upon the college, the work of the Lyceum commanded respect and interest beyond the borders of Williamstown. Professors at Rutgers, Columbia, and Genesee wrote to ask how they might go about setting up similar organizations at their own colleges.[18] Specimens were exchanged with Harvard—which had little that the Williams Lyceum wanted—Rensselaer, and the Smithsonian Institution, with the latter at its own suggestion.[19] James Dwight Dana at Yale was the recipient of duplicate specimens from the Lyceum's coral collections, and Asa Gray at Harvard took on the job of identifying botanical specimens for the Lyceum in return for the privilege of retaining duplicates.[20] Specimens were given to the cabinet of Mount Holyoke Female Seminary, whose resident steward was a former member of the society, and sold to Ripon College, whose president would have preferred an exchange.[21]

The recognition by scientists elsewhere of the work the students at Williams were doing was in part warranted by the interest which members of the Lyceum themselves took in the activities of professional scientists. In February 1847 Freeman Josiah Bumstead of the senior class returned from hearing Louis Agassiz in Boston and treated the members to a series of lectures based upon notes which he had taken while Agassiz discoursed at the Lowell Institute on embryology.[22] Undergraduate members of the Lyceum

15. At Pennsylvania College (now Gettysburg College), Linnaean Hall, which housed a natural history museum as well as academy classrooms, was completed in 1847. Students were active in helping to raise the funds, but they do not appear to have achieved the success of the students of Williams, who shared their building with no one and who raised all of the funds.

16. The story of the erection of Jackson Hall, of the student committees that tended to such matters as architecture, painting, etc., may be traced in "Records of the Lyceum of Natural History," *1;* 1854–55 *passim.*

17. *Williams Quarterly, 5* (1858), 345–6.

18. See "Records of the Lyceum of Natural History," *2;* Oct. 24, 1855; June 24, 1857; May 26, 1858. The correspondent from Rutgers was George Hammell Cook, later state geologist of New Jersey; from Columbia, Charles A. Joy.

19. "Records of the Lyceum of Natural History," Apr. 13, 1853; July 19, 1864; Sept. 27, 1860; June 21, 1864.

20. *Ibid.,* June 10, 1857, and Jan. 16, 1861.

21. *Ibid.,* Apr. 5, 1861, and Sept. 16, 1869.

22. *Ibid.,* Feb. 10 and 24, 1847.

attended meetings of the American Association for the Advancement of Science at Montreal in 1857 and Baltimore in 1858.[23] Sir John Lubbock's pioneer work in anthropology was the subject of a student report in 1870.[24]

Although the Williams student's curiosity about scientific matters and his penchant for a practical education were thus satisfied by the Lyceum, the society fulfilled yet other functions. A romantic respect for the exotic led members into discussions of volcanoes, giraffes, condor hunting, icebergs, and the discovery, in 1854, of an entrance to the interior of the Sphinx. The shelves and cabinets of the society's museum, in addition to providing a similar outlet for youthful admiration of the strange and beautiful, answered a storage problem created by an equally youthful passion for collecting. Housed with as much respect and care as the collections which exhibited the natural life of Williamstown (in one year William Dwight Whitney of the Class of 1845 shot and stuffed forty birds for the museum) were specimens which provoked dreams of distant places. Reaping scientific rewards from the Christian impulse which had sent Williams men into foreign missions, the Lyceum became, in 1851, the first American museum to own examples of Assyrian bas-reliefs.[25] An Arab tent, a monkey skin, and miscellaneous oddities from Natal, Hawaii, and Kamchatka also found their way into the society's collections as the gifts of foreign missionaries. In 1851 a circus impresario turned over to the Lyceum the carcass of a six-ton elephant named Columbus, who, having broken through a bridge in Adams, had died on a farm at Lenox. Unable to find a taxidermist capable of handling so large a carcass, the Lyceum interred Columbus where he had died, intending one day to mount his skeleton in Williamstown.[26] As late as April 1857 a committee took a look and changed its mind.

If the student museum had failed to inspire enterprising undergraduates to undertake novel pranks, Mark Hopkins himself would undoubtedly have been surprised. There is no record of the

23. *Ibid.*, Sept. 16, 1857, and May 26, 1858.

24. *Ibid.*, Nov. 3, 1870.

25. See MH to AL, Dec. 21, 1851, and June 29, 1852; MHS, MH-AL MSS. Selah Merril, "Assyrian and Babylonian Monuments in America," *Bibliotheca Sacra and Theological Eclectic, 32* (1875), 322–3. The donor of the Assyrian relics was Dwight W. Marsh, Class of 1842, missionary for the ABCFM at Mosul in 1850–51, who acceded to a suggestion of Albert Hopkins that he send some of the ruins of ancient Nineveh to the Lyceum. The Lyceum was the sole American possessor of such antiquities until 1854, when Yale, Union, and Amherst were similarly blessed.

26. Richard V. Happel, "Notes and Footnotes," *Berkshire Evening Eagle,* Aug. 15, 1951. "Records of the Lyceum of Natural History," *1;* 1851, *passim.*

"apples killed by the frost in May, 1794, picked May 1851" having
been served at a local boarding house, but the Lyceum's great black
bear appeared opposite Mark Hopkins on the chapel stage one
day in 1852 carrying the placard, "the last honor man, barely
eligible." [27] The Lyceum, therefore, was something much more than
a criticism of the curriculum or a course in the application of nature
to the work of the world. It was also—as Egyptian mummies, an
Arab tent, and the lamented Columbus suggest—something of a
circus, meeting all the demands traditionally placed upon the fair,
bazaar, or Barnum sideshow.

The concept of the well-rounded college graduate, which was a
part of the official jargon at Williams during the days of the
society's prosperity, received a powerful assist from the Lyceum.
Whether he knew it or not, Mark Hopkins was turning out young
men who had happily combined the pursuit of knowledge with the
satisfaction of youthful romanticism. That they had had fun doing
it made them that much "rounder," but that they had done it at
all was of their own choosing, not the administration's. The college
participated in the career of the Lyceum and in the development of
enterprising independent young men in the one way of which it
was perhaps most capable: it did nothing—partly from lack of
interest and from financial embarrassment—and the more it did
nothing, the more it helped its undergraduates to the self-education
which Hopkins had so highly esteemed in his inaugural address.

No college religiously oriented and financially situated as was
Williams would have considered the sending out of expeditions an
obligation which it owed to the cause of science. Indeed, colleges in
sounder financial condition felt no such responsibility. The students
of Williams College, however, did. The expeditions which the
Lyceum sent to Nova Scotia in 1835, Florida in 1857, Greenland
in 1860, South America in 1867, and Honduras in 1871 are un-
paralleled in the history of American education.

Credit for inspiring the first student expedition in the annals
of American science, that of the Lyceum to Nova Scotia in 1835,
properly belongs to two members of the Williams faculty, Ebenezer Emmons and Albert Hopkins. Their own plans to undertake
a two-man expedition in 1831 had miscarried, but the interest

27. *Catalogue of the Lyceum of Natural History of Williams College, Instituted
A.D. 1835* (Williamstown, Lyceum of Natural History, 1852), p. 40. A. D. Axtell to
E. J. Peck, June 29, 1852; WCL, Peck MSS.

aroused in their minds by the publication in 1828 and 1829 of
accounts of the explorations of Charles T. Jackson and Francis
Alger in Nova Scotia persisted.[28] Remarks which they made at a
meeting of the Lyceum on June 27, 1835, resulted in the appointment of a committee, composed of Emmons and Thompson Kidder
of the Class of 1836, secretary of the society, to ascertain the probable expenses of "a proposed naval expedition for scientific purposes." Hopkins, of course, contemplated religious dividends from
the excursion, while both he and Emmons, in their published reports
of the expedition, agreed that the lure of scenery, fogs, and tides
and "that love of adventure which is so natural to young men"
conspired to make their suggestion popular among the members of
the Lyceum.[29] The twenty-man expedition which they led to Nova
Scotia during the fall vacation of 1835 owed its inspiration to
them, but the sustaining interest which the Lyceum maintained in
scientific expeditions was the work of the students themselves.[30]

Although the next expedition did not set forth until 1857, meetings of the Lyceum in the intervening years were frequently devoted to the contemplation of expeditions not taken. An 1846 expedition through the Connecticut Valley failed to materialize for
lack of a faculty member to lead it; a similar plight befell expeditions of unrecorded destination in 1849 and 1851, and another to
the Pennsylvania coal regions in 1855.[31] In the meantime, however,
two undergraduate members of the Lyceum took an excursion of
their own to Nova Scotia after their freshman year: Henry Ward
of the Class of 1855 later laid the foundations of the natural history collections of Ward's Natural History Establishment at
Rochester and the Field Museum in Chicago; and James Orton
became a pioneer explorer in South America and, in 1869, the first
professor of natural history at Vassar.[32] In 1854 Orton and Professor Chadbourne were employed by Cyrus Field to undertake a

28. Ebenezer Emmons, "Notice of a Scientific Expedition," p. 330.
29. *Ibid.* Albert Hopkins, "Scientific Expedition of Students of Williams College," p. 1.
30. See "Records of the Lyceum of Natural History," *1;* June 27, July 11, and
July 25, 1835.
31. *Ibid.,* Apr. 8, 1846; Apr. 18, 1849; Apr. 2, 1851; Mar. 2, 1855. A similar fate
befell projected expeditions to Newfoundland in 1864 and the Windward Islands
in 1870. *Williams Quarterly, 11* (1864), 285; *18* (1870), 47-8.
32. *Williams Alumni Review, 14* (1921), 27-8. Also see sketches of Ward and
Orton in *Dictionary of American Biography* and Roswell Ward, *Henry A. Ward,
Museum Builder to America* (Rochester, Rochester Historical Society, 1948), pp.
45-8.

geological survey of Newfoundland, preparatory to his first attempt to lay the Atlantic cable in 1855.[33] Orton's exertions as president of the Lyceum in 1855 resulted in the benefactions of his uncle, Nathan Jackson, who provided the funds for the erection of the Lyceum building. As an alumnus, Orton joined the Lyceum on later expeditions, leading the one to South America in 1867.

The 1857 expedition to Florida in the fruit schooner *Dew Drop* was suggested by John Darby of the Class of 1831, then professor of natural science at East Alabama Male College; the expedition was headed by Chadbourne with Darby's assistance, and was financed largely by friends of science from outside the college. Although the trustees of Williams authorized a contribution of fifty dollars toward the undertaking, major contributions were made by Boston philanthropists like Nathan Appleton and scientists like Louis Agassiz.[34] One contributor was Major Amos B. Eaton, a son of Amos Eaton, whose only stipulation was that his own son, Daniel, a senior at Yale, be permitted to join the expedition, there being no similar opportunity available to students in New Haven.[35] The son, Daniel Cady Eaton, in 1864 became the first professor of botany at Yale and attained a reputation as an eminent student of American ferns. Samuel H. Scudder, a member of the senior class at Williams, rounded up three contributors to the funds of the expedition in Boston, thus guaranteeing a place for himself in the group.[36] Scudder, whose interest in nature had been aroused during his freshman year by a case of butterflies he had seen in the room of a friend, became the greatest American orthopterist of his time. Of the sixteen Williams undergraduates who took the two-month trip "for the cause of science," seven later pursued careers to the advancement of which tramping through Florida in search of plants, bugs, and rocks was an asset. Four became professors of materia medica and botany and one a paleontologist for the United States Geological Survey.[37]

33. "Records of the Lyceum of Natural History," *1*; Aug. 1, 1854. Henry M. Field, *The Story of the Atlantic Telegraph* (New York, Charles Scribner's Sons, 1892), pp. 45 ff. Paul A. Chadbourne, "Wanderings in Newfoundland," *Williams Quarterly*, *3* (1855), 52–60, 105–13, 213–21; *4* (1856), 27–32, 162–70. Arthur C. Cole, *A Hundred Years of Mount Holyoke College: The Evolution of an Educational Ideal* (New Haven, Yale University Press, 1940), p. 141. Chadbourne lectured on his Newfoundland experiences at Mount Holyoke in the spring of 1855.

34. "Records of the Lyceum of Natural History," *2*, Mar. 12 and 26, Nov. 12, 1856; Jan. 14, 28, 31, and Feb. 7, 11, and 14, 1857.

35. *Ibid.*, Feb. 7, 1857.

36. *Ibid.*, Jan. 14, 1857.

37. An interesting history of the Florida expedition could be written on the basis of the Lyceum minutes and other records available at Williams, including Samuel

Expedition of the Lyceum of Natural History to Florida, 1857. Seated at left: Professor Paul A. Chadbourne, leader of the expedition; second from right, with butterfly net: Samuel H. Scudder, Class of 1857, who became a prominent orthopterist. Photographed with their trophies, including Spanish moss, on their return to Williamstown.

Excitement, ingenuity, and scientific curiosity were also evident in later expeditions of the society, which continued to make its work tell, not only in the future careers of its members but also outside Williamstown. The 1860 expedition to Greenland was joined by two students from Bowdoin.[38] The 1867 expedition to South America received some assistance from the Smithsonian Institution and resulted in the publication in 1871 of a lengthy account of the expedition by two of the student members, H. M. and P. V. N. Myers' *Life and Nature under the Tropics.* To a revised edition of this work was appended an account of the 1870 expedition to Honduras.[39] Similar expeditions did not originate at any other college, let alone student natural history societies, until Yale University sent an expedition to the Rockies under the leadership of O. C. Marsh in 1870.

By way of its expeditions to distant places—and the more domestic activities that led Ebenezer Emmons to suppose that Williamstown had been "as carefully explored as almost any equal portion of our country"—the Lyceum performed a major role in the education of young men at Williams during the presidency of Mark Hopkins. Although a friend of the college objected in 1860 to the Greenland expedition as manifesting an overrated interest in what he called "the most fascinating & least valuable department in the collegiate course," another was so intrigued by the Lyceum's activities as to offer up to $3,000 if the college would round up a fund of $30,000 to endow biennial expeditions.[40] The college stood

E. Elmore's MS "Journal of the Florida Expedition," a daily record of the expedition from Feb. 19 to Apr. 26, 1857; *Williams Quarterly, 4* (1856), 191–2; (1857), 287–8, 293–328.

38. In addition to the Lyceum records, the following would be useful in reconstructing the story of the Greenland expedition: Edward P. Hopkins' MS, "Account of the Travels of E. P. Hopkins in the North," a journal kept from June 27 through Aug. 27, 1860. *Williams Quarterly, 7* (1860), 284–5; *8* (1860), 75–98. William P. Alcott, "The Physical Geography of Southern Greenland," *University Quarterly, 2* (1860), 304–9; *3* (1861), 76–84.

39. For these two expeditions, see H. M. and P. V. N. Myers, *Life and Nature under the Tropics; or, Sketches of Travels among the Andes, and on the Orinoco, Rio Negro, Amazon, and in Central America,* New York, D. Appleton and Co., 1871. James Orton, *The Andes and the Amazon,* New York, Harper and Brothers, 1870. *Williams Quarterly, 14* (1867), 205; *15* (1867), 120–8; (1868), 73–84, 191–6. And, of course, the Lyceum records. The Myers' book appears to have been necessary in order to counteract the implication in Orton's account that the expedition was entirely a Smithsonian affair; Albert Hopkins' introduction to the Myers' book sets the record straight.

40. Luther Halsey to MH, June 8, 1860; MHS, Hopkins MSS. Jared Curtis to MH, Jan. 16, 1860; HP, *4.* Curtis refers to a letter which he is enclosing from an

somewhere between these two gentlemen, letting the students do what they would but expending no energy of its own in search of a permanent endowment for scientific expeditions. William J. Walker's contribution of $10,000 in 1861, which set as one of its conditions the sending out of expeditions, was inspired by what he knew of the Lyceum. That the gift was no larger must be attributed in part to the lack of official interest in science that he found at Williams, compared with that at Amherst, Tufts, and the Massachusetts Institute of Technology, which he liberally endowed.

As for the Williams undergraduate, using the Lyceum as a vital supplement to the curriculum, he learned to look at nature in far broader terms than those conceived by the college. He found in nature satisfaction for a curiosity about what made things work. He thought in terms of how nature might be exploited for man's benefit and for his own material improvement. He took to the woods or to the seas out of a sheer search of excitement, making his own discoveries as he went along. For the Williams student who engaged in the activities of the Lyceum nature was not a great book to be contemplated but a limitless expanse in which to roam, dig, and gather curiosities.

In addition to directing into productive channels the fervor of young men who later became eminent scientists, the Lyceum also advanced the cause of science by making it popular. Its collecting, as well, surely deserves to be recognized as a contribution in the sense that museums and the laboratories of men like Asa Gray and James Dwight Dana were enriched by the work which these young men performed. By acting as if nature were as rich and full of life as it actually was, the Lyceum subverted the emphasis which the college placed upon nature as a static panorama in the service of evangelical orthodoxy. In dedicating his account of the 1867 expedition to Charles Darwin, James Orton exhibited the degree to which the pursuit of nature might indeed lead away from Christian orthodoxy. For the members of the Lyceum nature became also an object of study in which the services of men of science beyond the walls of Williams were enlisted. If nature was didactic local scenery for Mark Hopkins, for the members of the Lyceum it was an invitation to the Boston lectures of Louis Agassiz or the assistance of Frederick Putnam on the identification of fishes. And with it all, they had fun.

---

unnamed Boston gentleman offering the college up to $3,000 if others would band together to make a fund of $30,000 for biennial scientific expeditions.

In 1868 the Lyceum turned its library over to the college, and in 1871 a large portion of the specimens from Honduras went to the college instead of to the society's own museum.[41] These acts suggested not that the Lyceum was being overtaken by paralysis but that the college itself was beginning to awaken and the pursuit of science could in reality no longer be left to the enthusiasm of youthful amateurs. The professionalization of scientific study and the broadening of the Williams curriculum destroyed the Lyceum. Its gradual decline and eventual extinction amounted to a victory in which the students of Williams College succeeded in substituting their view of nature for that which had been for so long officially held by the college. Their victory, as was the case with so many of their victories, also robbed them of an opportunity to exhibit their individualism and to try their hand at self-development. For as the college came to do more and more for the student, there was clearly less and less that they needed to do for themselves.

41. "Records of the Lyceum of Natural History," *2;* April and May, 1871. "Agreement between Lyceum of Natural History and Williams College Library, Nov. 6, 1868"; WCL, Misc. MSS, *12.*

10. Nature Is Muscular: Organized Athletics

USING THE LYCEUM OF NATURAL HISTORY as a vehicle for exploiting and organizing the physical universe, the Williams student at the same time adopted new instruments for the exploitation and organization of physical man. In 1851 a student-operated gymnasium took its place beside the Lyceum in the extracurriculum, where it revealed the same undergraduate inventiveness and the same intrusion of student values and purposes upon the official scheme of things. The distance between the official view and the student view was as great as that which separated an Albert Hopkins lecture on the godliness of electricity from the student inspiration which wired East College for telegraphic communication in 1871.[1] For Mark Hopkins, the human body was a storehouse of strength and skill to be spent in the glory of God and the relief of man's estate.[2] For the undergraduates this was not enough.

Even before disclosing the score of an 1864 baseball game between Williams and Princeton, a reporter for the *Nassau Quarterly* suggested a contrast between the official view and the use to which young men in American colleges were putting their bodies. "The Williams boys presented a fine appearance," the Princeton writer reported, "all being about medium sized, heavy set, and with well developed muscles." For the Princeton reporter, the fine appearance of the Williams boys was important in itself and bore no relationship to the role which participants in "manly sports" might one day play in the relief of man's estate. The muscular development of the Williams undergraduate was related in the mind of the Princeton student to that same set of values which led him to conclude his account of the baseball game with the judgment: "The Williams boys . . . sang splendidly . . . and left the impression on all that they were a jolly, pleasant and gentlemanly set of fellows."[3]

Manners, charm, and a well-turned physique—they were all of

1. *Vidette, 6* (Oct. 28, 1871), 44.
2. *Public Exercises at the Laying of the Corner Stone of the People's College, at Havana, N.Y. Thursday, September 2d, A.D. 1858* (New York, John F. Trow, 1858), p. 23.
3. Quoted from a *Nassau Quarterly* report of the game which was played Nov. 22, 1864; in *Williams Quarterly, 12* (1865), 221-2.

the same parcel. As a package they were, as students at Williams knew, the attributes most desirable in prospective fraternity members. In sum, they were the attributes of a successful gentleman. As the 19th-century undergraduate, at Williams and elsewhere, laid the foundations of organized college athletics, the body itself became a thing of beauty, capable in large measure of self-creation in the gymnasium or on the playing field. Man the image of God became man competitive, boisterous, muscular, and physically attractive. Because the colleges themselves quite properly took their self-denying evangelism seriously, the 19th-century American college appeared to be little more than a framework in which the students discovered this world and erected institutions that permitted them to enjoy the discovery. The human body, in this sense, was one of their discoveries, and the gymnasium and the ball team were the institutions they adopted for its enjoyment.

As was so often true where the extracurriculum was concerned, the college was not actively hostile to the new developments. Basically, it was lethargic. Williams, however, was among the first American colleges to fall under the influence of the outdoor gymnasium movement, an importation from Europe which arrived with the baggage of a trio of German refugees in the 1820's. In 1825 Charles Beck, one of the trio, built the first outdoor gymnasium in the United States at the Round Hill School in Northampton; the next year Charles T. Follen, like Beck an exile from Metternich's Europe, provided Harvard with the first college gymnasium and the city of Boston with the first public gymnasium in American experience. These beginnings were paralleled at Williams in 1827, when the board of trustees appropriated $150 and detailed Mark Hopkins, then a tutor, to set up a gymnasium in Williamstown. After visiting the gymnasium at Northampton, Hopkins erected a swing and some parallel bars in an open clearing south of one of the college dormitories.[4]

Like its contemporaries, the Williams gymnasium proved to be premature. It lacked the military inspiration on which the movement had fed in Prussia, where Friedrich Ludwig Jahn had conceived of gymnastic exercises as a means of providing German youth with the physical equipment necessary to liberate the Fatherland from Napoleon. The Puritan ethic, too, objected to the kind

4. TR, *2*, 79; May 9, 1827. *Ibid.*, p. 82; Sept. 5, 1827. Faculty Records; June 15, 1827. MH, *A Discourse Delivered at Williamstown June 29, 1886, on the Fiftieth Anniversary of His Election as President of Williams College*, p. 12. Hopkins left Williams before finishing the job; it was completed by his brother Albert. Albert Hopkins to Harry Hopkins, Oct. 27, 1827, and Apr. 12, 1828; HL, *3*.

of frivolity and play suggested by an outdoor gymnasium. None was more definite in his strictures than William Paley, the 18th-century English theologian whose works were read in the Williams classroom. Referring to "the pleasures . . . of active sports," he had said that "the young are always too active in their pursuit of them." Human happiness, he had argued, consists in devoting the body to useful work, although "*any* engagement which is innocent is better than none; as . . . the laying out of a garden, the digging of a fish-pond,—even the raising of a cucumber or a tulip." [5] Appropriately, official Williams later attempted all of these engagements, even to digging a fish pond, with much more success than that which met the outdoor gymnasium of 1827.

In an America full of dreams yet to be fulfilled, unproductive physical exercise of the sort suggested by an outdoor gymnasium appeared to be unnecessarily trivial. Paley had implied as much; even more important, Williams students early in the 19th century were drawn from farms where they were trained to work but not to play. Young men did not need to be reminded that Americans judged their neighbors by their industry, not by their capacity for enjoyment. When the Reverend Alvan Hyde spoke to his sons, at Williams in the 1820's and 1830's, of the desirability of some bodily exercise, he advised them to limit their exertions to such activities as chopping wood and walking to and from their boarding houses. And to one he warned, "I hope you will not be seen with the ball-club in your hand this summer." [6] Hyde's point of view prevailed at the early Williams, where boarding house distances and wood chopping together necessarily provided sufficient physical exercise.

To supplement these practical exertions the college in the 1830's gave Albert Hopkins a free hand in adapting the more typically American manual labor system to the Williams scene. [7] The effort to combine physical development and self-support with practical accomplishments, which first appeared in the United States in 1820 at Captain Alden Partridge's school at Norwich, Vermont, took the form at Williams of the Horticultural and Landscape Gardening Association. The gymnasium of 1827, however, appears not to have lasted more than a year—if that long. Repugnant to practi-

5. *The Works of William Paley, D.D.* (Philadelphia, J. J. Woodward, 1835), pp. 31–4.

6. To Joseph, Oct. 26, 1820, and to Alexander, July 7, 1831; in *Memoir of Rev. Alvan Hyde, D.D. of Lee, Mass.*, pp. 202, 288.

7. See Harry Hopkins to MH, June 16, 1833, and Mary Hubbell Hopkins to Harry Hopkins, Mar. 28, 1833; HL, *5*. TR, *2*, 146; Aug. 20, 1833.

cal-minded and hard-working Americans, the outdoor gymnasium seemed a bit foolish to men who were accustomed to thinking of physical energy in terms of planted corn or sawed wood. Until another wave of German immigrants brought the gymnasium movement to the United States once again, in 1848, the Williams undergraduate channeled his energies into physical activity appropriate to his surroundings. Swimming, hunting, fishing, and sledding kept him out of doors in the course of a year. Walking, sawing wood, and early variations of football and baseball helped to keep him in vigorous enough health to warrant a student's boastful observation in 1847 that "the deathbell seldom tolls, and then, usually to announce the death of some aged person." [8] A study of 1870 showed that Williams alumni lived longer than those of any other college in New England.[9]

At the annual alumni meeting in 1848 David Dudley Field, undoubtedly influenced by the beginnings of the Turnerian movement, asked what the college was doing to provide gymnastic training for its students. His question met with an enthusiastic response from the undergraduates, who were now prepared to support the development of more formal athletic endeavor. In 1851 the college erected a seven-hundred-dollar gymnasium building, leaving to the students the problem of equipment and operation. As Mark Hopkins explained, "We let them manage it which they do better than we could." With characteristic inventiveness the students poured five hundred dollars' worth of equipment into the building and levied a tax of $1.25 upon all undergraduates who wished to enjoy the physical opportunities available there.[10] "The students are taking a strong interest in it, & will furnish it well," said Hopkins. "I feel perfectly sure that attention enough is not paid to the physical training of our young people, & I am glad to see any signs of increased attention to it. The time must come when it will enter into the scientific training in all our institutions." [11]

Hopkins, in advising the graduating seniors in 1871 to place themselves under the regimen by which athletes trained, departed far enough from traditional views to warn them against the dangers which flowed from neglect of exercise. But his interest was not in sport for the sake of sport: he admitted, for instance, that to many

8. Wells and Davis, *Sketches of Williams College*, p. 7.
9. Cole, *A Hundred Years of Mount Holyoke College*, p. 155.
10. MH to AL, Oct. 21, 1851; MHS, MH-AL MSS.
11. MH to AL, June 8, 1851; MHS, MH-AL MSS.

his moderate views toward athletics would seem to encroach "too much on the enjoyment of life." Athletics with moderation, but never as an end in itself. Athletics with regularity, even, but not in the service of competitive skill. For Mark Hopkins, athletics— like the classroom, mountain scenery, and college tutors—should serve God, and God alone.[12]

The students subscribed to a broader purpose for athletics, and they were less willing than the college authorities to condone a slow and faltering development of gymnastics at Williams. When, for instance, the gymnasium built in 1851 burned to the ground in the following February, the students and not the college erected another building on the ashes. Two days after the fire David Coit Scudder of the sophomore class wrote home to ask his parents how much he might subscribe toward a student gymnasium fund. Twelve members of his class had already subscribed ten dollars apiece.[13] On the other hand, on the day of the fire Mark Hopkins wrote to the college's most generous benefactor, "I hear they are talking already about getting up a new one. But we have done without it a long time, & can do so again." [14]

The students were altogether unwilling to do without a gymnasium, and before the year was out, they had gathered sufficient funds, let contracts, and given a mortgage upon a building to which the college contributed the total of only $100.[15] That they had Hopkins' sympathies there can be no doubt, but the college was itself unwilling to assume the responsibility for giving gymnastics a permanent home in Williamstown. Student interest managed to maintain this second Williams indoor gymnasium until in 1858 it, too, burned to the ground. Like its predecessor, the new gymnasium built that year was a student institution, completed and equipped in 1859 with perpendicular poles, vaulting bar, ring swings, and dumbbells.[16]

By 1860, however, the gymnastic and athletic movement had so captured the American college undergraduate that the Williams student was no longer satisfied with what he could provide for himself.[17] Unable to finance the operations of the new gymnasium,

12. MH, *The Body the Temple of God: A Baccalaureate Sermon, Delivered at Williamstown, Ms. June 25, 1871* (Boston, T. R. Marvin and Son, 1871), pp. 10–18.
13. Scudder, *Life and Letters of David Coit Scudder,* p. 37.
14. MH to AL, Feb. 19, 1852; MHS, MH-AL MSS.
15. MH to AL, Mar. 30, 1852, and July 29, 1852; MHS, MH-AL MSS.
16. *Williams Quarterly, 6* (1858), 93–4, 188; (1859), 381.
17. The collegiate gymnastic movement was widespread. New gymnasiums were in operation at Yale, Harvard, and Amherst in 1860. Agitation for new facilities

students complained of buck passing in the faculty and the board of trustees. "It is a disgrace," a student wrote of the situation, adding that it "does not rest with the students." [18] The college appeared to agree when in 1861 it paid off the gymnasium debt and took title to the building, and the next year took charge of the gymnasium and began to put its apparatus in repair.[19] Its new concern for athletics was brought to a climax in 1865 and 1866 with the erection of another building, the appointment of a professor of physical education, and the establishment of a Department of Physiology and Vocal and Physical Culture.[20]

The college's assumption of responsibility for gymnastics in the 1860's symbolized the widespread deterioration of the previous official view of man and nature. Undergraduate dissatisfaction with the old dispensation left its imprint almost everywhere. In the 1830's, for instance, there were no college songs at all. What music there was took the form of the devotional offerings of the Handel and Haydn Society. In 1859, however, Washington Gladden published in his senior year a collection of Williams songs that offered new evidence of the transformation which Williams was undergoing.[21] Not only had song entered the life of Williams—the mountains now assumed a new role. Gladden's own Alma Mater song, "The Mountains," testified that scenery was still important but its didactic interpretation was missing.[22] For Gladden and his fellow contributors the mountains were no longer summits from which to contemplate the divine but instead a setting for the jollity and fraternal life that took place within the valley. In his prize song, replete with scenic allusions, George L. Raymond of the Class of 1862 concluded:

> We love the might of each giant height,
>   The Peace of thy quiet valley,
> But more than all, in the time-worn hall,
>   The homes where brothers rally.[23]

was disrupting life at Trinity, Dartmouth, Middlebury, Bowdoin, and Oberlin. *University Quarterly, 2* (1860), 271, 342, 367, 380; *3* (1861), 371, 426.

18. C. L. Hutchins, "Amusements," *Williams Quarterly, 8* (1860), 8–9. See also *Williams Quarterly, 8* (1861), 208; *9* (1861), 143.

19. TR, *2*, 385–6; Aug. 5, 1861. *Ibid.*, p. 402; Aug. 4, 1862.

20. See *Williams Quarterly, 11* (1863), 143–6; (1864), 286; *12* (1864), 141; *13* (1865), 62, 143. TR, *2*, 421, 431, 441; Aug. 1, 1864, July 31, 1865, and July 30, 1866. *Ibid., 3, 5*; July 27, 1868.

21. Gladden, *Songs of Williams*.

22. Gladden, "The Mountains," *Williams Quarterly, 6* (1859), 278–9.

23. *Songs of Williams*, p. 16.

Only two songs in the collection spoke of the joys of climbing Mount Greylock: both were contributions of a clergyman of the Class of 1827.[24] In 1859, in fact, Mountain Day was calling few students to the mountains, and Chip Day, which had given institutional recognition to wood sawing, had recently been abandoned.[25]

Ralph Waldo Emerson would not have thought of himself in connection with gymnastics or college athletics, but his student-sponsored visits to Williams in 1854 and 1865 delivered the same verdict upon the orthodox construction of man and nature as did the student gymnasia. James A. Garfield could not sleep after hearing Emerson in 1854.[26] Another revealed the master's influence when he complained in the *Quarterly:* "The schools of our time . . . tell [young men] to be crammed with Euclid—learn from Locke, Paley, and Edwards that you are possessed of a soul, conscience, and will; but never to *think* that their false philosophy reduces the soul to physical sensation, conscience to calculation, free-will to mechanics, immortality to an eternal sleep, man to brute, and God to matter." What did the young Williams student suggest as a remedy? In language and thought right out of Emerson he proposed simply that man be "his own masterly and giant self," that he be "natural." [27]

Emerson returned to Williams to address the Adelphic Union for a second time at commencement in 1865, his one lecture on that occasion being sufficiently tantalizing to induce an independent group of students to invite him to return in November to deliver a series of six lectures on "American Life." Official recognition was, of course, resolutely withheld, as was use of the college chapel, the only campus building capable of containing the crowds which Emerson attracted. The students procured from the local Methodist clergyman the largest meeting house in town, and for a week Emerson held court in Williamstown, while lessons went unprepared and devotees worshiped at the master's feet.[28] Looking out of

24. A. D. Wheeler, "Away to the Mountain" and "The Return"; *Songs of Williams,* pp. 23–4.
25. See *Williams Quarterly, 3* (1856), 378–80; *10* (1862), 63.
26. Garfield to C. E. Fuller, Aug. 22, 1854; in Smith, *The Life and Letters of James Abram Garfield, 1,* 76.
27. O. V. Tousley, "Be Natural," *Williams Quarterly, 1* (1854), 236–9.
28. Emerson's visit to Williamstown in 1865 may be best traced in *Journals of Ralph Waldo Emerson,* eds. Emerson and Forbes, *10,* 107, 116–18; *The Letters of Ralph Waldo Emerson,* ed. Ralph L. Rusk (New York, Columbia University Press, 1939), *5,* 433–4; and Charles J. Woodbury, *Talks with Ralph Waldo Emerson,* New

the window of the room of one of his student hosts, Emerson one day caught a glimpse of the college chapel and asked how many faiths there were in Williamstown. Before young Charles Woodbury could respond, Emerson supplied his own answer: "Three thousand, five hundred people; three thousand, five hundred faiths in the village of Williamstown! Let yours not come from tradition. . . . Widen the circle, so as to admit ventilation." [29]

The kind of ventilation of which Emerson spoke derived from a more romantic view of nature and less circumscribed view of man than that purveyed by the college. Emerson spoke to the idealism of American youth and to its ready love of action. His popularity with the students suggests that for them there was a certain dryness in the intellectual diet that offered nature by way of the Bible, Locke, Paley, and Jonathan Edwards. In Emerson they found a richer fare which, while abandoning the conventional texts, encouraged them to be as independent in their approach to nature and self as they dared. Emerson at Williams was, in truth, a voice from the outside, but a voice that echoed wherever Williams students busied themselves in the enjoyment of nature and the expression of self. One such place was the playing field in Pittsfield, upon which intercollegiate baseball was born in 1859.

By the time the college was ready to take a serious interest in a gymnasium, the Williams undergraduate had found in baseball another instrument for the display and development of muscle, skill, and competitive prowess. The college hurried on its way, paying new attention to the gymnasium, introducing gymnastic exhibitions in 1867, levying an annual fee of three dollars upon all students for the use of the gymnasium in 1868.[30] Already, however, it was out of step. "The best the Colleges can do, is to give to the muscles a training . . . having for its end their symmetrical development, and perfection; that is, to give them a liberal education," Mark Hopkins said in 1858.[31] Ten years later the Williams catalogue, recognizing the importance of the gymnasium by extolling its equipment at the beginning of the section on departments of instruction, repeated Hopkins' sentiments. "It is believed," an-

York, Baker and Taylor Co., 1890. See also *Williams Quarterly, 12* (1865), 221; *13* (1865), 139, 140, 146.

29. Woodbury, pp. 33–4.

30. *Williams Quarterly, 15* (1867), 162.

31. *Public Exercises at the Laying of the Corner Stone of the People's College, at Havana, N.Y.,* p. 26.

nounced the catalogue, "that the body can as fittingly receive education as the mind. . . . Vocal Culture, following naturally from Physical Culture, is made the basis of . . . thorough and complete instruction in Elocution." [32]

That it had occurred to the Williams undergraduate to think of physical development in terms of elocution is rather doubtful, but it was characteristic that the college, in introducing gymnastics into the curriculum should tie the new to the traditional. Since 1793 Ebenezer Fitch and his successors had been preparing Williams undergraduates for eloquent action in the pulpit or at the bar, and it was a neat solution that grafted an old utility upon the new dispensation. Charles Russell Treat, the first professor of gymnastics at Williams, not only gave vocal training to Williams students but rehearsed them prior to their weekly elocution performances in the college chapel.[33] While the college combined elocution with chest expansion, however, the students pioneered in new directions, laying the foundations of intercollegiate athletic competition.

To the students of Amherst belongs credit for the suggestion which placed the Amherst and Williams baseball teams upon the field of the Pittsfield Base Ball Club on July 1, 1859. This first game of intercollegiate baseball, played according to rules which had prevailed for many years on New England sand lots, treated Pittsfield to a new spectacle in American life, the college weekend centered upon a sporting event. Carloads of students taking advantage of half-rate railroad fares, the presence of many young ladies at the game, an Amherst-Williams chess match on July 2, and a concert by the Mendelssohn Society of Williams at Burbank's Hall conspired to provide a holiday setting for the game. In both the baseball and the chess contests Williams lost; the baseball game lasted for three and a half hours, and the score was 73–32. But the enthusiasm generated by the game among Williams undergraduates bore fruit in the organization of a rash of class and college ball clubs in Williamstown.[34]

The contests of 1859 were repeated at Westfield the following

32. *Catalogue of the Officers and Students of Williams College. For the year 1868–9* (Williamstown, 1868), pp. 21–2.

33. Charles R. Treat, MS report to the board of trustees [1869?]; WCL, Misc. MSS, *2*.

34. An account of the Amherst-Williams baseball game of 1859 was carried in the *Adams Transcript,* an extra edition without date but carrying a story datelined Pittsfield, July 1, 1859. See also *Williams Quarterly, 7* (1859), 95. For the resulting enthusiasm for baseball see *ibid.,* and *8* (1860), 62, 69–72; *9* (1862), 293.

The Williams baseball team, 1869, ten years after Williams and Amherst played the first game of intercollegiate baseball.

July, and the college, recognizing the hold of baseball upon its students, provided a playing field adjacent to West College.[35] By 1862 interclass games were being played according to the so-called New York rules, from which the modern game of baseball developed. In 1864 intercollegiate competition, based upon the New York game, took a Williams team into play against Princeton and Harvard for the first time.[36] In 1865 the idea of a college team was sufficiently ascendant over that of class teams that the necessity of having a color to identify the college in intercollegiate competition was met by the selection of royal purple by some feminine summer visitors.[37]

Intercollegiate competition, involving as it did the fair name of the college and the pride and honor of its athletic representatives, demanded the development of the means of victory. Since the college was unwilling to provide more than a playing field, the undergraduates supplied such other necessities as money and professional coaching. "It is hoped that the good feeling existing between Nassau and Williams may ever continue," pronounced a Princeton student upon the occasion of the Princeton-Williams baseball game of 1864.[38] But two years later a sour note was heard in Cambridge, where a Harvard student reported: "Our Williams friends learned base ball from New York professionals, we are told, and that is where they got their manners, too. Their way of crowing over any especially bad luck on our side, with a 'Yi, yi, yi,' and a howl, are unmistakably borrowed from the firemen and roughs." [39] Whether the Harvard charges were true no one now can say, but it is a matter of record that a student subscription sent the Williams team to Worcester for the game in which Harvard was defeated, 39-37.[40] In 1868 a trainer was imported from New York, and the following year members of the Williams team contributed $300 for the hire of a trainer named Flanly.[41]

Student-hired coaches probably *were* of such character as to warrant raised eyebrows in Cambridge. Professional athletes in the 1860's were not likely to be college graduates; it was more probable that they were products of the city streets or, as the Harvard re-

35. TR, *2*, 375; July 30, 1860.
36. *Williams Quarterly, 12* (1864), 138; (1865), 221-2.
37. *Ibid., 13* (1865), 63, 72.
38. Quoted from *Nassau Quarterly* in *Williams Quarterly, 12* (1865), 221-2.
39. Quoted from *Harvard Advocate* in *Williams Quarterly, 14* (1866), 128.
40. *Williams Quarterly, 13* (1866), 277.
41. *Ibid., 16* (1869), 268.

porter so nicely put it, "firemen and roughs." Coaching raised a
new problem in the administration of American colleges. Richard
Henry Dana, Jr., after two years before the mast, wrote to Mark
Hopkins from Boston in 1872 that of course coaching and friendly
training were all right, as long as the coaches and trainers were
college graduates or good friends of the college. "The objection is
to . . . 'professionals,' " he maintained, expressing the hope that
Williams would not give way to pressure but would insist that
coaching be left in the hands of "an educated and respectable
gentleman." [42]

Like so many new problems that arose in the course of the 19th
century, this was another which had been provoked by the undergraduates, whose imagination and quest for thrills created intercollegiate athletic competition before there were enough alumni of
sufficient inclination to make athletics their profession. "To
be sure," a Yale student wrote in 1860, "the walks about New
Haven are delightful. . . . But, after all, walking is but milk-
and-water exercise, and something more stirring is needed to make
the 'Red river of life' course swift and strong." [43] No one more
thoroughly agreed with him than did the students of Amherst and
Williams. As late as 1855 they had gone to Charlemont to join in
an intercollegiate mountain dedication. In 1859 their inauguration
of intercollegiate baseball did indeed make the red river of life run
more swift and strong.

Acutely sensitive to the appearance of every new form of athletic
recreation, the students of Williams did not permit their interest in
baseball to interfere with the adoption of other diversions, some
ephemeral, some lasting. The publication of *Tom Brown's School-
days* in 1857 and the much heralded visit of an English cricket club
to America two years later were greeted at Williams with the
formation of a sophomore cricket club in 1859. No sooner had Dio
Lewis, founder of a school of gymnastics, published his popular
guide to physical development in 1862 than it was being avidly read
and practiced on the Williams campus. Croquet developed into a
national craze in 1865; it appeared on the Williams campus the
same year. In 1869 a team of circus velocipedists put on the market
the first popular model of a velocipede; in February of that year
students were learning how to operate "that new wonder" from
the Messrs. Topliff and Keith, at ten cents a lesson. In 1869 Princeton and Rutgers played the first game of intercollegiate football,

42. Richard Henry Dana, Jr., to MH, Nov. 1, 1872; HP, *6*.
43. *University Quarterly, 1* (1860), 217.

and in May 1871 a Williams reporter announced that "foot ball is beginning to engage attention here." [44]

Attention was being engaged in so many directions it is a wonder that a student body so small could sustain an athletic program so diverse. From 1863 through 1868 William C. Dole, director of gymnastics at Bowdoin, annually visited Williams, where, at the request of the students, he gave lessons in boxing. In October 1868 forty students paid him five dollars apiece for a series of twelve lessons.[45] The same year another itinerant athlete, a Major Beatty, found twenty students to take lessons in horsemanship and the use of the broadsword.[46] Fraternity boat clubs appeared in 1869, followed by a college crew with a three-hundred-dollar paper boat in 1871.[47]

The day of the full-scale college athletic program was still in the future when Mark Hopkins retired from the presidency of Williams in 1872. His students, however, had fashioned out of their respect for muscle and excitement and competition a whole new department of higher education. "It has been found somewhat embarrassing," an observer reported for the *American Journal of Education* in 1833, "to maintain, at the same time, and in the same institution, a strong interest in intellectual and physical education." [48] The interest in physical development in the 1830's was so slight, however, as to cause little difficulty, and during the Hopkins administration it bored into long-standing practice only enough to cause the abolition of Wednesday and Saturday evening prayers, in the interest of long afternoons on the playing fields. The real embarrassment, like the real athletic program, still lay in the future.

The future, nonetheless, owed much to Mark Hopkins' students. Wherever they confronted the world of nature they gave it a secular purpose. The Lyceum of Natural History and the development of a program of athletics at Williams were their robust answer to the mild and didactic construction of nature offered by the col-

44. See *Williams Quarterly, 7* (1859), 190. Samuel Warren Dike to his sister Mary, Oct. 1, 1862; WCL, Dike MSS. *Williams Quarterly, 13* (1865), 63. *Vidette, 2* (1869), 3. *Ibid., 5* (1871), 233. For athletic developments in the United States during these years see John Allen Krout, *Annals of American Sport* (New Haven, Yale University Press, 1929), pp. 129, 145, 149, 173, 237.

45. See *Williams Quarterly, 11* (1863), 141; *12* (1864), 141; *13* (1866), 211; *14* (1867), 207; *16* (1868), 122. *Vidette, 2* (Sept. 26, 1868), 3.

46. *Williams Quarterly, 15* (1868), 305. *Vidette, 2* (May 9, 1868), 2.

47. *Vidette, 4* (Dec. 4, 1869), 1–3. *Williams Quarterly, 18* (1871), 171.

48. *American Journal of Education, 5* (1833), 35–6.

lege. Even in as remote an area as the care of college grounds, student views in the end prevailed. "I doubt if there is any institution that has such grounds as these might be made by some expense and labor," Mark Hopkins remarked in 1852, concluding, "they are highly pleasing—there is a way in which they are improving, but they are not essential." [49] The very next year Charles A. Stoddard of the Class of 1854 recommended in the *Quarterly* that a competent landscape gardener lay out the college lands and that $2,000 be set aside for the endowment of the care of lawns.[50] His suggestion was repeated by students and faculty in ensuing years, but the college preferred to look upon its grounds as a sort of religious laboratory where, through the instrumentality of the Horticultural and Landscape Gardening Association, students might bend body and soul toward an awareness of God.

As early as the 1840's, under the particular influence of Andrew Jackson Downing, a New York horticulturist and architect, Americans began to take a more widespread interest in landscape gardening. The Williams Landscape Gardening Association, founded in the 1830's, undoubtedly owed its inspiration to William Paley, for whom gardening was, at best, an innocent diversion. Downing and his followers went beyond Paley and the Williams Gardening Association and consciously proposed to humanize and civilize nature by combining homes and public buildings with trees and formal gardens. The demands voiced by Williams students, beginning early in the 1850's, that the college pay more attention to its grounds were a part of a growing movement which hoped to create pleasant and beautiful vistas of rural charm in a nation undergoing a period of rapid urbanization. Even before the Civil War, Americans were seeking a certain kind of simplicity and relief from the city in a carefully cultivated ruralism.

In 1853, for instance, the trustees of Hamilton College busied themselves in surrounding their institution with a park, in which well-graveled paths and quiet groves of maples were blended in an effort to create a kind of rural paradise.[51] The works of Downing, urging that attention be paid to landscaping and to the conscious creation of a rural charm in which civilization and nature would be happily combined, began to appear in the student libraries at Williams in the early 1860's and in the library of the college itself

49. MH to AL, July 13, 1852; MHS, MH-AL MSS.
50. *Williams Quarterly, 1* (July, 1853), 64–8.
51. *Documentary History of Hamilton College* (Clinton, N.Y., Hamilton College, 1922), pp. 253–9.

before the end of the decade.[52] During the same years the great city parks, like the Central Park of Frederick Law Olmsted in New York, began to take form, in answer to the sense of loss which an agrarian and outdoor people were experiencing in their movement to the cities.

The old Horticultural and Landscape Gardening Association was tied to another set of purposes, and thus, when Williams fell under the spell of the new interest in parks and rural charm, it appropriately turned to other auspices. Harvey Rice, a graduate of the Class of 1824 and a leading citizen of Cleveland, ushered the park movement into the life of the college. At his suggestion, a ten-acre maple grove was set aside as a monument to the young men who had caught a vision of foreign missions under the haystack in 1806. At the dedication exercises of the park in 1867, Rice, who himself contributed a monument which was erected in the center of the maple grove, revealed his indebtedness to the work being done in such places as Central Park when he disclosed plans which would "embellish the park with specimens of trees, and shrubs, and flowers of every foreign land to which missionaries have been sent." Mission Park, he said, would "become a place of delightful resort." [53]

The demand that Williams College itself become such a place grew more insistent, and in 1872 the board of trustees authorized the unprecedented sum of $5,000 for improving the college grounds.[54] Their appropriation was not inspired by the purposes that had sustained the Landscape Gardening Association. Neither God nor college discipline nor student health was expected to benefit necessarily from their appropriation. The improvements for which they provided in 1872 were called forth by an awareness that the outside world was judging Williams College by externals. Well kept college grounds would convey an impression of urbanity in combination with rural simplicity. Carefully trimmed lawns and neat gravel paths would impart a sense of material well being, a goal that had become paramount in American life. Nature could be tamed, as the railroad builders and cable layers had proven. Now, colleges, too, were expected to do their part in creating little pockets of charm, where civilization and nature were blended— carefully, studiously, reverently—into a series of quiet landscapes:

52. In particular, his *Rural Essays*, New York, George P. Putnam, 1853; and *A Treatise on the Theory and Practice of Landscape Gardening, Adapted to North America*, 6th ed. New York, A. O. Moore, 1859.

53. Durfee, *Williams Biographical Annals*, pp. 185-6.

54. TR, *3*, 47; June 24, 1872.

a maple grove and a marble monument, a row of elms and a chapel tower, the soft shadows of a college dormitory on a neat, green lawn.

The last creation of the old order was the organization by Albert Hopkins in 1863 of a town-and-gown mountain climbing and nature study club.[55] Whether he thought so or not, the Alpine Club was in a way a last desperate protest against the secular movements which had taken young bodies off the mountain and into the gymnasium, off the summits and into the laboratories. And yet, as a protest it carried the seeds of its own destruction. Richard Townley Haines of Elizabeth, New Jersey, who in the 1830's took his family to Williamstown in the summer in order to be near his sons, may have given the town the first suggestion that it might one day be a summer resort.[56] By 1850 Williamstown in the summer was attracting numbers of city people who were seeking fresh air and scenic delights in the Berkshires, and from this group Albert Hopkins drew many members for his Alpine Club.[57]

He probably did not question what it was that brought people from the cities to Williamstown in the summer. And he may not have seen in the annual hegira any reason to relate Williamstown as a summer resort with Williams College as a baseball team. But the relationship was there. The city folk whose wealth permitted them to indulge in the material enjoyment of a summer vacation were hardly looking for God in Williamstown. What they sought was escape from the crass and busy world in which they made their living. They asked of Williamstown that it repay them in rural vistas, fresh air, and health for the lives they spent in the competitive acquisition of wealth and honor during the rest of the year. These were the kind of people, indeed, whom the gymnasium and ball club were fashioning out of the Williams undergraduate. By 1872, in fact, Williamstown enjoyed a two-way traffic in which candidates for success in this world were sent forth at each commencement while their predecessors, who had made their way, were arriving to take up residence for the summer. The graduates of the later years of the Hopkins era recommended themselves to material success by virtue of the spirit of independence and ingenuity which they had turned toward the creation of a program

55. Perry, *Williamstown and Williams College*, pp. 579–81.
56. Durfee, *Williams Biographical Annals*, p. 77.
57. *Williams Quarterly, 1* (1853), 85–6; *2* (1854), 186. *Vidette, 5* (Oct. 29, 1870), 59. Also, the following letters in WCL: William Pitt Palmer to MH, Jan. 27, 1857, in HP, *4;* MH to Lawrence Hopkins, Sept. 14, 1864, in HP, *2;* Samuel Warren Dike to his brother, July 9, 1862, in Dike MSS.

of competitive athletics at Williams. In addition, who could say that a manly physique and a skill at games might not one day lead through the paths of business success and social approval to a summer home in Williamstown?

Part Four: MATTER

11. Amos Lawrence and the Stewardship of Wealth

ONE COLD DAY in January 1846 the president of Williams was enjoying a drive through Boston with Amos Lawrence, the millionaire merchant-manufacturer and philanthropist who four years before had decided to spend his declining years translating his fortune into good works. Did Hopkins want anything for the college, Lawrence wondered. No, the Williams president could not think of a thing. The next day, however, he remembered that the trustees *had* voted to build a library if it could be done for $2500. He then told Lawrence, yes, come to think of it, the college had been thinking about building a library; perhaps Mr. Lawrence might be interested. "I will give it" was the ready answer with which Lawrence, in the course of a year, added a seven-thousand-dollar library to the plant of Williams College.[1]

Lawrence, a self-made Yankee merchant whose career mirrored the growth of New England merchandising and manufacturing, discovered Williams in 1844. In 1841, it is true, his hundred dollar contribution toward the rebuilding of East College, which had gone up in flames in October, was more generous than any other support the college was able to muster in Boston on that gloomy occasion.[2] But from the winter of 1844, when Lawrence heard Hopkins deliver his first series of lectures before the Lowell Institute in Boston, until his death in 1852, Lawrence moved from the periphery and became the leading private benefactor of Williams College.

If he played the role of benefactor more in the guise of good fairy than demanding patron, he did so because he was as able a practitioner as was Hopkins an advocate of the Christian stewardship of wealth. Seldom in history have the advocate and the practitioner fashioned a friendship as warm or productive as that which Hopkins and Lawrence erected upon their mutually held views on the acquisition, right estimate, and right use of property. The esteem in which they held each other grew until in 1851 Lawrence was writing to Hopkins, "Our *intercourse* has been of such a character

1. Hopkins told this story in *A Discourse Commemorative of Amos Lawrence, Delivered by Request of the Students, in the Chapel of Williams College. February 21, 1853* (Boston, T. R. Marvin, 1853), p. 18.
2. *Ibid.*, pp. 16–17.

as to allow *you* to be my father confessor." [3] And Hopkins was writing to Lawrence, in appreciation of the latter's well-timed gifts, "If it had not been for you . . . I do not see that I could have worked here at all." [4]

Lawrence's major benefactions to Williams began with a visit by Lawrence's son, Amos Adams, to Hopkins' hotel room in Boston in January 1844. The message which the younger Lawrence carried was simple and direct: his father liked what he had seen and heard when Mark Hopkins spoke from the rostrum of the Lowell Institute; he would like to give Williams College $5,000.[5] In August 1844 came another $5,000 from Amos Lawrence, "a great thing for us," Hopkins wrote, which would put "the college in a better position than it has been since I have been connected with it." [6] Indeed, the position of the college was so greatly improved that the trustees found it possible to create a Lawrence Professorship of Languages the same month.[7] An additional $10,000 was forthcoming the following January, with the stipulation, gladly accepted, that the first thousand dollars' income be paid to Albert Hopkins, in six semiannual installments, for uncompensated services rendered to the college.[8] Complementing these welcome checks were books for the college library and, on one occasion, a skeleton brought home from Paris by Lawrence's son William, who was pleased enough with this addition to the college natural science collections to describe it as "so clean and beautiful, I should almost be willing to take it to bed with me." [9]

In January 1846 Lawrence authorized Hopkins to begin work on the new college library about which they had talked in Boston. "Prepare *such* a building as you will be satisfied with & as will do credit to your taste & judgment *fifty years* hence," he wrote, urging that the project be accomplished with dispatch.[10] At his suggestion the original plans were enlarged, bringing the cost of the building to an eventual $7,000—a sum which Hopkins regretted spending but accepted as unique, in that he was certain that no other library in the United States capable of housing 30,000 books had been

3. Jan. 7, 1851; MHS, MH-AL MSS.

4. July 30, 1851; MHS, MH-AL MSS.

5. MH to Mary Curtis Hopkins, Feb. 6, 1844; HP, *6*.

6. *Idem*, Aug. 7, 1844; HL, *6*.

7. TR, *2*, 239; Aug. 20, 1844.

8. AL to MH, Jan. 28, 1845; MHS, MH-AL MSS.

9. TR, *2*, 251; Aug. 19, 1845. AL to MH, Apr. 17, 1845; MHS, MH-AL MSS.

10. Jan. 26, 1846; WCL, Misc. MSS, *10*. Characteristically, Lawrence urged that precautions be taken to keep his own name out of any publicity which the new building might inspire.

built for less than three times that amount.[11] When the brick octagonal building was two years old, Hopkins pronounced the verdict that "it will hold all the books the Institution will ever be likely to want." [12]

To his larger gifts Lawrence added in 1847 a two-thousand dollar scholarship fund for students from Lawrence Academy, and in 1852 he gave $1,000 with which to enlarge the college grounds and $1500 with which to buy a new telescope for the Observatory.[13] In December 1845 he sent Hopkins the first of what became an annual series of checks for $100, to be used as Hopkins decided in easing poor students through financial difficulties. Distributing the money with discretion, Hopkins gave ten dollars here, fifteen dollars there, seldom more, to boys for whom, as he put it, "a *little* money may often be the weight in the scale that shall give a favorable turn" to their destinies.[14]

This "encouragement money," as Lawrence called it, endeared him to the undergraduates, so much that when he died in 1852, they asked Hopkins to deliver a sermon on his life.[15] Soon after the father's death, William prepared a volume of extracts from the benefactor's diary and letters for private distribution, and the students at Williams successfully prevailed upon him to permit a wider publication.[16] *Extracts from the Diary and Correspondence of the Late Amos Lawrence* was something of an early-day success guide, in which the career of Amos Lawrence was an open invitation to American youth to go out and do likewise.

In the last months of his life, Lawrence busied himself among his friends in Boston, interesting them in the good work that was being done at Williams, encouraging them to contribute to a college fund drive which was then underway. In a letter to Hopkins, six weeks before his death, he wrote, "I yesterday had a charming ride & talk with good old Uncle Jonathan Phillips. The old gentleman is *oppressed* with more money than he knows what to do with,

11. See AL to MH, May 15, 1846; MH to AL, May 24, 1846, and May 30, 1846; AL to MH, July 21, 1847—all in MHS, MH-AL MSS.
12. MH to AL, Oct. 17, 1848; MHS, MH-AL MSS.
13. TR, *2*, 268; Aug. 17, 1847. *Ibid.*, p. 303; Aug. 16, 1852.
14. MH to AL, Dec. 25, 1845; MHS, MH-AL MSS. For these benefactions see MH to AL, Dec. 25, 1845; Mar. 24, May 1, 30, June 17, Oct. 19, 27, 1846; Mar. 25, Apr. 11, June 24, July 30, Sept. 28, 1847; May 4, June 1, Oct. 24, 1849; Sept. 23, 1850; Oct. 21, 1851; June 1852—all in MHS, MH-AL MSS.
15. AL to MH, Apr. 6, 1847; MHS, MH-AL MSS.
16. *Extracts from the Diary and Correspondence of the Late Amos Lawrence; with a Brief Account of Some Incidents in His Life*, ed. William R. Lawrence, Boston, Gould and Lincoln, 1855.

& is I believe earnestly desirous to use it as a good *steward*. . . .
When you come here, I shall wish him to make your acquaintance." [17]

Williams did not hide its appreciation. When Lawrence sent for
distribution among the students 200 copies of James Hamilton's
Life in Earnest, a guide to material success the title of which suggests its message, Professor Joseph Alden organized a voluntary
class of forty students who met on Sunday afternoons for discussions and recitations.[18] At Lawrence's request Hopkins preached,
as was hardly his custom, in the Unitarian church in Boston which
Lawrence attended.[19] Lawrence himself was asked by the trustees
to sit for a portrait which, when completed, became the first portrait of any of its friends or benefactors, let alone the founder, to
adorn the college walls.[20] These manifestations of appreciation were
kindly received, but Lawrence did not accept them as an invitation
to participate in the conduct of college affairs. He remained a model
benefactor. Occasionally he sent a clergyman friend, perhaps a
Williams alumnus, to represent him at commencement.[21] Only once,
however, did he visit the Williams campus—in July 1851, a little
more than a year before his death and, characteristically, while
the college was not in session. "All my anticipations have been
more than realized," he wrote to Mark Hopkins upon his return
to Boston, in what must have been one of the most welcome bread-
and-butter notes in the history of American education.[22]

To the Hopkins family, as well as the college, Amos Lawrence
was a constant provider. He showered bouquets upon Mary Hopkins when she visited Boston. He introduced Mark, who had never
lost a country boy's tendency to be impressed by very important
people, into the elegant society of Boston. At the home of Abbott
Lawrence, Amos' brother, Mark wrote to his wife, he saw more sil-
ver plate than he had ever seen before. To the Hopkins children—

17. Nov. 20, 1852; MHS, MH-AL MSS.
18. AL to MH, Oct. 9, 1852, and MH to AL, Oct. 1, 1852; MHS, MH-AL MSS.
19. MH to his wife, Feb. 16, 1844; HP, *1*.
20. TR, *2*, 251; Aug. 19, 1845. MH to AL, June 17, 1846; MHS, MH-AL MSS.
Chester Harding painted the portrait from an earlier portrait of Lawrence which
he had also done; it now hangs in the old college library, Lawrence Hall, which
houses the college art museum.
21. See AL to MH, July 30, 1847; MHS, MH-AL MSS. Also, AL to Calvin Durfee, July 19, 1849, and C. S. K. Lathrop to Durfee, Aug. 17, 1849; WCL, Williams
College Autographs, *1*. AL to ———, Aug. 21, 1849; WCL, Misc. MSS, *6*.
22. July 26, 1851; MHS, MH-AL MSS. For preparations for the trip see, in
the same collection, AL to MH, July 12, 1851; MH to AL, July 15, 1851; AL to
MH, July 19, 1851.

and, indeed, to their mother and father—he was known as Uncle Amos. Upon them he endlessly bestowed gifts, ranging from tops and whips and dolls to gold watches and clothing. The president of Williams he kept in tailored suits, making the arrangements himself for the fittings in Boston. His gifts were so frequent and so varied that Hopkins once reminded him, "Men are rare enough who endow colleges, but this endowing of kitchens too is quite unprecedented." [23] Nothing symbolizes so well the pervading presence of Lawrence in the Hopkins home as the career of a plaster bust of himself, a gift to Mrs. Hopkins in February 1844.

"I suspect that he took a fancy to you" is the way that Mark announced to his wife Mary that she could look forward to the arrival of a replica of Amos Lawrence in Williamstown.[24] When the bust arrived, he reported to Lawrence that Uncle Amos was "looking fresh and smiling and not seeming to have suffered at all from the journey." [25] Within two months, however, the carelessness of an Irish maid and the pardonable curiosity of two-year-old Archie had put an end to the plaster bust. "This was a source of mortification to us, as well as of regret," Hopkins wrote with obvious embarrassment. "And what were we to do? . . . We have a fine little boy . . . and if you do not object to it, we propose to call him *Amos Lawrence*." [26] On the occasion of the little boy's birth, which occurred before the fatal accident, only Mark had objected to the chorus of proposals within the family that the new baby be named for Uncle Amos. At the time he suggested Hugh Nicodemus, Ichabod, or Ephraim Williams—all, young Mary Louisa thought, "very homely names." [27] For a college president to name his son for its most generous benefactor would have its complications, Hopkins confessed to Lawrence. "It might be liable to misconstruction." The faculty, the alumni, the friends of the college did not know that Amos Lawrence had been prompted in his benefactions less by his interest in Williams than by his admiration for its president. If they did know, Hopkins was certain, "It would be felt that I could in no way more properly manifest my sense of the kindness and the honor done me in that act."

23. MH to AL, Nov. 30, 1848; MHS, MH-AL MSS. For reference to Lawrence's generosity to the Hopkins family see MH to Mary Curtis Hopkins, Feb. 1, 1844, Feb. 19, 1847, and Mar. 15, 1847, in WCL, HL, *6; idem,* Feb. 7, 1844, and Jan. 24, 1846, in HP, *1;* Mary Louisa Hopkins to Mary Curtis Hopkins, Aug. 7, 1844, in HL, *6.*
24. Feb. 16, 1844; HP, *1.*
25. Mar. 2, 1844; MHS, MH-AL MSS.
26. MH to AL, May 7, 1844, and AL to MH, May 11, 1844; MHS, MH-AL MSS.
27. Mary Louisa Hopkins to Mary Curtis Hopkins, Apr. 4, 1844; HL, *6.*

Mark once admitted to Lawrence that the benefactor's movements reminded him of "the campaigns of Napoleon in Italy where
he always came down upon them sooner and more powerfully than
they expected." [28] Hopkins' proposal that the boy be named Amos
Lawrence developed into such a campaign. On the eleventh of May
Lawrence cheerfully granted permission. On the sixteenth he proposed that young Amos Lawrence Hopkins be made, at his expense,
a life director in the American Bible Society.[29] On the twenty-third
a second bust arrived in Williamstown, wrapped in "checked cloth
fit to make summer clothes for children . . . cotton cloth . . .
petticoats . . . calico . . . books . . . a splendid edition of Pilgrim's Progress for Master Amos Lawrence. . . . I then took the
bust into the parlor," Mark wrote his wife, who was visiting her
family in Troy, "but just as I was setting it down I happened to
put my hand up to the head on the inside and felt something and
pulled and out came mousselin de Laine . . . and Shalley . . .
and crepes . . . and spools of thread . . . and tape and little
books." [30] Young Mary's eyes had grown large, and as the plaster
bust of Amos Lawrence disgorged its contents, she had repeated,
"What an odd gentleman! What an odd gentleman!" And in July
Lawrence suggested another gift to the college, which he later gave,
of $5,000, the first thousand dollars' income of which was to be
paid to Mark Hopkins and held in trust for the education of
Amos Lawrence Hopkins.[31] An odd gentleman, indeed!

To young Mary Hopkins what made Amos Lawrence odd was
his munificence. To a later generation it would be the motive. For,
like almost everything else in the mid-19th century, benefactions
in the day of Amos Lawrence were tied irrevocably to the Almighty.
Puritan New England had learned more than how to make a dollar;
it had combined with Yankee shrewdness not only the patience of
Job but that stewardship of wealth which permitted Job in the Old
Testament story to say, "I caused the widow's heart to sing for
joy." The small New England college depended heavily upon successful men who had taken to heart the story of Job. If Williams
had its Amos Lawrence, whose total gifts of $40,000 were not sur-
passed by a private benefactor until 1875, men enough of similar

28. Feb. 4, 1845; MHS, MH-AL MSS. The occasion was the receipt of a draft
for $10,000, an unexpected and unsolicited gift to the college.
29. AL to MH, May 11, 16, 1844; MHS, MH-AL MSS.
30. May 23, 1844; HP, 7.
31. MH to AL, Aug. 2, 1844, and AL to MH, Aug. 29, 1844; MHS, MH-AL MSS.

inclination were available to relieve the other colleges of New England from constant financial embarrassment. At Amherst, for instance, there was Samuel Williston, a Connecticut Valley button manufacturer; at Wesleyan, Isaac Rich, a Boston fish merchant. "What shall it profit a man, if he gain the whole world, and lose his own soul?" went the biblical text to which these men subscribed. Amos Lawrence, for one, scribbled it on a piece of paper and carried it in his wallet.[32]

"My property imposes upon me many duties, which can only be known to my Maker," Lawrence had confided to his account book on the first day of January 1828. "May a sense of these duties be constantly impressed upon my mind." [33] He thus entered upon his friendship with the president of Williams in no need of the encouragement or reminders which Hopkins, like others, was sometimes called upon to deliver. Hopkins was altogether honest, however disingenuous his words may seem in retrospect, when he thanked Lawrence for his first gift of $5,000. "It is, my dear Sir, painful to receive from some men, but a pleasure to receive from you," he wrote, "because you know the meaning and spirit of that scripture which says that it is more *blessed to give than to receive.*" [34]

Basic to their mutual awareness of the obligations of wealth, of course, was an inherent respect for property. Not until a still later series of Lowell Lectures, in 1868, did Hopkins find the occasion to state, at length, his complete case for property, but its postulates were contained in the attitudes which he held in common with Lawrence. These attitudes were the ordinary intellectual equipment of New England conservatives; they had experienced a great flowering under the impact of Jacksonian democracy; by the 1850's they were standard fare. "The Right to Property reveals itself through an original desire," Hopkins said. Without it, "society could not exist. With no right to the product of his labor no man would make a tool, or a garment, or build a shelter, or raise a crop." Indeed, the president of Williams concluded, "There could be no industry and no progress. . . . The general well-being and progress of society has been in proportion to the freedom of every man to gain property in all legitimate ways, and to security in its

32. *Extracts from the Diary and Correspondence of the Late Amos Lawrence,* pp. 146–7.
33. *Ibid.,* p. 51.
34. Jan. 27, 1844; MHS, MH-AL MSS.

possession." In language not unlike that which he used in discoursing to Williams students on the death of Lawrence, he argued that the acquisition of property should be encouraged, as long as acquisition remained subordinate to the higher value of love, a love which benefited others out of a devotion to God. With a common sense characteristic of the Scottish philosophers who were his guides, he remarked, "There is no giving without a previous getting." [35]

As Hopkins pointed out to Lawrence upon more than one occasion, however, the steward of wealth did not arrive at a station of grace merely by being dutifully beneficent. There was a difference, he insisted, between benefactions inspired by a sense of privilege and those motivated by "an onerous & self-denying duty." [36] Not every college president, to be sure, cared about the difference, but Mark Hopkins was one who did. "You spoke of the great idea of stewardship—that is well," he wrote to Lawrence after visiting him in Boston in 1847, "but the time ought to come when even that shall become subordinate to the greater idea of *love*, or rather shall be swallowed up in it." He warned that to recognize a Christian duty and to perform it were not enough. To find peace, the steward must also find "the love of God in Jesus Christ our Lord." [37]

It was this cultivation of peace that he urged upon Lawrence in the last years of his life, and not without some justification. For Lawrence was human, too, and the impulse to contribute to Williams again in 1845 was born of something not altogether in keeping with the refinements of the doctrine of stewardship as it was preached by Hopkins. "I desire to do *something* by which the remembrance of me in the circle *my friend Hopkins* blesses, to make my memory worthy of being cherished, & if I can do *this something*, I shall not have been spared *thus long* in vain," he scribbled on a letter he received from Hopkins in January of that year.[38] Again, in 1847, when congratulating his brother Abbott for the benefactions to Harvard which became the Lawrence Scientific School, he was guilty of deviation from genuinely orthodox stewardship. On that occasion, in reminding his brother that their talents were "to be accounted for when the Master calls," he emphasized a fear of

35. MH, *The Law of Love and Love as a Law: or, Moral Science, Theoretical and Practical* (New York, Charles Scribner, 1869), pp. 182–3.

36. Jan. 20, 1851; MHS, MH-AL MSS.

37. Aug. 31, 1847; MHS, MH-AL MSS.

38. Lawrence's notation of Jan. 14, 1845, is on a letter from MH of Jan. 10, 1845; MHS, MH-AL MSS.

God rather than that simple love which Hopkins sought to incul-
cate.[39]

In Hopkins' estimation, therefore, the death of Lawrence's son
Robert in November 1845 was a heavenly warning to Lawrence to
turn from all things earthly to God. The benefactor's own poor
health was intended to turn him "more fully from all selfish and
ostentatious methods of spending wealth, to the better example and
higher enjoyments of a benevolence that has blessed so many." [40]
Mark Hopkins, too, was human, and he wished that the infirmity
might be removed, "but perhaps," he felt called upon to add, "it is
the thorn in the flesh lest you should be exalted above all measure." [41] When Lawrence died on December 31, 1852, Hopkins went
on to Boston, staying at the Lawrence home, attending the funeral
as a friend—there was no preacher. To his mother he expressed the
belief that Amos Lawrence had succeeded in moving beyond stewardship to love. "His death was sudden," he lamented, "but he
lived in a constant state of preparation, having the fullest reliance
upon the atonement, which he cordially received." [42]

Certain as they were of the sanctity of property, the individual
incentive and effort which created it, and the Christian way to dispose of it, Mark Hopkins and Amos Lawrence were, not surprisingly, of similar political persuasion. Lawrence, who thought of
Thomas Jefferson as a "sad infliction," was as much Whig as was
Mark Hopkins, who upon thinking of the Democratic administration of James K. Polk decided that "we must do what we can for the
young and trust in God." [43]

To both Hopkins and Lawrence the rise of democracy as well as
the Democracy was a chilling sight to behold. "*Politics* . . . is
dirty *work* . . . mainly done by *knaves* & *blockheads*. . . . The
open-mouthed lovers of the *dear* people are self-seekers in most
instances." Such were the political opinions of Amos Lawrence.[44]
If Hopkins was less vituperative, he was in no sense less conservative. In a sermon before the legislature of the Commonwealth in
January 1839 he warned the legislators that they must not act as
if government were responsible to the people instead of to God. In
an obvious challenge to the equalitarianism of Jacksonian politi-

39. June 9, 1847; MHS, Lawrence Papers.
40. Nov. 5, 1845; MHS, MH-AL MSS.
41. MH to AL, Aug. 2, 1844; MHS, MH-AL MSS.
42. Jan. 11, 1853; MHS, Hopkins Family MSS.
43. AL to MH, May 11, 1844, and MH to AL, Mar. 11, 1845; MHS, MH-AL MSS.
44. AL to MH, May 11, 1846; MHS, MH-AL MSS. *Extracts from the Diary and
Correspondence of the Late Amos Lawrence,* p. 47.

cians, he charged that "men are upon an equality only as they are equally upon trial in the sight of God, and nothing will ever reconcile them to the unavoidable inequalities of the present state, but the consciousness that their circumstances were allotted to them by Him who best knew what trials they would need." [45] The protection of industry and of property, the ignorance of the masses, the sordidness of politics, the perilous road to Heaven of the wealthy, the easier path of the poor, education as the only permissible social equalizer—these were the conservative shibboleths of the day, and Mark Hopkins embraced them all.

Hopkins viewed with as much alarm as did men of great property the leveling tendencies of the age, because he expected very little from "the unhappy and unavoidable working of our poor human nature." [46] In his last letter to Lawrence he stated the fears and the apologetics of men of property in all times. "There is clearly a tendency everywhere towards a more direct exercise of power by the masses," he lamented. "This may go on . . . till it shall be felt that there is an unbalanced and irresponsible power in the hands of the masses, & then there will only need to come up a *populace*, assuming to be the people, & imbued with agrarian & infidel notions . . . to bring about a direct physical struggle for property & power, & a state of things which would make despotism a blessing." [47]

Lawrence's political opinions certainly stemmed from an appreciation of his own struggle for material success in a young nation where freedom of action was less curtailed than elsewhere in the civilized world. On the other hand, Hopkins' politics grew out of the same Christian thinking which accepted property both as a right and as a necessity and which went on to elaborate its uses in the doctrines of stewardship and love. The Thomas Jeffersons and Andrew Jacksons, the Tammanys and the labor unions were one with Hopkins in their zeal for the possession of property. He left them, however, when they sought to usurp the privileges of the Lord, in whose hands alone rested the power to give property or to take it. God had willed that Amos Lawrence be an instrument

45. MH, *A Sermon Delivered before His Excellency Edward Everett, Governor, His Honor George Hull, Lieutenant Governor, the Honorable Council, and the Legislature of Massachusetts, on the Anniversary Election. January 2, 1839* (Boston, Dutton and Wentworth, 1839), p. 15.

46. MH to AL, May 1, 1846; MHS, MH-AL MSS. MH to Ray Palmer, Apr. 14, 1862; WCL, Palmer MSS.

47. Nov. 18, 1852; MHS, MH-AL MSS.

for good, and Lawrence had cooperated. Others could do the same, if they would. "Who," he asked urgently of the students of Williams College, "will not work together with these noble benefactors? Who will not be a co-worker with God?" [48]

Amos Lawrence, who had worked so admirably with God, also imparted to Williams a vision of a greater college—in his library plans, in his purchase of property in Williamstown—a vision which was lacking in a board of trustees whose ambitions were narrowed by a tradition of financial struggle and geographic isolation. The trustee who tried to imagine in 1852 what Williams would have been like without Amos Lawrence exaggerated only slightly when he said, "We shouldn't have been able to do much more than vegetate." [49] Yet an even more important work was done by giving unsolicited encouragement to its president. Lawrence's benefactions to Williams coincided with the decade in which Mark Hopkins was most ardently wooed by tempting offers to leave the Berkshires for pastoral, professorial, or presidential fields elsewhere. Every offer he received promised greater opportunity and prestige than that which was, in those days, attached to the presidency of a country college. Between 1847 and 1852 he was twice offered a professorship at the Andover Theological Seminary. He was asked to become the pastor of important urban churches—Pilgrim Church in Brooklyn in 1844 and Mercer Street Church in New York in 1851. Union Theological Seminary asked him in 1851 if he would come down from the hills and lend a hand in its important work. In 1850 the chancellorship of New York University was his for the taking, and in 1852 he could have become the president of the University of Michigan. [50]

To all these offers Hopkins answered no. Although he was fearful of sectarian and political interference at the new University of Michigan, he was almost persuaded to try his skills in the West by the entreating letters which came from Charles H. Palmer of the Michigan board of regents in the early months of 1852. [51] The Michigan offer happily coincided with an offer to his brother Albert of the principal's chair at Mount Holyoke Female Seminary, an

48. MH, *A Discourse Commemorative of Amos Lawrence*, p. 36.
49. MH to AL, July 29, 1852; MHS, MH-AL MSS.
50. MH to AL, Jan. 20 and Feb. 10, 1851, and Dec. 6, 1847; MHS, MH-AL MSS. MH to Mary Curtis Hopkins, Oct. 21, 1850; HL, *6*.
51. See the letters of Palmer, dated Jan. 10, Feb. 12, 16, Mar. 20, and ——— 16, 1852; also, H. D. Kitchel to MH, Mar. 1, 1852—all in HP, *8*.

offer that Albert was seriously entertaining. At this point in time, the Hopkins tradition at Williams most nearly approached a premature death.

Mount Holyoke not only promised Albert Hopkins more salary and more freedom from classroom duties than Williams could offer—its representatives spoke of the milder climate of the Connecticut Valley and the helping hand which the ladies of South Hadley would gladly lend to comfort Albert's invalid wife. "If he should go," Mark wrote to Lawrence, "it would almost seem as if we might as well break up. Indeed I told him I thought I should go too, as I have recently had an official communication inquiring whether I would accept the presidency of Michigan University." He promptly, and it would seem sincerely, added, "It would be certainly pleasanter to be among these mountains & to work with you & with men here." [52]

Into this smoldering crisis Amos Lawrence moved with his usual dispatch. In June 1852, when Albert had just about made up his mind to leave Williamstown, Lawrence sent a thousand dollars to Mark, to be applied at his discretion in keeping Albert at Williams. Although Holyoke indicated its willingness to give Albert another year within which to make up his mind, the thousand dollars of Amos Lawrence appears to have turned the trick.[53] The Hopkins brothers stayed, and the tradition and the legend put down new roots.[54]

Family and regional ties and a sense of loyalty to a college with which he had been associated as student or teacher, with the exception of four years, since 1822, certainly helped to keep Mark Hopkins at Williams. In addition, Hopkins freely admitted—in a

52. MH to AL, Feb. 19, 1852; MHS, MH-AL MSS.

53. MH to AL, June 1852; AL to MH, June 10, 1852; Albert and Louisa Payson Hopkins to Lawrence, July 13, 1852; MH to AL, July 29, 1852—all in MHS, MH-AL MSS. See also Cole, *A Hundred Years of Mount Holyoke College,* pp. 180–1, 369. The official offer from Mount Holyoke was voted on Aug. 5, almost two months after Lawrence had, in effect, ruined the preliminary efforts of the Mount Holyoke board of trustees.

54. Mark, having decided against Michigan, lent his efforts, fruitlessly, to getting the job for Absalom Peters, the Congregational clergyman (then fund-raising for Williams) whose refusal to become the president of Williams had opened the way for Hopkins in 1836 (MH to AL, Apr. 5, 1852; MHS, MH-AL MSS). The Michigan board of regents settled on Henry Phillip Tappan, who, as its first president, gave Michigan a more dynamic sort of administration than the regents had had in mind when H. D. Kitchel, urging Hopkins to accept the post, wrote: "We want New England ways—especially in college matters. We desire to make our university to us what your colleges are to the Eastern States" (Mar. 1, 1852; HP, 8). Tappan, instead, attempted to pattern Michigan after the Prussian universities.

letter to Lawrence in 1850—the importance of the role their relationship played in holding him to the job in Williamstown:

> There has been an impression that I was bound to you to remain here, & I have been inquired of by letter to know if that was not so. But while I would not make, & you would not wish, any engagement of that kind, I have no hesitation in saying that I feel great satisfaction in that I am working with you, & that it would be a strong motive with me to remain here, if you would feel that the proper results of what you have done would be better realized in that way.[55]

Lawrence, for his part, had already made clear his position in an earlier letter, in which he wrote, "The reports *of* & *from* your college make me feel that my labours in getting it on *'its legs,'* have been *repaid fourfold.*" [56]

Amos Lawrence ably symbolized one of the most dependable and important sources of financial support of the 19th-century American college. His willing and eager devotion to the stewardship principle enabled Williams College to share in his wealth, as other colleges shared in the wealth of other benefactors who themselves had not gone to college. But the stewardship of wealth alone could not—and did not—sustain the small liberal arts college. To this worthy Christian sentiment were also added the generosity of the state and an increasingly complex apparatus designed to play upon alumni loyalty. Williams depended upon all three. Yet none was as pleasant to contemplate or as rewarding in human relationships as the kind of financial support represented by Amos Lawrence. A good man who desired to meet his God, he needed no special proddings, he asked no special favors. "Uncle Amos," the Hopkins children and the students of Williams College called this gentleman, who deserves to be thought of as one of the last of the old-time college benefactors.

55. Nov. 27, 1850; MHS, MH-AL MSS.
56. Nov. 11, 1850; MHS, MH-AL MSS.

12. The Hand of the Commonwealth: State Aid

THE ARRIVAL of Amos Lawrence upon the scene in 1844 permitted Williams to remove the accumulated deficits of ten continuous years, and during the eight years of his benefactions a comparative sense of relief pervaded the college. Yet compared to the sums that were going elsewhere, Amos Lawrence's $40,000 was not large. Educational benefactions of the period were larger, it seemed, when they went elsewhere than Williams. The roll of wealthy men who took their stewardship seriously was impressive, but what comfort was there for Daniel Dewey, the college treasurer, in knowing that John Lowell's $250,000 established the Lowell Institute in 1836, or that Amherst had found, in Samuel Williston, the source of at least $150,000? John Jacob Astor poured $400,000 into a library for the city of New York in 1848, and beginning in 1856 Isaac Rich made a series of gifts to Wesleyan totaling $150,000. Eliphalet Nott turned $600,000 over to Union College in 1854, and three years later Peter Cooper contributed $300,000 toward the creation of the Cooper Institute.[1]

At Williams, Amos Lawrence—with $40,000—remained the greatest private benefactor until 1875. As late as 1852 the permanent endowment of the college was a little over $30,000; five years earlier, Amherst's endowment passed $150,000.[2] As late as 1871 Hopkins could say that for fifty years Williams had not received a single bequest that had paid off.[3] No Williams treasurer could afford to be smug, even if for a change he could pay the college bills.

A part of the problem which confronted Williams was common to other institutions of higher learning. The benefactions which founded the Lowell Institute, the Astor Library, and the Cooper Institute revealed not only a yearning for self-monumentation but also a concern for educating the masses in things practical as well as classical. Men of property, sensing the discontent that was manifest in the infant labor movement and in the growth of popular democracy, were making their investments carefully. A dollar spent

1. For biographical sketches of these 19th-century benefactors see appropriate entries in *Dictionary of American Biography*.
2. TR, *2*, 314–15; Aug. 17, 1853. Stanley King, *A History of the Endowment of Amherst College* (Amherst, Amherst College, 1950), p. 48.
3. MH to Joseph E. Lockwood, reported in *Vidette, 5* (Mar. 4, 1871), 161–2.

in giving a mechanic a sense of self-improvement and self-impor-
tance was, to a man of hard sense, a better and more immediately
rewarding investment than was a dollar contributed to higher
learning. In this sort of giving, of which there was much, the college, whether it was Amherst or Williams or Princeton, was forgotten.

Chance, it must also be admitted, played a large part in deter-
mining which colleges were to benefit from the largess which flowed
from new fortunes in manufacturing, speculation, and merchandising. A Wesleyan president, not a Williams president, had been
kind to the boy Isaac Rich. Eliphalet Nott, who was the president
of Union College for sixty-two years, could not have been expected
to give his fortune to Williams. Chance alone, however, will not
explain the degree to which the endowment of Williams lagged
behind that of other colleges or the degree to which it failed to
attract large and frequent benefactions.

Basic to the difficulties of the college, of course, was its location.
As late as 1864 John Z. Goodrich, in proposing an energetic fund
drive in Berkshire County, expressed the opinion that it was distance "from the great money centers" which partially accounted
for the meager endowment of Williams.[4] Amherst College, by
virtue of its closer proximity to Boston, some undoubtedly argued,
held a geographical advantage over Williams in the constant search
for endowment. And the argument would have had some foundation, for between 1844 and 1867 the endowment of Amherst was
increased by $236,000 from four friends of Amherst in Boston.
The Connecticut Valley in which Amherst was situated, moreover,
was less tied to agriculture and more advanced in manufacturing
than was Berkshire County. Consequently, while Amherst found in
Samuel Williston of Easthampton and Samuel Hitchcock of Brimfield the source of an additional $325,000, Williams looked almost
in vain among the men of western Massachusetts for financial
support.[5]

To the obvious geographical advantage at Amherst must be
added the careful work of such Amherst presidents as William A.
Stearns, who might have fumbled his first interview with one
prospective benefactor, had he chosen to recognize the fact that his
host, then practicing nudism, was absolutely naked. It is questionable whether Mark Hopkins would have been equal to such a situation. "That ugly business of begging," as he described a mission

4. To MH, July 30, 1864; HP, *3*.
5. King, *A History of the Endowment of Amherst College*, pp. 38, 61-4.

to Boston in 1849, challenged him not at all.[6] Hopkins had a penchant for the unsolicited contribution—enough of them came his way to warrant some sense of satisfaction—but his lack of zeal as a money raiser must also be considered an impediment in the way of the development of a sizable endowment at Williams.

In 1872, when the endowment of Amherst was approximately $600,000, that of Williams was just short of $300,000, a ten-fold increase over the endowment of twenty years before.[7] This decided improvement in the financial position of Williams, while warranting no relaxation in the constant effort to save the college, was the work of three agencies—the reputation of the college and of Mark Hopkins for sound Christian influence, the activities of the Society of Alumni, and the financial assistance of the state. Of these three the most important, in one sense, was undoubtedly reputation. For very few men, and certainly not the members of the General Court of Massachusetts, would have showered gifts upon an institution devoted to infidelity and radical political or social theory. The endowment which Hopkins turned over to his successor in 1872 was a reflection of his own reputation, but the bald fact is that over a third of that endowment was bestowed by the Commonwealth of Massachusetts and another third was raised under the necessity of equaling the grants of the state in order to secure them.

Would it be an exaggeration to suggest that Williams College was enabled to survive all of its vicissitudes only because the state was generous? Of course, every dollar, whatever its source, gave the college sustenance—but subtract the assistance of the state, its encouragement, its incentive for greater exertion, and then ask where the college would have been. No one can answer with exactness, but the conclusion is inescapable that the "independent, privately supported" American college has perpetrated a fiction upon itself and upon society by ignoring the degree to which it is a creature of the state. For better or worse, the blood of the state of Massachusetts runs through the veins of Williams College. In these respects, the history of Williams is not unique, and on more than one occasion that blood was the difference between life and perhaps death—certainly between life and hopeless infirmity.[8]

6. MH to AL, Feb. 17, 1849; MHS, MH-AL MSS.

7. King, p. 64. Carter, *Mark Hopkins*, p. 75.

8. A study of federal and state aid to higher education, published in 1890, recorded the following state assistance to so-called independent institutions; Columbia, $140,130; Hobart, $63,000; University of Pennsylvania, $287,267; Bowdoin, $52,500; Union, $358,111; Hamilton, $120,000; Dartmouth, $35,000

To place the financial assistance of the state in a proper relationship to the history of the college is not to deprecate the role of Mark Hopkins. For whatever the state gave, it gave in the knowledge that the president of Williams was Hopkins. At the same time, although some gifts found their way into the Williams coffers because of widespread respect for its president, they were not frequent. The $5,000 with which Amos Lawrence's widow endowed the library in 1857 and the $30,000 with which William E. Dodge, a founder of Phelps, Dodge, and Co. and co-worker with Hopkins on the American Board of Commissioners for Foreign Missions, endowed the president's salary in 1867 were certainly acts of devotion.[9] A gift of $25,000 in 1864 from John Z. Goodrich, the husband of Hopkins' cousin Mary, could have been considered a vote of special confidence in Hopkins, but the gift, at the suggestion of cousin Mary, was returned by the board of trustees when Goodrich fell into financial difficulties soon after it was made.

A campaign in Boston and eastern Massachusetts which ran from 1852 through 1855, coming as it did on the heels of the Lawrence gifts and the many offers to Hopkins of positions elsewhere, might have been expected to approach its fifty-thousand dollar goal on the reputation of its president alone. When Absalom Peters, the Congregational clergyman who conducted the campaign, wrote from Boston in October 1852 giving his first report, he could say, "My courage is up." His report, which is a model of frankness, conveyed the impression that the campaign was certainly being conducted with exemplary finesse and technique:

> I spent a night at Ware with our good friend Mr. Hyde, who subscribed $100, & introduced me to his father in law, Orrin Sage who put down his name for $500. I arrived at Boston Friday evening & on Saturday obtained a handsome introduction from Mr. Walley to his Uncle Jonathan Phillips. . . . I suggested to him the founding of a Professorship with $20,000. . . . I went immediately to Mr. Lawrence & reported.

plus $101,000 in land grants. Yale received financial support from Connecticut later than 1890, and Harvard, aided at its founding in 1636 with a grant of 400 pounds, benefited from 102 further appropriations before 1789 and was awarded ten annual grants of $10,000, beginning in 1814. To Harvard's Museum of Comparative Zoology the Commonwealth of Massachusetts had contributed $235,000 by 1890. See Frank W. Blackmar, *The History of Federal and State Aid to Higher Education in the United States,* Washington, Government Printing Office, 1890.

9. For Dodge's benefactions see his letter to MH, July 26, 1867; HP, *3.* TR, *2,* 456; July 29, 1867. Said Dodge: *"This fund* I can but hope may prove a comfort to you in freeing you from any anxiety as to your support."

He is delighted with the prospect, & we are bringing influences
to bear upon Mr. Phillips. . . . But we must have patience.
. . . I have today had a pleasant interview with Amos A. Lawrence, who has given me a line to his father in law, Hon. William
Appleton. I am thus breaking into a circle of great wealth,
with some hope of success, & feel the need of the utmost discretion and carefulness. . . . Write me a letter & give me your
views. . . . Mr. Dewey [Daniel N. Dewey, college treasurer]
suggested the getting up of a Diploma for Abbott Lawrence.
I think it would be well. It would please Uncle Amos, & do us
good. . . . I have this day made the acquaintance of the late
Mayor, Bigelow & his br. Rev. Dr. Bigelow. They have both
thought of visiting Williamstown . . . this week or next. They
are put up to this by Mr. Lawrence [who] thinks [their] talk
to these rich men, on [their] return will be of service to us.
You will treat [them] accordingly. . . . So you see I have
got some "glorious nibbles" & that my operations look hopeful.
But I dare not boast at this mere putting on of the hands. . . .
But my courage is up. . . . I trust the Lord will direct & bless.
. . . I may have to wait here some weeks before I can begin to
reap the large sums which I have in view. . . . P.S. . . . Mr.
Phillips called on Mr. Lawrence yesterday & said he would give
$1,000, & spoke in a manner which leads us still to hope he
may be induced to do more. He said he *was rich enough & was
seventy-five years old.*[10]

The nibbles, however, never became glorious catches. Three years
later, when the Peters agency was concluded, it was possible to
report total donations of $13,000, of which $3,000 was absorbed
in the expenses of solicitation.[11] Not every campaign at Williams
went so badly; those that were more successful were inspired by the
state or by the Society of Alumni. The 1852–55 campaign, if it
proved nothing else, demonstrated that having Mark Hopkins in
the presidency was not enough to open the coffers of Boston.

In 1872 a Williams undergraduate voiced the opinion that "colleges ought not be left wholly to private beneficence. They ought
to be the constant wards of the state, as much, at least, as penal and
corrective institutions." [12] His opinion was neither revolutionary

10. Peters to MH, Oct. 25, 1852; HP, *3*.
11. The history of the Peters agency can be traced in TR, *2* for the years 1852–
55, as well as in "Gifts to Williams College," a MS record of gifts received by the
college treasurer.
12. *Vidette, 6* (Mar. 28, 1872), 184.

nor unpopular, and at no time, at least through 1872, is there any indication that the presidents and trustees of Williams College would have disagreed with him.

Indeed, Williams College could hardly have survived even until 1836 had not the Commonwealth of Massachusetts, between 1793 and 1823, injected awards amounting to $53,000 into the struggling institution, a sum exactly equal to that which the college itself had been able to raise in subscriptions, state-authorized lotteries, and bequests during the same period.[13] After 1836 a series of petitions to the General Court for assistance are ample testimony of the degree to which the trustees of the college subscribed to the idea, as they voiced it in a petition of 1839, that the legislature of the Commonwealth was "the constitutional guardian and patron of education." [14] On five occasions during the Hopkins administration—1837, 1839, 1842, 1849, and 1863—they reminded the General Court of its obligations to Williams College.[15] On two occasions, in 1859 and 1868, the Commonwealth appropriated a total of $100,000 for Williams. With these contributions the state of Massachusetts became the largest single contributor to the funds of Williams College until the benefactions of Frederick Ferris Thompson in the 1890's.[16] Until the sons of Williams were able to devote to the college a share of the earnings accumulated in post-Civil War finance and manufacturing, however, the Commonwealth of Massachusetts sustained the institution.

Although the petitions of 1837, 1839, 1842, 1849, and 1863 were fruitless in immediate rewards, they symbolized the dependence of the college upon the state for assistance. And the response of the state demonstrated the sympathy of the Commonwealth, even though funds were not forthcoming. In 1837 the trustees

13. In 1793 the Commonwealth authorized four annual payments of $1,000 each, and in 1813 ten annual payments of $3,000 each; in 1796, 1804, 1805, and 1809 the college was granted townships in Maine, upon which it realized approximately $19,000. Prior to the incorporation of the college in 1793, the trustees had raised $3,500 by lottery and $2,000 in subscriptions; in 1811 and 1813 they received a total of $5,700 from Woodbridge Little for a charity fund, in 1820 they raised $17,500 by subscription, and in 1826, $25,000. See TR, *1, 2*; "Gifts to Williams College"; *Quarterly Journal of the American Education Society, 2* (May, 1830), 242–3; "Statement of the funds of Williams College, Jany. 1827," MS in WCL, Misc. MSS, *9; Massachusetts Legislative Papers*, Senate Document No. 38 (1839), pp. 6–12.

14. Senate Document No. 38 (1839), pp. 3–5.

15. TR, *2*, 187; Aug. 1837. MH to Daniel Dewey, Jan. 11, 1839, and to Mary Curtis Hopkins, Jan. 1 and 5, 1839: HP, *1*. MH to Mary Curtis Hopkins, Jan. 11, 1842; HP, *1*. Edward Everett to MH, Dec. 3, 1847; HP, *12*. MH to AL, Dec. 20, 1848 and Apr. 2, 1849; MHS, MH-AL MSS. TR, *2*, 418; Aug. 3, 1863.

16. *Acts and Resolves Passed by the General Court of Massachusetts in the Year 1859* . . . (Boston, 1859), chap. 154, pp. 314–16. *Ibid.*, for 1868, chap. 64, pp. 289–90.

asked for relief on the grounds that they had been encouraged to expect it when the state of the Commonwealth treasury permitted. They reminded the General Court of its obligation to "diffuse useful knowledge and raise the general standard of education," suggesting that Williams, on its part, might prove more worthy of state assistance if it opened its doors in the winter to neighboring farmers for free courses in such subjects as agricultural chemistry and mineralogy.[17] In 1839 Hopkins, on behalf of the trustees, acknowledged to the General Court that Williams College felt that it was its "duty" to report on the "condition and wants" of an institution which had been so carefully preserved by the Commonwealth in the past. "Your petitioners," he concluded, "can at present look only to the Legislature for the means of putting [modern languages, civil engineering, and practical mechanics] on the footing their importance demands." [18]

When East College was consumed by fire in 1841, the committee on zoology of the Lyceum of Natural History lamented the disappearance of the bats which occupied the rooms there, and students generally observed that bed bugs were freely destroyed.[19] To Mark Hopkins and his trustees, however, the fire was another challenge to survival, and soon another appeal to the state was made. They reminded the General Court that the destroyed building had been a monument to the generosity of the Commonwealth, having been erected in 1797 from the sale of land in Maine which had been conveyed to the college by the General Court. "When the calamity occurred," Hopkins confessed, the trustees "determined to look first to private aid, but were met on every hand with the inquiry why they did not apply to the Legislature. . . . Thus they were compelled . . . to look, as the Constitution teaches them to do, to your Honorable body." [20]

Although deeply moved by the petitions of the college, the General Court refused to vote the sums demanded. In February 1837 a committee to which the petition of that year had been referred agreed that Williams had "reached almost the summit of usefulness, and there faints, and falters, and needs . . . the reviving appliances of the [state] treasury, to enable it to ascend." The Committee recommended an annual appropriation of $1,000 for ten years, ending, in a final burst of prose, with full confidence

17. Senate Document No. 39 (1837), "Petition of the President and Trustees of Williams College, and Report Thereon," pp. 3–5.

18. Senate Document No. 38 (1839), pp. 3–5.

19. "Records of the Lyceum of Natural History," *1*, 66; Nov. 6, 1841.

20. MS copy of petition in handwriting of MH; WCL, Misc. MSS, *12*.

that with these grants Williams would "rival, in purity, the snow upon its surrounding mountains, and in healthful and invigorating influences, the winds that fan their summits." [21] The prose was glorious but the report of the committee was rejected.

The legislative committee which handled the petition of 1839 was equally impressed by the arguments of the college. It agreed that an increase in tuition to nine dollars a term would "probably reduce the number of scholars . . . [from] the middling classes." It admitted that "private liberality has been applied to till it is deaf to the appeals of the institution." It confessed that aid from the Commonwealth would not enrich the college but simply protect it from exhaustion. The Committee was sympathetic but referred the petition to the next legislature for further consideration. [22]

In 1842 the committee which had been asked by the General Court to consider the Williams petition seeking funds to rebuild East College reported that it had been impressed by the fact that Williams had done an able job in giving "persons of small pecuniary means, opportunity of obtaining a liberal education." Furthermore, the committee believed that it was the obligation of the Commonwealth to sustain its educational institutions, to which, indeed, Massachusetts was indebted for its "high moral and intellectual character." Indifference to the petition of Williams College, the committee declared, would "betoken a departure from that ground whereon our civil institutions and our freedom can alone be securely based." It concluded with the recommendation that a sum of $15,000 be contributed for the rebuilding of East College. The committee was rebuffed in the General Court.

The trouble with the petitions of Williams College was thus not that they failed to provoke sympathy but that the sympathy and understanding demonstrated by select committees could not be translated into effective action upon the floor of the legislature. In the popular mind, to which politicians in Massachusetts as well as elsewhere were wont to pay increasing deference, a college inevitably inspired thoughts of rich men. Agrarian and urban discontent in the 1820's and 1830's, which had been reflected in the rise of the Democratic party under Andrew Jackson, was accompanied by a profound mistrust of institutions whose alumni were the conservative pillars of society. Popular democratic unrest in Massachusetts during the period was mirrored in the strong position of the Democratic party in state elections from 1835 to 1846,

21. Senate Document No. 39 (1837), pp. 6–13.
22. Senate Document No. 38 (1839), pp. 6–12.

and particularly in the grasp which the Democrats held upon the depressed agricultural western counties.[23]

There was interest in education, but funds and energies were poured into such popular manifestations as the creation of a State Board of Education in 1837, the development of a system of free common schools, and the chartering of state normal schools as a source of teachers for the common schools. Free to dispose of a $1,300,000 share in surplus revenues of the United States treasury, the Massachusetts General Court in 1837 turned a deaf ear upon the pleas of Williams College and in true democratic fashion distributed the money among the towns of the state, where in many cases it was further distributed among the people.[24] The problem which confronted an institution of higher learning seeking state aid was well understood by Charles Sedgwick of Lenox, who wished Mark Hopkins well in his 1842 petition for the rebuilding of East College and expressed the hope that "the *Democracy* may distinguish itself in this [committee] from what it is in many other places—the perversion of a name that ought to be synonimous with universal humanity—for base & selfish purposes." [25]

Sedgwick's hope was unwarranted. The Democracy, as well as the people whose political power was beginning to be felt with increasing sensitivity in Massachusetts, were the very same men of whom Hopkins had spoken in his inaugural address at Williams in 1836 when he remarked, "It is objected to colleges that they are aristocratic." On that occasion Hopkins had charged that "nothing but a return of society to a savage state could satisfy" these enemies of collegiate education who could "conceive of no improvement except by levelling every thing down." [26] A petition from the citizens of Williamstown to the General Court in 1837 asking that the college be deprived of its tax exemption and another in 1842 seeking to prevent students from voting in town elections were manifestations of the spirit which Hopkins viewed with alarm.[27] But it was the spirit of the age, feeding in western Massachusetts, in addition, upon a general resentment against academies and col-

23. See Arthur B. Darling, *Political Changes in Massachusetts 1824-1848* (New Haven, Yale University Press, 1925), *passim*.

24. Edward Everett, *Speech in Support of the Memorial of Harvard, Williams, and Amherst Colleges, Delivered before the Joint Committee on Education, in the Hall of the House of Representatives, Boston, on the 7th of February, 1849* (Cambridge, Metcalf, 1849), p. 13.

25. Sedgwick to MH, Dec. 20, 1841; WCL, Misc. MSS, *2*.

26. MH, *An Inaugural Discourse*, pp. 21-2.

27. Fuess, *Amherst: The Story of a New England College*, p. 95. MH to Mary Curtis Hopkins, Jan. 16, 1842; HP, *1*.

leges for taking young men off the farms and turning them into
lackeys of the growing wealthy manufacturing class.[28] The whole
range of popular prejudice against the colleges received the attention of Edward Everett when, speaking for Harvard, Amherst,
and Williams before the Joint Committee on Education of the
General Court in 1849, he asked that their petition for the creation
of a state fund to benefit collegiate education be granted:

> We do not desire to build up the Colleges to the neglect of the
> Schools. . . . We submit that it is not quite fair, to attempt
> to raise a prejudice against us, by saying that we seek to endow
> them richly at the expense of the Schools. . . . We are still
> told,—and this objection in some form or other meets us at
> every turn,—that Common School education is a popular in-
> terest, and College education is not. . . . It is . . . said, The
> Schools are for the many; the Colleges for the few. . . . The
> Colleges are not pleading their own cause, on this occasion;
> they are pleading the cause of the people.[29]

The people and their elected representatives, however, did not
hear the pleas. As Edward Hitchcock of Amherst wrote to Hopkins
in 1848, sensing one source of their difficulty, "We must get at the
country members." [30] The country members could not be had. And
Mark Hopkins responded, "The State is a politician & I fear our
colleges are to get nothing more from her." [31] In a previous letter
to Hopkins, Hitchcock had touched upon another problem that
must have disturbed the legislators—the emergence of denominational colleges, all of which would, in time, be knocking on the
doors of the legislative chamber. Referring to a proposal of the
Harvard authorities that the state create a fund which would benefit colleges that might be incorporated in the future, as well as
existing institutions, Hitchcock remarked: "I have little doubt that
if after five years they could be sure of an income . . . the Baptists, the Methodists, the Episcopalians & Universalists would at
once establish a college, and the Catholics already have one." [32]
The prospect of an annual migration of college presidents to Bos-

28. Oscar and Mary Flug Handlin, *Commonwealth: A Study of the Role of Government in the American Economy: Massachusetts 1774–1861* (New York, New York University Press, 1947), p. 201.
29. Edward Everett, *Speech in Support of the Memorial of Harvard, Williams, and Amherst Colleges*, pp. 6 ff.
30. Dec. 7, 1848; HP, 7.
31. To AL, May 8, 1848; MHS, MH-AL MSS.
32. Dec. 20, 1847; HP, 7.

ton for funds to balance their budgets must certainly have been a chilling possibility to some legislators.

During these years, however, the Commonwealth was not totally deaf to pleas for help from collegiate institutions. Harvard, like Williams, had received its last previous assistance from the Commonwealth in 1823. Amherst, on the other hand, although refused in 1827, 1831, 1837, and again in 1849, did succeed in partaking of the fruits of the state in 1847. Both Williams and Harvard had benefited handsomely from previous state grants, and thus the $25,000 which the General Court authorized for Amherst in 1847 was in a sense a payment long overdue.

Hopkins was altogether wrong in supposing in 1848 that an end had come to state aid. Williams would be remembered again. Referring to an action of the General Court on April 2, 1859, an undergraduate editor gleefully reported, "The Old Commonwealth . . . opened her purse for us . . . counting out a cool twenty-five thousand." [33] The gift was apparently unsolicited. At any rate, it was not the result of a petition from the college. On this occasion, as a matter of fact, the Commonwealth's purse was opened in five directions—to the Museum of Comparative Zoology at Harvard, to Tufts, to Amherst, to the Wesleyan Academy at Wilbraham, and to Williams.[34] And for the first time the state told the college what it was to do with at least part of the money— establish scholarships for worthy sons of Massachusetts.

The state grants in 1859 requiring the establishment of scholarships at Amherst, Tufts, and Williams revealed a desire to place state aid to education upon a popular footing. The omission of the College of the Holy Cross, the only other institution of higher learning in the state, from the grants of 1859 may be another story. In 1854 the anti-Catholic, nativist American party had so completely captured the state of Massachusetts that in the legislature of 1855 only three members were not affiliated with this immigrant-hating Catholic-baiting group. From 1855 through 1858 Henry J. Gardner, an affirmed Know Nothing, was governor. His successor, although a Republican with a Republican legislature, was Nathaniel P. Banks, who had been an ardent Know Nothing. By 1859 the American party had been destroyed by the political realignments inspired by the slavery controversy, but it would be foolish to suppose that the animosities upon which the movement had fed were in fact any less strongly held. More than

33. *Williams Quarterly*, 7 (1859), 187.
34. *Acts and Resolves . . . 1859*, chap. 154, pp. 314–16.

one legislator, casting his vote for the appropriations of 1859, must have thought that he was making at least a small gesture toward preserving old Massachusetts from the ruin which Irish immigration seemed to foreshadow.

The generous appropriation of the General Court in 1868, contributing another $75,000 to Williams, not only proved that Hopkins had underestimated the possible future generosity of the Commonwealth but demonstrated as well that Williams alumni had attained positions of influence in the Commonwealth.[35] The announcement of the appropriation was met in Williamstown by a "jollification," in which the students toured the town, demanding speeches from members of the faculty and from President Hopkins, who told them that he supposed that the gift "was owing to zealous friends of the college in the legislature." [36] He was not wrong. Samuel W. Bowerman and Marshall Wilcox, both of the Class of 1844, both representatives of Berkshire County in the Senate, had worked hard. Their efforts met with the warm approval of the secretary of the Massachusetts Board of Education, Joseph White of the Class of 1836, a Williams trustee since 1848 and treasurer of the college since 1859.[37] Moreover, the cause in which they succeeded in enlisting the support of their fellow legislators was particularly convincing: in 1868 Williams College looked very much as if it might become a casualty of the Civil War. In the legislature the only outspoken opposition came, quite appropriately, from a former Universalist minister and a young Irish Democrat. Western Massachusetts was almost solid in its support.[38]

Generous as the Commonwealth was, the grant of 1868 brought to an end its financial assistance to Williams College. The state did not give again, nor did the college ask. The final separation was accompanied by no formal announcements. The state did not say that henceforth it would refrain from subsidizing the small private colleges of the Commonwealth. The trustees of Williams College did not issue a statement expressing fear of continued state aid, nor did they declare that in the future they would seek financial security independent of the state. Indeed, as the assistance

35. *Acts and Resolves . . . 1868,* chap. 64, pp. 289–90.
36. *Williams Quarterly, 16* (1868), 70. *Vidette, 2* (June 20, 1868), 4.
37. Carter, *Mark Hopkins,* pp. 70–2.
38. H. G. Knight to MH, Jan. 6, 1868; WCL, Misc. MSS, *12.* The importance of the state grant of 1868 cannot be overstated. As Hopkins himself said in 1886: "But for an unexpected gift by the State . . . I do not see how the College could have got on." *A Discourse Delivered at Williamstown June 29, 1886,* p. 19.

itself had been haphazard and irregular, so its disappearance was characterized by a mutual willingness to allow matters to move on as they would, under the impetus of new developments.

The Commonwealth discovered that it had more important functions to perform in the realm of education, functions which could be tied to the practical business of American industrial development, the agricultural rebirth of Massachusetts, and the provision of popular higher learning in an institution of its own. Thus in 1863 the newly chartered Massachusetts State College and the new Massachusetts Institute of Technology became the favorite beneficiaries of the state. In its first twenty-five years Massachusetts State College received grants of almost $600,000 from the Commonwealth; by 1890 MIT was indebted to the Commonwealth for donations of over $200,000.[39] Both of these institutions seemed to provide an opportunity for more practical—and certainly more popular—investments than did a place like Williams, tied to the classical curriculum and devoted not to teaching young men how to make a living, but to the impractical considerations of how to live fully.

The college, on the other hand, apparently did not complain. It, too, was being exposed to new forces, the most important of which was the desire of its alumni to capture the college in its entirety for themselves, coupled with the appearance of alumni with funds enough to undertake the capture. The college was thus enabled to move into a more secure financial future, without the slightest regret over the termination of the state assistance which had for so long sustained it. In time its administrators would boast of its independence of the state.

In its parting gifts to the college in 1859 and 1868 the Commonwealth did not fail to attach strings to its grants. With characteristic respect for the New England virtues of determination and energetic application, the state insisted, in both instances, that Williams College would have to prove its worth by matching the appropriations of the Commonwealth through its own efforts. If this was bribery, the college was not unprepared, for in 1821 it had given birth to a unique American institution, the Society of Alumni, which was designed to bail the college out of financial difficulties. The Society of Alumni was to be more important in the future, but in 1859 and 1868 it was not found wanting.

39. Blackmar, *History of Federal and State Aid to Higher Education in the United States,* pp. 98–100.

13. Sons and Lovers: The Society of Alumni

THE SOCIETY OF ALUMNI, which was organized at commencement in 1821, was a product of the movement to transfer the college to the Connecticut Valley. Ironically, the meeting from which the society sprang was called at the behest of Emory Washburn of the Class of 1817, a young man who had recently been admitted to the Berkshire bar and who, in time, would become governor of the Commonwealth. Washburn had transferred to Williams from Dartmouth in 1815, in order to be under the tutelage of his uncle, Zephaniah Swift Moore, who took the road from Hanover the same year to become the president of Williams. In 1821, Moore was on his way to become the first president of Amherst, a road which, this time, Washburn was unwilling to take.[1]

In their call to the alumni, issued in the newspapers in late August, Washburn and his associates declared that "the meeting is notified at the request of a number of gentlemen educated at the Institution, who are desirous that the true state of the College may be known to the Alumni, and the influence and patronage of those it has educated may be united for its support, protection, and improvement." [2] College alumni had met before: since 1792 most Yale classes had been organized with permanent secretaries, and reunion classes of alumni had become a characteristic social fixture of commencement week at many eastern colleges, including Williams.[3] But never before had college alumni met for such purposes as those of the Williams alumni, nor had any similar organization developed at any of the English or continental universities. The first constitution of the society, which was adopted on September 5, 1821, gave to it three aims—the "promotion of literature," the development of "good fellowship among ourselves," and the advancement of "the reputation and interests of our Alma Mater." [4] The desire to perform good works, combined in this instance with love of college, was thus given an organizational

1. See reminiscences of Washburn in the introduction to Durfee, *A History of Williams College*, p. 19. Also, Perry, "Recollections and Diaries," *1*, 64.
2. Quoted from an unnamed newspaper of Aug. 25, 1821, in Wells and Davis, *Sketches of Williams College*, pp. 34–5.
3. See *The Manual of Alumni Work* (Ithaca, Association of Alumni Secretaries, 1924), p. 5.
4. SOA Records, *1;* Sept. 5, 1821.

form, as was indeed the case with every other good work in early 19th-century America. Washburn and his contemporaries, assisted by a tradition of class organization, turned a humanitarian impulse and a respect for the institution which had nurtured them in their youth into a uniquely American organization. Theirs was the first effort to give permanent form to the great untapped reservoir of alumni loyalty and alumni resources.

Although the Williams society was certainly inspired by the grim necessities of a dark moment in the history of the college, the idea was too good not to be transferred to other colleges. In 1826 the alumni of Princeton organized along similar lines; in 1832 Miami in Ohio and in 1834 the University of Georgia at Athens followed suit.[5] By 1850, an alumni society was an accepted component of the apparatus of higher education in the United States.

Slowly the purposes which the alumni of Williams set before themselves and their counterparts elsewhere in September 1821 were translated into action. In 1826 the Society of Alumni voted to offer commencement prizes in elocution. In 1830 it undertook an abortive campaign to provide funds for a fellowship; in 1835 it appealed to all alumni for books for the college library.[6] And in 1836 it completed a successful campaign for funds, which provided approximately $4500 for additions to the philosophic and chemical apparatus of the college.[7] At the conclusion of the campaign the executive committee of the society issued a report, signed by Mark Hopkins and Jonathan Keys Paige, which expressed the inspiration that motivated the society throughout the period: "The best security for the continued prosperity of the college is found in the attachment and devotion of its sons." [8] The spirit of this aphorism lay at the basis of the activities of the society during the Hopkins administration, when its major efforts were devoted to a cultivation of the college's past, to the development of the society as a body of influence in the government of the college, and to raising funds.

At or near the center of these activities walked David Dudley Field, a native of Stockbridge, a boyhood companion and college contemporary of Mark Hopkins. Field, who made a distinguished name for himself as a lawyer and law reformer, also deserves to be recognized as one of the first professional college alumni. Sus-

5. *The Manual of Alumni Work,* p. 6. E. Merton Coulter, *College Life in the Old South* (Athens, University of Georgia Press, 1951), p. 139.
6. SOA Records, *1;* Sept. 1826; Sept. 1830; Sept. 1831; Sept. 1835.
7. *Ibid.,* Sept. 5, 1832; Sept. 1834; Sept. 1836. TR, *2,* 260; Aug. 18, 1836.
8. SOA Records, *1;* Sept. 1836.

pended from Williams in 1824 for his "leading part" in an especially violent and destructive undergraduate riot, Field was told
that he might be readmitted at the end of six months upon "exhibiting a proper temper." [9] He never returned, but in the course
of time he was restored to the rolls of his class, and in 1855 he
received an honorary degree of Doctor of Laws. "The only men
who make any lasting impression on the world are fighters," he
once said, revealing a characteristic which must have made him an
object of both respect and fear at the annual alumni meetings.[10]

In 1843, on the fiftieth anniversary of the chartering of Williams, the Society of Alumni organized a celebration to commem-
orate the occasion.[11] Its activities in that year signalized, in a
sense, a coming of age for the college and warranted these beginnings at a careful cultivation of a sense of historic tradition. Not
until 1853, however, did the promise of the celebrations of 1843
begin to bear fruit. In that year David Dudley Field inaugurated
an era of monument building in the history of the college, with
his proposal that the alumni erect a monument to Ephraim Williams on the spot where he fell at Lake George in 1755 and "find if
possible his remains and erect over them a monument on the college
grounds." Under Field's guidance, a monument was erected at
Lake George in 1854, and although the remains of Ephraim Williams could not be found—it was supposed that the empty grave
had been rifled by an antiquarian descendant of the Colonel twenty
years before—a large boulder, weighing a ton, was placed upon
the grave.[12]

9. MH to Harry Hopkins, July 28, 1824; HP, *2*. Faculty Records for July 26 and
28, and August 2 and 5, 1824.
10. Cited by Frederick C. Hicks in his sketch of Field in *Dictionary of American
Biography, 6*, 362.
11. SOA Records, *1;* Aug. 1842; Aug. 1843.
12. *Ibid., 2;* Aug. 16, 1853; Aug. 15, 1854; Aug. 15, 1855. The Colonel's remains
have always been a source of some mystery. In 1867, for instance, a student reported that they had been turned up by a ploughshare in the vicinity of Glens Falls,
New York, near the monument which had been erected by the alumni in 1854;
Williams Quarterly, 15 (1867), 158. In 1920 the college somehow convinced itself
that by transporting a spadeful or so of earth from the area of the Lake George
monument it could bury the Colonel in Williamstown. It was during the elaborate
ceremonies, at which the Colonel was allegedly interred in the college chapel, that
one of the official mourners, Calvin Coolidge, then governor of the Commonwealth,
is supposed to have looked down upon the casket splendidly draped with Old Glory,
and said, in effect, "Here, under the flag for which he so nobly fought, lie the
remains of a great American soldier." No one reports having heard a rumble from
the casket, but the soldier who had fought so long for his king and who had met
death in the uniform of the British army must certainly have turned over, if indeed
he was there at all.

During the next fourteen years, spurred on by the unrelenting determination of Dudley Field, Williams College vigorously went about the business of creating material symbols of its historic past. Monuments were erected in the college cemetery to the memory of its early presidents—to Ebenezer Fitch, whose remains were removed from Bloomfield, New York, and to Edward Dorr Griffin.[13] The land which once held the haystack under which Samuel J. Mills and his contemporaries pledged their word to God to Christianize the heathen of far-off lands was purchased and christened Mission Park. So well had Williams learned to cultivate its past that the Civil War was hardly over before a monument was erected to the memory of the college dead and before Field himself was orating at its dedication.[14] So strongly had the alumni come to think of themselves as the college that the monument was originally intended to bear only the names of bona fide graduates. A chorus of student protests caused the alumni to change their minds and include among the heroes of Williams young nongraduates who had left college during the war to find death on the battlefield.[15]

In introducing historic symbols into the life of the college, Field and the Society of Alumni performed a task that until their exertions had been altogether left undone. With subsidies from Field and other alumni, Calvin Durfee of the Class of 1825, sometime financial agent of the college and permanent secretary of the Society of Alumni, embodied the traditions and glorified the heroes of the college in a series of pioneer volumes. *A History of Williams College*, published in 1860 and appropriately dedicated to David Dudley Field, was followed in 1865 by his *Sketch of the Late Rev. Ebenezer Fitch, D.D.*, and in 1871 by the *Biographical Annals*, which undertook to assemble sketches of all of the graduates, trustees, and benefactors of the college. Durfee laid the foundations of the college's manuscript collections relating to its past and in 1875 prepared the first number of the *Obituary Report*, which supplemented the *Annals* of 1871.

Neither Durfee nor the Society of Alumni gave to Williams College its traditions, its heroes, or the struggles and the ideals that had characterized its past. They did, however—with their monu-

13. SOA Records, *2*; Aug. 2, 1864. *Williams Quarterly, 8* (1860), 22–3; *11* (1863), 138; (1864), 135; *13* (1865), 146.

14. *Williams Quarterly, 11* (1863), 136. *Speeches, Arguments, and Miscellaneous Papers of David Dudley Field*, ed. A. P. Sprague (New York, D. Appleton, 1884), *2*, 275. Spring, *A History of Williams College*, p. 191.

15. Dexter A. Knowlton, "The Monument," *Williams Quarterly, 13* (1865), pp. 27–30.

Griffin Hall; chapel and classroom building completed in 1828; as seen *ca.* 1856.

ments and their publications—so incorporate the past into the present that a cult was created and a sense of tradition fostered. In short, they embodied in a religion the relationships of the alumni to the college. If the college was the church, they were its faithful communicants. They created the supports and forms of an established church—the shrines (at each commencement alumni gathered in prayer at the monument in Mission Park); they created the inspired history, the book to which alumni might turn for solace and for the undisputed record (first Durfee's *History* and then the story retold for later generations by Arthur Latham Perry in 1899 and Leverett Wilson Spring in 1917). Before long, regional alumni associations were propagating and sustaining the faith on the far-flung frontiers where Williams men were gathered.

If the Society of Alumni nurtured a tradition, it also created one. In the process of carrying the weight of the college's past upon its shoulders, it developed new strength, asserted itself, and in time began to demand a proportionately larger share in the government of the college. At its 1856 meeting it voted to raise $10,000 for a new college building. The next year the college board of trustees voted to build a new chapel, "if it can be done without involving the college in debt," and went so far as to ask Field to join the committee of trustees to which the job had been referred. Before the weekend was over, the alumni at their annual meeting had subscribed $6,000 toward erecting the new building, which by then had become a chapel *and* an alumni hall. Heading the list of donors was David Dudley Field, and when the building was completed in 1859, it was in reality both a chapel and an alumni hall.[16] By such means the old religion which the college had long fostered and the new religion which the alumni had first institutionalized in 1821 were brought under the same roof.

Alumni Hall became, thereafter, the setting for the deliberations and demands by which the alumni penetrated the actual government of the college. In August 1862 Dudley Field demanded from the rostrum of Alumni Hall that the college provide compulsory "instruction and exercise in the military art" for the duration of the Civil War. "All peaceful pursuits must accommodate themselves to the demands of the war," he argued, and the Society of

16. SOA Records, *2;* Aug. 5, 1856. TR, *2*, 346; Aug. 3, 1857. *Massachusetts Argus,* Aug. 6, 1857. *Williams Quarterly, 5* (1857), 188; 7 (1859), 96. The alumni of Yale erected an alumni hall in 1853.

Alumni passed an appropriate resolution.[17] In November the undergraduates were drilling an hour a day. The alumni, however, were not to be satisfied with the role of adviser.

At their 1866 meeting they called upon the board of trustees to apply to the General Court of Massachusetts for the creation of a board of overseers, "the members of which shall be elected by the graduates of the college." [18] They thus sought to repeat the accomplishment of the alumni of Harvard, who had the year before won the right to elect members to the Harvard board of overseers. Comfortable in the knowledge that influential regional alumni associations had been created in the course of the year in Boston, New York, and Troy and aware of the efforts to form similar organizations in Chicago and on the West Coast, the Society of Alumni broadened its demands at the annual meeting of 1867.[19] The board of trustees was asked to elect to the board annually, for a five-year term, a member of the body of alumni to be nominated at each commencement by alumni ballots. Furthermore, the society demanded the right to appoint, as a board of visitors, six alumni to attend the senior examinations and annual examinations, to "make inquiries into the instruction and discipline of the college, offer suggestions to the Faculty," and "present an annual report to the Alumni." On its part, the Society of Alumni pledged its members to raise a fifty-thousand dollar fund with which to endow scholarships. With an acute sense of history, the society called upon Emory Washburn to present its demands to the board of trustees.[20]

The board of trustees, which in 1867 was equally composed of Williams alumni and non-Williams men, acquiesced, and at the annual meeting of 1868 the alumni elected their first representative.[21] At the same meeting they heard their first examining-committee report from John W. Dickinson of the Class of 1852, who had been distressed to discover that not every Williams instructor could claim a classroom of his own. "If the teachers are located, each having an exclusive use of his own room," he argued, "then each can locate the doctrine he teaches, so that the student in after years can the better recall what was taught, and the better keep

17. SOA Records, 2; Aug. 5, 1862. Williams Quarterly, 10 (1862), 140.

18. SOA Records, 2; July 31, 1866.

19. Ibid., July 30, 1867. Williams Quarterly, 15 (1867), 153–4; 16 (1868), 71.

20. TR, 2, 465–6, July 29, 1867. SOA Records, 2; July 30, 1867.

21. The alumni of Yale and of Amherst succeeded in gaining representation on their respective governing bodies in 1872. Princeton alumni won their struggle for elective power in 1900.

distinct from one another the different topics he has learned."
Dickinson's suggestion may have doubtful pedagogical value, but
the alumni had arrived, and when college opened in the fall, every
instructor had his own classroom.[22]

The penetration by the alumni was now complete. They had
transformed the government of the college, which had, in the past,
rested in the hands of the trustees and the president, who made
policy, and remotely in the hands of the faculty, who executed it.
It would be incorrect to accuse the alumni of infiltration, for they
had subscribed to the cult so well that they had not the slightest
doubt that the college belonged to them. They were proud to be
sons of Williams and sought, by demanding a role in controlling
her destiny, to do their part in preserving her health, taking care
of her in her old age, and seeing that her neighbors did not out-
distance her. It was well that they thought as they did. The General
Court in 1859 and 1868 passed legislation designed to test their
manliness. Could the sons of Williams College manifest sufficient
perseverance, devotion, and energy to send $100,000 home to Alma
Mater to match the sums allotted by the Court? That was the test,
and it was successfully met.

The Society of Alumni from its birth had concerned itself with
the financial condition of the college. Its 1832–36 campaign
realized over $4,000, and with it Albert Hopkins purchased in
Europe the scientific equipment that went into the college astronomical observatory. In 1843 the society appointed a committee
to look into measures for liquidating the perennial college debt
and asked the board of trustees to issue an appeal to the public. As
yet, neither the Society of Alumni nor the alumni body were full-
fledged financial arms of the college, and thus their request that
the board of trustees undertake a general appeal in 1843 was an
admission that the college must look beyond the Williams alumni
body for essential support. When, for instance, Philip Van Ness
Morris of the Class of 1813 gave the college $10,000 in 1859, he
was acclaimed as the son who had given the largest gift of any
alumnus in the history of the college.[23]

Nonetheless, the Society of Alumni continued to give indications
of the function it would perform with increasing success in the
future. In 1864, with Field leading the way, the society resolved
to raise $110,000 in endowment in order to provide for an assort-

22. *Williams Quarterly, 16* (1868), 108–13, 120–1.
23. SOA Records, *2;* Aug. 2, 1859.

ment of needs which it felt confronted the college, including a full-
time professor in gymnastics.[24] In 1870 class committees were
created to solicit funds for the endowment of class scholarships, in
order to meet, at Williams, the success with which other colleges,
particularly Dartmouth and Harvard, were increasing their scholarship funds.[25] In 1874 the society created the Century Association, membership in which obliged an alumnus to pay up to $100
of the annual deficit of the college.[26]

Active in the giving and the soliciting which these many efforts
prompted was Dudley Field. No drive, no cause, failed to receive
financial support from him. His proposal that the alumni provide
a purse for the use of Mark Hopkins during his trip to Europe in
1861 and his challenge to contribute as much as any alumnus, his
gift of an organ for the college chapel in 1862, his gift of $25,000
to endow the professorship in astronomy in 1864—these benefactions demonstrated the versatility of his generosity.[27] His contributions to the college totaled forty thousand dollars.[28] In addition,
he presided at New York alumni dinners, called to listen to Mark
Hopkins plead for funds with which to guarantee the promises of
the Commonwealth.[29] And even when a nonalumnus was concerned,
Dudley Field was at hand, negotiating the transactions, encouraging the benefactor in his giving.

Field, for instance, hovered over the benefactions of Nathan
Jackson, a son of Berkshire who had been a successful innkeeper
and real estate speculator in New York. Intrigued by a circular
sent from Williamstown by his undergraduate nephew, James Orton, Jackson was inspired to defray the costs of erecting a building for the Lyceum of Natural History in 1855, and he continued
to be a warm and cheerful contributor to the college until his death
in 1863.[30] In 1858, with Field on hand, he bought a large dwell-
ing place on Main Street and presented it, with land to spare, as a
home for the presidents of the college.[31] The same year he created

24. *Ibid.*, Aug. 2, 1864. *Williams Quarterly, 12* (1864), 142–4.
25. SOA Records, *2;* June 30, 1870. TR, *3,* 27; June 27, 1870. Charles F. Gilson
and others, "To the Alumni of Williams," a printed circular, dated Nov. 1871. (The
one addressed to David Ames Wells by the agent for his class, J. L. T. Phillips,
is in the Wells Papers, LC.)
26. SOA Records, *2;* June 30, 1874.
27. *Williams Quarterly, 10* (1862), 144; *8* (1860), 141; *13* (1865), 141.
28. Henry M. Field, *The Life of David Dudley Field* (New York, C. Scribner's
Sons, 1898), p. 353.
29. *Williams Quarterly, 16* (1869), 259–62.
30. See Jackson to MH, May 17, 1855; HP, *10. Idem,* Aug. 28, 1855, and Sept.
19, 1855; WCL, Misc. MSS, *8.*
31. Jackson to MH, Mar. 11, 1858; WCL, Misc. MSS, *8.* TR, *2, 354–7;* Aug. 2, 1858.

the Jackson Theological Foundation to support a professorship in theology and aid the sons of missionaries.

Uneducated as he was, Nathan Jackson appreciated the values of a liberal education and did what he could to give comfort to student and faculty alike as they struggled to make something of Williams College. On one occasion he sent to Williamstown 400 pounds of dried fish and forty gallons of New Orleans molasses for distribution among the faculty. "Reminded by the severe cold weather," as he put it, he gave fifty dollars to Hopkins and instructed him to buy firewood for the students. He purchased the chair in which the presidents of King's College (later, Columbia) had presided at commencements before the Revolution and sent it to Williamstown in order to lend dignity to the commencement proceedings of a country college. He provided student boarding houses with "cheap and holsum food" at less than cost. Noticing during a visit to the college that several faculty houses were in need of paint, he sent quantities of oil and white lead to Williamstown to do the job.[32]

Jackson's imagination knew no bounds. He proposed, for instance, that he provide a sum of money the annual income of which was to be used by the president in entertaining groups of students and members of the faculty at Sunday dinners—Sunday because Ephraim Williams, the founder and a distant ancestor of Jackson's, was born on a Sunday. Although Mark Hopkins apparently discouraged him in this particular project, his intentions were indeed sound. With this fund he had hoped to make educated men a bit more worldly. "One grate fault with our Lerned men is the want of graucefull and easy appearance," he wrote to Hopkins. "By a firmilliar association with the Polite Part of the world they are all wais asqued in society [where they are not] at Ease & [are] out of thair Naturall Ellement." Apologizing for his lack of education, he excused his suggestion for faculty-student dinners on the grounds that "I have had grate experience with Human Nature. . . . I think I have some good ideas a Bout man & the world."[33]

And that he did. In answer to a letter from Hopkins disclosing the latter's inability to dispose of a shipment of sugar from Jackson among the unmarried professors at Williams, he quickly responded: "I supposed them being men of education would of course be men of common sense and would know enough to know that a wife

32. Jackson to MH, Dec. 24, 1857; Feb. 1, 1858; June 12 and July 18, 1860; WCL, Misc. MSS, 8. Jackson to Calvin Durfee, Jan. 21, 1858, and Sept. 10, 1857; HP, 10.
33. Jackson to MH, Jan. 31, 1858; WCL, Misc. MSS, 8.

in that cold region would be highly necessary. [They are] not friends of multiplycation. . . . Such men if they wont have wimn . . . they should not have sugar. . . . Let them [take] the sour and cold this winter." [34] Seldom have scholars been more soundly or deservedly put in their place.

As for Jackson, he obviously was no friend of the sour and the cold. Beginning in 1857 he contributed $100 annually for a college dinner in February, honoring the birthday of the founder, and before his death, he provided a fund of $2,000 for its perpetuation. In proposing the first dinner, he characteristically ordered, "Give those young men who are living on pudding and molasses a good hearty dinner this cold winter." [35] When he thought about the dinner which was about to take place in 1860, he wrote, "It makes me happy to make so many happy and, in the words of a certain writer, to send 'an explosion of innasant laughter echoing thrugh a community.' " [36] If Jackson is but a footnote in the story of David Dudley Field's exertions for Williams College, he indeed looms large as that happy man who alone among its benefactors endowed laughter and frivolity with a two-thousand dollar foundation.

Field, of course, was not alone in demonstrating that the sons of Williams were loyal. The ten-thousand dollar gift of Philip Van Ness Morris in 1859 was of powerful consequence in assuring the state's grant of that year. While not in a position to give more than $1,000 himself, William Hyde of the Class of 1826 was instrumental in guaranteeing the grants authorized by the Commonwealth in 1868: the contributions of his father-in-law, Orrin Sage, amounted to over $50,000 and happily a large share of that sum fell during the years when the college was meeting the challenge which had been issued by the state. Although nonalumni trustees like Samuel D. Warren, and associates of Hopkins in his religious work like William E. Dodge, were helpful, fully three-quarters of the $100,000 which the college was required to raise in order to receive an equal sum from the state was either contributed by alumni or can be attributed directly to their efforts.[37]

By insisting that the college raise funds equal to the grants from

34. Dec. 19, 1855; WCL, Misc. MSS, 8.

35. Jackson to Calvin Durfee, Feb. 18, 1856; HP, 10. Jackson's proposal in 1856 was apparently too late to be acted upon, and thus the first dinner did not occur until 1857.

36. Jackson to Calvin Durfee, Feb. 20, 1860; HP, 10.

37. See "Gifts to Williams College," pp. 34–67; MS record of benefactions, in the office of the treasurer, Williams College.

the state, the General Court of Massachusetts was responsible for increasing the endowment of the college by $200,000.[38] The Commonwealth's incentive gifts of 1859 and 1868, combined with the coming of age of the Society of Alumni, put the college upon the strongest financial base it had known, although their combined efforts were more in the nature of a salvage operation than some friends of the college preferred to admit. The Society of Alumni had in reality only begun to give evidence of the power which had been contained in the idea which Emory Washburn had imparted to the alumni of Williams—indeed, of all colleges—in 1821. A child of necessity in that year, the Society in fact never lost the aura which a sense of financial urgency had first cast upon it. For as the college grew older, as it was forced increasingly to compete with the many new colleges and the developing universities, it needed more of all that the alumni offered—the cultivation of a tradition, the welding of the sons of Williams into a band of loyal men, and money. Washburn, Durfee, Field, and their contemporaries elevated the college alumnus to a position of extraordinary power, in recognition of the degree to which American higher education depended upon him for survival.

Williams, which in its early years had been nonsectarian in inspiration, although financially dependent upon its religious reputation, never in its history felt the weight of church domination. In all of its relations with the Commonwealth—in its charter, which left the college free to pick its trustees as it wished and among whom it wished, and in the successive grants which totaled $153,000 —the college never experienced what is referred to as the interference of the state. But when these less meddlesome supports dis-

38. Actually, all of the $100,000 received from the Commonwealth and the $100,-000 raised to guarantee the grants was not turned over to the endowment funds of the college. The books of the treasurer and of the trustees are not easily deciphered, but it is certain that the endowment of the college increased from approximately $50,000 in 1859 to about $300,000 in 1871. Thus, although some of the $200,000 was consumed in current expenditures and in building repairs, the increase in endowment can appropriately be attributed to the joint contributions of the state and of the alumni drives, since the size of those contributions permitted the college to add other benefactions to its permanent endowment. For instance, in 1864, after the grant of 1859 had been assured and before that of 1868 had been projected, Alfred Smith of the class of 1810 gave Mark Hopkins $10,000 to be used as he desired. Because the state grant of 1859 had permitted the trustees to expend approximately $12,000 for equipment and building repairs, Hopkins felt free in 1865 to recommend to the trustees that Smith's donation be used to endow a professorship in modern languages, which was established at the annual meeting in July. See TR, 2, 381, 416; Aug. 5, 1861, and Aug. 3, 1863. Alfred Smith to MH, Oct. 25, 1864; WCL, Misc. MSS, 2. MH to Lawrence Hopkins, Nov. 9, 1864; HP, 2. TR, 2, 431; July 31, 1865.

appeared—the church for lack of wealth, the state for lack of interest—they were replaced by the alumni, to whom Williams was, by then, both mother and kept woman. Thus, while Dudley Field could weep silently in his old age as he remembered how, when he looked from his window as a student, he could see how the moonlight "lay like a transparent, celestial robe upon the sleeping valley and the waking hills," he could also, upon occasion, stir the college community by insisting, at annual alumni meetings, that Williams adopt military training, or abolish fraternities, or introduce co-education.[39] The alumnus became, particularly as the college produced more lawyers and businessmen and fewer clergymen, the little boy, grown up and successful, who had learned how to get on in the world. As a consequence of his love for the college and its dependence upon him for its very breath, he became an instrument of interference of such proportions that, in a sense, "the independent college" became a hollow phrase.

By 1872 alumni interference had become so institutionalized (in the vigorous Society of Alumni) and so legalized (in the election of alumni trustees) that the loss of independence to the college implicit in this interference was hardly recognized for what it was. The composition of the board of trustees itself began to reflect the kind of inbredness and parochialism that developed as a corollary to the arrival of the alumnus as a man of power. By 1872 alumni outnumbered nonalumni on the board of trustees. Such a development mirrored, of course, the aging of the college and the availability of an aging alumni body to draw upon. The first alumnus to be appointed to the board of trustees was Daniel Noble of the Class of 1796, whose election occurred in 1809, when he was thirty-three years old. Other alumni followed him—in such numbers, indeed, that after 1876 only three men who were not alumni of the college were appointed to the board, the last being Albert Charles Houghton in 1891.

Of course it would be misleading—indeed inaccurate—to assume that alumni preponderance in the councils of the college was intentionally subversive of institutional independence. While one kind of independence was surely lost when the college came under the sway of an active minority of alumni, another kind was gained when the college was thereby freed from financial uncertainty.

39. The quotation is from "Williams, The Beautiful," an address which Field delivered before the Adelphic Union in Williamstown on July 5, 1875. It is reprinted in *Speeches, Arguments, and Miscellaneous Papers of David Dudley Field*, *2*, 302. See also Spring, *A History of Williams College*, pp. 234, 289.

Moreover, a board of trustees composed entirely of alumni did not necessarily mean that a college was "captured" by its alumni. Certainly, however, such a board acted in reference to a vested interest —in nothing more than memories and devotion, perhaps—which a board of more catholic composition would have lacked.

The alumni came to power, too, as the result of tendencies toward fragmentation in the modern world. At the Williams of Edward Dorr Griffin, the president, faculty, and trustees were predominantly men of similar background and persuasion. But the Williams that was taking shape toward the end of the Hopkins era clearly demonstrated that this particular kind of unity was on the wane. As the instructors became more professionalized, as the trustees came to be drawn more and more from the ranks of successful businessmen and corporation lawyers, a dichotomy was introduced which lent substance to the impression that the alumni had taken control of the college in a way that had neither been feasible nor even imaginable in the past. For in the early 1800's no one connected with Williams cared to dispute whether the good life was the religious life. Religion itself was life—for professor and for trustee. But when religion was no longer central in importance, when professors began to approach the good life by way of scholarship, and alumni found the good life in the pursuit of material success—when these developments took place, the old unity was lost. And the vacuum which it left had somehow to be filled. Given the values which American society then respected, the vacuum *was* filled by successful businessmen and not by successful scholars. Toward the end of the Hopkins era, the alumni were beginning to fill the vacuum.

The growing reliance of the college upon a certain kind of alumnus for financial support would also contribute to a loss of independence. The most successful men would be the wealthiest, and the wealthiest, ordinarily, would be those who could speak with greatest authority on what should or should not be done. They would be those busy men who, perhaps, most needed and most desired the refreshing experience of renewing their youth by participating actively in the life of the college.

During the Hopkins period, moreover, Williams was so small, the need of the college to adjust to new circumstances was so negligible, and the means of communication between Williamstown and nonresident trustees were so difficult that the president and faculty were very much left to their own devices. In a rather stable situation the stakes of power were relatively low. As the stakes increased—as they certainly did when questions of significant change were raised—the locus of power became more important. And then, not surprisingly, power gravitated to the alumni—to those who were most indispensable to the survival of the college. Swifter means of travel contributed, eventually, to a greater assertion of that power. At least until 1872, only with difficulty could the board of trustees be assembled except at its annual meeting during commencement week; the effort was seldom made. In time, aided by improved conditions of travel, the number of meetings would grow correspondingly with the number of problems which a changing world forced upon the college.

Improved travel conditions meant, too, that more alumni returned for class reunions and annual alumni meetings, which provided them with a means of escaping from harsh responsibility and a humdrum existence, an excuse for returning to the haunts of remembered pleasures. Of those who returned to raise their voices at alumni meetings, none was more typical than the alumnus who insisted in 1873 that something be done to encourage the undergraduate boating club.

And what of the majority of alumni who did not return? No one seemed to care; nor, perhaps, should anyone have cared. After all, the college now required, as it never had before, the financial support of its alumni, their efforts to recruit students, and their active representation of the college in communities all over the country. By 1872 the alumni who filled these needs were well on the way toward a share in the control of the college which neither the state nor the church had ever demanded. To some observers the degree of control may have seemed high, but in fact there was no apparent alternative.

14. Moss on the Log

FIFTY YEARS after his election to the presidency of Williams, Mark Hopkins, then eighty-five years old, addressed the alumni of the college for the last time. Their beloved "Prex," although still conducting Williams seniors through the paths and byways of moral and intellectual philosophy, had turned over his office to Paul Ansel Chadbourne, one of his former students, in 1872. He had lost some of his vigor. Just the previous year, for the first time in his long career of teaching, he had forgotten to meet a class.[1] His stoop was more apparent than ever, and only a few white wisps remained of the hair which he had arranged in such a way as to conceal his baldness. But his fame had grown, his brown eyes still sparkled, and all over the world his sons sang his praises.

Those who returned to Williamstown in 1886 welcomed the opportunity to hear once more his serene and confident pronouncements, to participate in his obvious enjoyment at being an elder statesman of the college they all loved. By then, he had twice been succeeded in office—for the second time when another of his students, Franklin Carter, followed Chadbourne in 1881. He had missed but four of the twenty trustee meetings held during their administrations. He could not help succumbing to nostalgia or indulging in a not unbecoming pride, as he reviewed for the benefit of the alumni his fifty-eight years of service to the college—the two years as tutor, six years as professor before the memorable thirty-six-year term as president, and then the fourteen years as professor since his retirement from the presidency in 1872.

Yet one or two alumni in his audience must have revealed a sense of shocked surprise when he remarked, "After the crisis caused by the [Civil War] the College was slowly recovering itself till my resignation in 1872." [2] Not everyone could have forgotten that the college enrollment in 1871 had fallen to 119, a nadir that it had not known since 1836, the year when Mark Hopkins had succeeded Edward Dorr Griffin. Nor could they have forgotten the great soul-searching of those last years of his presidency, when the college was

1. MH to Dr. Ballard, Nov. 18, 1885; HP, 2.
2. MH, *A Discourse Delivered at Williamstown June 29, 1886 on the Fiftieth Anniversary of His Election as President*, p. 21.

agitated by a concern for its future that rivaled in intensity the anguish of the days early in the century when the trustees had hoped to abandon the institution altogether. The anxiety of those last years, after all, had called forth James A. Garfield's classic defense of the college as it had been. And the discovery which had provoked that anxiety was based upon the everywhere apparent evidence that the log was covered with moss.

The Civil War years at Williams were, as Mark Hopkins said, a period of crisis—and as the students would have said, of excitement as well. From an administrative point of view the stimulating aura of war was hardly a compensation for spiraling inflation or sudden enrollment losses. For the students, on the other hand, war was a new and stirring alternative to the classroom. Consequently, they enthusiastically abandoned themselves to daily newspaper accounts of the shifting tide of battle, to compulsory military drill, to articles in the *Quarterly* written by classmates who had put on uniforms or gone to work among the freedmen of the South. They hanged Jefferson Davis in effigy, and they welcomed the announcement in 1865 that because of Lee's surrender college would close a week early.

The war undoubtedly sharpened an awareness, long apparent among the undergraduates, that something was wrong at Williams. Enrollment decline seemed to symbolize the college's great difficulty, and the war seemed to account for that decline. But not all of the loss in enrollment, manifest in the drop from 233 in 1860 to 169 in 1862, was war-inspired. During the entire course of the war only 29 students withdrew for military service.[3] And although the average size of the freshman class fell from 59 for the four years before the war to 37 during the war, the freshman classes had actually been growing progressively smaller since 1853. Moreover, the wartime college enrollments were not consistently alarming and sometimes were embarrassingly high: the 1864 registration of 187 was not surpassed for another 12 years.

Of course a college accustomed to meeting most of its current expenses from charges levied against its students could little afford *any* enrollment loss. And it is certainly true that income from endowment was not adequate to cope with wartime and postwar inflation. These, however, were problems which Williams shared with all American colleges, and if they were the only difficulties which it faced, it had but to join its sister institutions in raising fees

3. Spring, *A History of Williams College*, p. 189.

and expectantly awaiting a return to prewar enrollment levels.[4] Fees were raised, but the waiting proved to be endless. No one who took a turn at facing up to the condition of the college denied that more students and more money would help matters considerably. But their searching analyses of the difficulties and their proposed solutions led them far astray from the war, until they had questioned the health of the college in all respects, including the effectiveness of Mark Hopkins himself.

As early as 1860, for instance, trustees of the college had begun seriously to question Mark Hopkins' approach to undergraduate discipline. Not every student had responded as desired to the rather loose construction which he placed upon college laws. Not every boy could be moved to perfect behavior merely by treating him like a man. Disturbed by reports of lax discipline, probably emanating from the faculty, the trustees called the professors before them at their commencement meeting in 1860 and inquired, "What is the matter with college discipline?" According to Arthur Latham Perry, who then had been a professor for seven years, the tenor of the faculty answers was substantially to the effect that "the executive officer of the faculty, the president, either softened down or ignored the decisions of the majority in cases of discipline brought before them, or took out of their hands altogether important cases, either patching them up himself or more likely letting them drift." The following day Perry was advised by two trustees that the board desired him "to pursue a policy in faculty meetings independent of the president's, more strenuous and steady in the line of good discipline," and to exert his efforts in holding Hopkins "strongly to a line of college conduct to which he was naturally and by habit disinclined." Perry decided to steer his own course, enforcing a stricter discipline wherever and whenever he could, requiring from his own students a closer attention to college duties and more regular attendance at classes.[5] Not until 1868, however, did the faculty as a whole take any formal action calculated to upset the concept of discipline by precept and moral suasion which had long prevailed. And then their action provoked a full-scale rebellion.

4. At Harvard, Yale, and Princeton enrollment moved steadily upward between 1865 and 1875, according to George W. Pierson, *Yale College: An Educational History* (New Haven, Yale University Press, 1952), *1*, 723. At Amherst enrollment surpassed 300 for the first time in 1874, an increase of 63 over the enrollment of 1855: Fuess, *Amherst: The Story of a New England College*, p. 171. In 1874, the Williams enrollment of 160 was 64 fewer than that of 1855.

5. Perry, *Williamstown and Williams College*, pp. 615 ff.

A young newcomer to the faculty and future president of the college, Franklin Carter of the Class of 1862, who had taken charge of instruction in Latin and French in 1865, was largely responsible for the tempest which swept the college in November 1868. Less willing than most of his colleagues to accept the disciplinary status quo, he became an advocate in faculty meetings of a more stringent rule on class attendance. A committee appointed by Hopkins to look into the matter reported in favor of the adoption of the following rule at a faculty meeting on the fifth of November:

> Each absence from any recitation, whether at the beginning of or during the term, whether excused or unexcused, will count as zero in the record of standing. In cases, however, in which attendance shall be shown by the student to have been impossible, each officer shall have the option of allowing the recitation to be made up at such time as he shall appoint; and no mark shall be given to such recitation unless it shall amount to a substantial performance of the work omitted.[6]

Patterned after a rule long in existence at Yale and obviously intended to promote class attendance by means of the marking system, the rule was a significant departure from the traditional Williams pattern. Nonetheless, it met with faculty approval and was announced to the undergraduates by the senior member of the faculty, John Bascom, on November sixth. Although he had appointed the committee which formulated the rule, Mark Hopkins was absent when it was promulgated. At the time he was at Marietta, Ohio, discoursing on the virtues of a liberal education.

Student reaction to the ruling was immediate and unmistakable. On the afternoon of November sixth the undergraduates met in Alumni Hall and adopted a petition asking the faculty to postpone the operation of the rule until after Hopkins' return from Marietta. Rebuffed by Bascom, who refused to consider their petition, they met again on November tenth, when all but three undergraduates signed a resolution announcing that they had withdrawn from the college and would refuse to attend classes until the rule had been repealed.[7]

The next day Carter, as secretary of the faculty, sent a circular to the parents of the striking students, explaining that the rule had been designed to prevent unexcused absences which had "long em-

6. *Ibid.*, pp. 642 ff. Faculty Records, Nov. 5, 1868.
7. *Williams Quarterly, 16* (1868), 133–4. *Vidette, 2* (Nov. 12, 1868), 1.

barrassed us and limited the value of our institution." [8] In the meantime, the undergraduates, while maintaining order, boycotted their classes. On November eleventh only two students appeared in the recitation rooms. On the fourteenth an undergraduate committee, having received no satisfaction at a meeting with the faculty on the previous evening, recommended that the revolt continue and that a committee of four students be sent to Cornell, the new university at Ithaca, to confer with the authorities there on admitting the Williams rebels. [9] At the same time, a college meeting accepted recommendations that a strike fund be created and that all students leave for home if the faculty should expel any one of them. In the eventuality that Mark Hopkins, who returned to Williamstown late that day, refused to meet with their committee, it was decided to confer directly with the trustees. Such an eventuality did not seem very probable. As *Vidette* had knowingly said on the twelfth, "We have a chance of success. Dr. Hopkins will return soon and he is opposed to such rigorous discipline." [10]

At chapel services on Sunday, the fifteenth, Hopkins asked the few students present, and through them the entire student body, to meet with him the next morning. They accepted his invitation and heard him speak in defense of the faculty for over an hour. While not committing himself to the rule in question, he scolded the undergraduates for their mistaken subversion of law and order and urged them to return to classes and to full standing in the college. Not until the students returned to their duties, thereby acknowledging the rightful authority of the college faculty, would he be willing to consider further action. At an undergraduate meeting later in the day, all but sixty-nine of the rebels decided to accede to the president's request, placing some hope in his suggestion that it was possible to change the rule lawfully. In the meantime Hopkins himself had been walking around the campus, informing the students whom he met that he found the ruling as obnoxious as they did and that surely something would be done about it. By nightfall the entire student body had capitulated, and on the morning of the seventeenth college returned to normal. [11]

At a faculty meeting on November twenty-fourth the rule was

8. *Vidette, 2* (Nov. 12, 1868), 2.

9. *Ibid.* (Nov. 21, 1868), p. 206. Typescript, "Diaries of Marshall J. Hapgood," entries of Nov. 6, 10, 11, 12; in WCL.

10. *Vidette, 2* (Nov. 12, 1868), 4–5.

11. Carter, *Mark Hopkins,* pp. 77–98; "Diaries of Marshall J. Hapgood," Nov. 16 and 17; WCL.

amended in such a way as to assure every student that any unavoidable or excused absence could be made up, guaranteeing him recourse to a full faculty meeting if he should be dissatisfied with the decision of any one member of the faculty.[12] To the students the amendment was an apparent victory: on the evening that the change was announced they collected outside Hopkins' home and treated him to an appreciative serenade.[13] To most of the faculty the change seemed to meet their original purposes as well as the rule which they had first announced. Not until the first case under the new ruling came before them, soon after, did they realize that the construction which Mark Hopkins was capable of placing upon it would substantially thwart their original intentions.[14] But a rule had been passed, a rebellion provoked, and the college, insofar as discipline was concerned, had apparently returned to the reign of family and moral government which had theretofore prevailed.

Not for many years had so much of the college's dirty linen been hung in public. Whatever the sympathies which reports of the rebellion evoked, evidence was at hand that something was amiss at Williams College. The congratulatory telegrams the rebelling students had received from the senior and junior classes at Yale and the editorial support they were given by the *Troy Times*, the *New York Evening Mail*, and the *New York World* had the effect of bringing into question the competency of the Williams faculty.[15] On the other hand, the quality of the Williams student body was questioned by editorials like that carried in the *New York Daily Tribune*, which said, "We have received a number of communications from the students of Williams College, several of which are neither polite nor grammatical. . . . It is clear that their education is not yet complete."[16]

Mark Hopkins' own mail was filled with expressions of shock and disappointment. The father of one undergraduate wrote, "My feelings of confidence have been rudely shocked."[17] An alumnus spoke of the faculty ruling as "undermining confidence of alumni in the college," and a trustee wrote that the faculty had imperiled "the future of the college."[18] Whether the observer chose to find

12. Faculty Records; Nov. 24, 1868. *Williams Quarterly, 16* (1869), 211.
13. *Vidette, 2* (Dec. 5, 1868), 4.
14. Perry, *Williamstown and Williams College*, p. 647.
15. *Vidette, 2* (Nov. 21, 1868), 2–6.
16. *New York Daily Tribune*, Nov. 18, 1868, p. 4.
17. W. S. Gilman to MH, Nov. 14 and 20, 1868; HP, *4.*
18. Everard Kempshall to MH, Nov. 24, 1868; HP, *4.* Robert R. Booth to MH, undated; HP, *3.*

his villain in an incompetent faculty, an ill-mannered student body, or a lax president, the total effect of the rebellion was to cast a shadow over the college during Hopkins' last years as president.

While the faculty of 1868 had hoped primarily to alter the disciplinary climate of the college, its ruling revealed a concern for standards of scholarship and academic performance. Although students sometimes thought so, the college had never demanded a level of performance or a degree of exertion which seriously impinged upon their time-consuming extracurriculum. Brilliant students were seldom challenged by the Williams course of study. "I find myself able to get my lessons without difficulty in study hours so I go to bed when I please which is half after nine," Mark Hopkins had written to his mother from Williamstown in 1822.[19] The next year, he shared with his brother an accurate impression of the final examinations: "The members of the Senior class have all passed their examinations successfully as is usual on such occasions.—They say that the Reverend and Honorable examiners [members of the board of trustees] nodded and slept half the time." [20] "College . . . is rather an easy life," William Dwight Whitney had written his cousin in 1842. "I never study more than an hour and a half a day, and plenty of time is left for reading, writing, hunting, and skinning and stuffing." [21]

Students in general were hardly overtaxed by the Williams regimen. Arthur Latham Perry, in the 1860's, was apparently the first Williams professor to adopt a class roll call and to pay strict attention to class attendance.[22] In a letter written in 1843 a student freely revealed his disenchantment with the Williams classroom: "At some of the recitations especially in [mathematics], half of those who were called on have made answer 'Not prepared.' [The faculty] frequently do not keep us more than ten or fifteen minutes, and once our recitation in mathematics lasted but seven." [23] In 1861 Samuel Chapman Armstrong received credit in astronomy for going to the college observatory on clear nights and looking at the stars. "I . . . am accountable to no one for my work," he wrote.[24] "Our studies are magnificent," he declared during his senior year,

19. Feb. 28, 1822; HL, 2.
20. Aug. 7, 1823; HL, 2.
21. To Dwight Whitney Marsh, Nov. 28, 1842; SML:YU, Whitney MSS.
22. Perry, "Recollections and Diaries," 1, 157.
23. Thomas Hyde to James Farrar, Oct. 17, 1843; WCL, Misc. MSS, 15.
24. To Richard B. Armstrong, May 17, 1861; in "Personal Memories and Letters of General S. C. Armstrong," pp. 52-3.

cheerfully approving the very slight demands which Mark Hopkins placed upon his students. "I'll tell you how I study my lessons,"
he continued. "My chum [Hopkins' son, Archie] takes up Sir
William Hamilton's metaphysics and reads it aloud. I take my arm
chair or the lounge and listen to him. In less than an hour he is
through and I am ready for recitations—that is all the preparation
I have, and we only recite twice a day." [25]

Whenever, for one reason or another, undergraduates did find
their lessons particularly demanding, they frequently resorted to
the "bolt"—a practice which might take the form of a boycott
of a particular class or a mass exodus from it if the professor
refused to accommodate himself to their objections. An undergraduate definition of an excessive assignment was given by the
Class of 1856, which appointed a committee to request that lessons
in history be confined to no more than eight pages.[26] To the "bolt"
they added English translations of Greek and Latin authors,
known in undergraduate parlance as "ponies" and "trots." In
1861 another student deplored the widespread classroom practices
of reciting from concealed books, copying from notes, and exchanging information with careful whispers.[27]

The absence of any overriding concern for the strengthening of
standards during the Hopkins era was not accidental. The college,
after all, was not preeminently interested in the intellect. As long
as sound Christian influence could permeate the community, the
college was almost ready to allow the mind to take care of itself.
Certainly for many years Mark Hopkins and his faculty worried
more about the character of their students than they did about
their scholarship. From the students' point of view, the classroom
was so secondary to the extracurriculum that it deserved the kind
of neglect they accorded it. In both instances neglect was inten-
tional.

Scholarship, moreover, had seldom been known to accomplish
the kind of success which Americans respected. As one student had
explained in 1858, "in a land so notoriously 'fast' as this, men
cannot afford *time* to plow up the soul or the mind in deep furrows
. . . but allow the plow of education to skim lightly over the sur-
face." [28] Among American undergraduates a sense of guilt often
attached itself to any undue scholarly exertion. At Williams the

25. To Mrs. C. C. Armstrong, Jan. 16, 1862; *ibid.*, p. 126d.
26. MS "Journal of the Class of 1856," June 29, 1854; WCL.
27. John H. Goodhue, "Do You Fakir?" *Williams Quarterly, 8* (1861), 22–5.
28. *Williams Quarterly, 5* (1858), 230.

valedictorian of the Class of 1809 was so eager to win the respect of his classmates that he lounged all day and left his studying for the small hours of the morning, when he would be undetected.[29]

Despite those tendencies of evangelical Protestantism and the national culture that reduced scholarship to a position of inferiority, countertendencies were at work which would free the intellect from some of the chains placed upon it. The declining force of evangelism, the steady urbanization of the nation and the characteristic flowering of intellectual institutions, the influence of German scholarship and the gradual transformation of teaching from a calling into a profession, the successful transfer of a competitive commercial spirit to the classroom, the patriotic urge to overcome the biting criticisms of foreign observers—these were some of the developments and motives which helped to turn Williams and other American colleges toward a consideration of scholarship and standards. The intellect would seldom, if ever, dominate the American college, but first it had to be given the chance to be recognized.

To the dismay of Mark Hopkins, intellect—in the form of standards and libraries and scientific equipment—was seeking recognition at Williams with an embarrassing persistence during the last years of his presidency. In a way, the path had been reasonably well prepared in the preceding decades, when bit by bit the college had raised its standards and revealed a growing concern for the quality of the work done by its undergraduates. Requirements for admission had been slowly strengthened, reflecting developments in the nation's academies and high schools. In 1836, for instance, an applicant for admission could meet the mathematics requirement by presenting himself in arithmetic. In 1842 he was expected to master algebra through simple equations, and in 1861 through two books of geometry.[30] Furthermore, in 1829 the trustees voted to abandon the practice of conferring degrees upon seniors who had neither been examined nor paid their tuition; in 1832 they first sent report cards to parents and guardians; in 1857 they informed the professors that they were expected to hold each class in session for a full hour.[31]

More rigorous examinations were instituted. In 1856 sophomores were required to take written examinations on the work of their first two years; in 1858 the seniors were examined upon the work of their junior year as well; in 1866 both of these practices were replaced

29. Oliver P. Buel, "Genius in College," *Williams Quarterly*, 6 (1858), 65–7.
30. Spring, *A History of Williams College*, p. 166.
31. TR, *2*, 104, Sept. 1, 1829; p. 136, Sept. 4, 1832; p. 343, Aug. 8, 1857.

by annual examinations for all classes at the end of the summer term.[32] In 1861 the trustees began to require lengthy reports from the professors on the status of scholarship and discipline in their classes, and in 1866 they appointed a committee to inform John Tatlock, who had been teaching at Williams since his graduation in 1836, that his instruction in mathematics was "not of that continued, thorough, and excellent character, nor conducted with the discipline, gravity, and good order, which the prosperity and reputation of the college require." [33] Despite the encouraging trend of these actions, after the war many of the professors and friends of the college were certain that the standards of the college could be further strengthened. Their criticisms and demands, even their successes, further complicated the process of returning the college to its prewar prosperity.

Returning the college to this prosperity became something of a crusade for the friends of Williams, a crusade that was fed by an awareness that the difficulties of the college were not simply matters of enrollment and finance. The faculty also gave indications of withering away. Salaries had moved steadily upward, from $1200 in 1863 to $2,000 in 1870, and yet Williams was experiencing a more rapid turnover in professors than it had ever known.[34] In 1867 vacancies existed in the professorships of natural philosophy, natural history, chemistry, and mathematics. Although these chairs were all filled in 1868, the next year brought forth a new rash of resignations, by the professors of rhetoric, mathematics, and physiology. In 1871 the professors of chemistry and modern languages departed for Yale and the professor of Greek resigned to become an academy headmaster. To complete the seeming disintegration of the Williams faculty, Albert Hopkins, professor of astronomy since 1838, died in May 1872.[35]

No common cause accounted for this unprecedented unsettling of the Williams faculty. Dissatisfaction, attractive offers elsewhere, and death all took their toll. The total effect of these many losses and the difficulty which was sometimes experienced in finding re-

32. Spring, *A History of Williams College*, pp. 167–8. *Williams Quarterly, 6* (1858), 96. TR, *2*, 445; July 30, 1866. *Williams Quarterly, 4* (1867), 81.

33. TR, *2*, 384, Aug. 5, 1861; p. 442, July 30, 1866.

34. TR, *2*, 417, Aug. 3, 1863; p. 422, Aug. 1, 1864; p. 446, July 30, 1866; p. 458, July 29, 1867; *3*, 27, June 27, 1870.

35. For faculty resignations during this period see especially TR, *2*, 457, July 29, 1867; *3*, 49, June 24, 1872. *Williams Quarterly, 15* (1867), 158; *17* (1869), 50; *19* (1872), 154; *19* (1871), 42. *Vidette, 6* (Sept. 16, 1871), *8*. *Williams Review, 3* (1872), 4.

placements were nevertheless disquieting to the Williams community. Whether true or not, so many changes gave the impression that either the college lacked confidence in its appointees or the professors lacked confidence in the college. In either case, Williams was not thereby made a more attractive institution to the inquiring parent of a prospective undergraduate. A student writing in *Vidette* in January 1872 disclosed neither the source nor the specific nature of published criticisms of the college which he had read, but the rapidly disintegrating Williams faculty may well have inspired some of the reports which led him to say: "It is evident, from certain articles which have recently appeared in some of our leading journals, that the feeling is prevalent . . . among [newspapermen] that Williams College is on the wane." [36]

Certainly statistics seemed to indicate that the college was experiencing a serious decline. In 1869 both Dartmouth and Amherst far outstripped Williams in enrollment and endowment.[37] In 1871, when Williams graduated forty men, Amherst graduated fifty-nine and Dartmouth sixty-eight.[38] Yet newspapermen did not have to search through college catalogues to come to the conclusion that Williams College was in trouble. They needed only to listen to voices of despair from the college itself. No occasion was more instructive for that purpose than the dinner of the New York alumni held at Delmonico's on the night of December 28, 1871.

The voice from Williamstown on that occasion was John Bascom, professor of rhetoric, who had been successfully prevailed upon to reconsider his resignation of 1869. Posterity remembers what James A. Garfield, then a relatively obscure Republican politician, is supposed to have said to the seventy or eighty Williams alumni, undergraduates, and newsmen gathered to partake of a six-dollar dinner. At the time, however, the remarks of Bascom were both more sensational and more easily remembered. Two weeks before the dinner Bascom had written to Garfield, seeking an appointment to the government Labor Commission in Washington, an appointment which they had discussed in Williamstown during commencement week in June. "I am quite willing to leave Williams," Bascom had volunteered. "My religious liberty has led the authorities to look upon me with distrust, and my opportunities are so straitened, that I can do comparatively little for the college. . . . I am out of

36. *Vidette, 6* (Jan. 27, 1872), 86.
37. *Ibid., 3* (Sept. 11, 1869), 4–5.
38. *Ibid., 6* (Sept. 16, 1871), 12.

sympathy with the present languid *executive* administration, and am unable to quicken it. Hence I am willing to withdraw as an impotent minority." [39] Garfield, therefore, was probably in no sense surprised at the volume of criticism which poured from the professor at Delmonico's on December twenty-eight. William Cullen Bryant, David Dudley Field, Henry Martin Field, Emory Washburn, Washington Gladden, and other distinguished alumni who were present may have been unprepared for the treat which Bascom had in store for them, but Garfield, who became Bascom's adversary of the evening, was well primed. [40]

An undergraduate reporter described Bascom's speech as "a brief resume of the disadvantages and disabilities of the College at present." However brief, it justified the announcement of the *New York Standard* that it "created a sensation." [41] Williams, Bascom said, was located too near Pownal and Petersburg and too far from Boston and New York. The trustees, he continued, were too old and too conservative—a remark which must have fallen uncomfortably upon at least two of his listeners; Erastus C. Benedict and Emory Washburn, both trustees, were approaching their seventy-second birthdays. The alumni, he charged, were neglectful of their duties; the professors were underpaid, and the college lacked the facilities necessary to do its job properly. Moreover, he pointed out, Mark Hopkins was not altogether the asset so many people assumed: his towering presence in Williamstown gave the world the erroneous impression that the college depended solely upon him for its reputation and usefulness. In addition, the president of the college was characterized by a want of enterprise which no institution could endure forever. [42]

No Williams alumni gathering had been similarly spoken to during the previous thirty-five years. Well might one undergraduate publication report that "this address . . . was manifestly not designed for the public ear." [43] *Vidette* refused to publish Bascom's remarks, and although its editors may have been alarmed when other student journals and New York papers did, they would have found some consolation in Bascom's letter to Garfield two weeks after the dinner. "I softened my real opinions

39. Bascom to Garfield, Dec. 15, 1871; LC, Garfield Papers.
40. *Williams Review, 2* (1872), 89–90.
41. Dec. 29, 1871; cited in Carroll A. Wilson, "Familiar 'Small College' Quotations, II: Mark Hopkins and the Log," *The Colophon, new ser. 3* (1938), 194–209. See below, n. 44.
42. For Bascom's remarks see *ibid.*, as well as *Williams Review, 2* (1872), 89–90.
43. *Vidette, 6* (Jan. 27, 1872), 92–3.

very much" was Bascom's own verdict on the speech which inspired
the response that has worked its way into the lore of education as
"The ideal college is Mark Hopkins on one end of a log and a student on the other." [44]

Whether Garfield's metaphor on that night at Delmonico's was
a brick shanty, a pine bench, a log cabin, a piece of birch bark, or
a simple unadorned and unidentified log—as were variously reported—, the meaning of his answer to Bascom was perfectly clear.
Garfield, who never forgot the encouraging letter with which Hopkins had invited him to enter Williams in 1854, placed on record
his firm conviction that the inspired teaching of Mark Hopkins
was at least equivalent to the libraries, laboratories, and other buildings which a critic like Bascom desired. It is doubtful, however,
whether he intended to convey the impression, which some of his
listeners gathered, that Williams College needed only Mark Hopkins in order to justify itself.

In letters written in January and again in February, Garfield elaborated upon his inspired remarks. He did not wish to
be misunderstood. Not even he was of the opinion that all was
well at Williams College. Although he would refrain from involving the college in a building program, he would certainly
urge that attention be paid to faculty salaries, food costs, and
the creation of more scholarships. "The two great supports of
the College are cheap bread and costly brains," he declared.[45] Apparently even the father of the aphorism—which Bascom many
years later described as "a pleasant and dignified casting of a rich
mantle over somewhat threadbare garments"—was ready to try
his hand at the current Williams pastime.[46] He, too, was disturbed.
He, too, would propose a remedy or so for the existing ills. The
ideal college was Mark Hopkins on one end of the log and a student on the other, but the General was also forced to ask, from
where were the students to come?

44. Bascom to Garfield, Jan. 13, 1872; LC, Garfield Papers. The late Carroll A.
Wilson of the Class of 1907 (above, n. 41) undertook the intriguing task of attempting to find out what Garfield really said at the dinner and of explaining the
final form which the aphorism took. He concluded, quite soundly, that while it is
impossible to determine exactly what Garfield said, the aphorism which is accredited
to him bears a reasonable resemblance to what he probably said. Wilson decided that
the standard version of the saying was undoubtedly popularized on the national
lecture circuit by John J. Ingalls of the Class of 1855, in the decades after the
deaths of both Garfield and Hopkins. His review of the materials available for his
piece of detective work is both illuminating and exhaustive.

45. See *Williams Review, 2* (1872), 113, and Smith, *The Life and Letters of James
Abram Garfield, 2,* 813.

46. John Bascom, *Things Learned by Living,* p. 106.

The answers given to that question by faculty, alumni, and students were quite as diverse as the problems which they hoped to solve. But no one can ever justly accuse the Williams community of 1871 of lacking imagination or singleness of purpose. Samuel Chapman Armstrong, speaking before the Boston Alumni Association, thought, for instance, that enrollment would benefit from a widespread advertising campaign in the nation's press.[47] One undergraduate spoke more prophetically than he knew when he wrote, "Now that athletic sports prevail so extensively among young men, that college whose ball nine or boat crew bears off the palm above all others may reasonably expect an increase in the number of future applicants." [48]

Other students said that they would welcome the opening of a preparatory school in Williamstown to serve as a sort of feeding station for the college, or a faculty whose publications would command a wide circulation, or perhaps the removal of the college to Pittsfield. The *Williams Review* bowed to the dictates of a characteristic American standard of judgment when it suggested that the college be carried on "as all business enterprises are, or go into bankruptcy." Its solutions: a college president with executive ability, and "a competent business man" to be known as Dean of the College, who would combine in one office matters of money, property, business, upkeep of grounds, alumni activity, advertising, college entertaining, and the procurement of students.[49]

The professors had their own set of suggestions. They petitioned the board of trustees for a twenty-thousand dollar appropriation for the beautification of the college grounds, warning that "the natural beauties of W'mstown are a strong and peculiar force among those influences which sustain the college. Visitors . . . are, consciously and unconsciously decided by them in sending their sons to college." [50] Professor William R. Dimmock argued for a closer approximation to the elective curriculum that was being developed at Harvard by President Eliot. And of course they subscribed to the notion that salaries might be raised and to the hope that the library and laboratories might be better equipped.

The faculty had already succeeded in banishing one vestige of the old Williams which they were certain had carried little attraction for most prospective Williams undergraduates. In 1869 the

47. *Williams Quarterly, 18* (1871), 127.
48. *Vidette, 5* (May 20, 1871), 229.
49. *Williams Review, 2* (1871), 51; (1872), 27 ff., 81-3.
50. "Petition of Faculty to Board of Trustees," June 24, 1872; WCL, Misc. MSS, *11.*

old six weeks' winter vacation disappeared from the college catalogue and was replaced by a winter vacation of two weeks, the usual
spring vacation of two weeks, and a summer vacation of nine instead of five weeks.[51] The old college calendar had been intended
to help poor boys pay their way through college by leaving them
free to teach at district country schools. The six-week winter vacation, and a readily granted permission to be absent from college
for three weeks on either side of the vacation, permitted many boys
to teach during the twelve-week winter term of the New England
district schools. In 1824, for instance, thirty-four students were
absent during the winter months.[52] Although some students continued to take advantage of the vacation for the purpose for which
it was designed, the changed complexion of the undergraduate body
made the old calendar an anachronism. In 1861 over half of the
students of Oberlin were reported to be teaching during its long
winter vacation, and a similar report emanated from Bowdoin as
late as 1871, but for Williams the long vacation was no longer
appropriate.[53]

From the point of view of a faculty that was increasingly concerned with raising the standards of the college, the interruption of
the long vacation and the absenteeism of the few students who
continued to teach were detrimental to their efforts. As for the
students, they were being drawn from a far wealthier segment of
society than was true when the calendar had been introduced. In
1868 the Williams trustees, in answer to a faculty petition, placed
Williams in the company of Yale and Brown, announcing in effect
that its vacation schedule would henceforth be more in accord with
the habits of students like the six Williams undergraduates who
spent the summer vacation of 1856 sailing their twenty-foot yacht
"Alpha" down the Hudson, from Hoosick Falls to New York.[54]

The alumni of the college responded to the new crisis with a
sense of concern and dedication appropriate to their recently won
power to elect members of the board of trustees. Alumni groups in
New York and Boston and various committees of the Society of
Alumni joined the fray—for that is what it had become—and

51. See especially TR, *3;* July 27, 1868. MS reports of John Bascom and Franklin
Carter to the board of trustees, apparently in 1868; WCL, Misc. MSS, *8.* Faculty
Records; July 22, 1868.
52. MS "Memoranda of Absences Allowed to the Students of Williams College
after September 1821"; WCL.
53. *University Quarterly, 3* (1861), 178, 377, 401, 431. *Vidette, 5* (Mar. 4, 1871),
162–3.
54. W. W. Williams, "The Yacht 'Alpha,' and Her Crew," *Williams Quarterly,
4* (1856), 102–11.

offered their own suggestions as to what Williams needed most. They focused their attention particularly upon the raising of funds, the existence of high board costs in Williamstown, and the advisability of making Williams a coeducational college.

"The continued increase of the price of board in Williamstown threatens serious injury to the college," the trustees had declared in 1805, in the first officially recorded awareness of the threat of high board costs to the security of the college.[55] Post-Civil War inflation once again raised the specter of board costs. Even the college catalogues, which sometimes were conveniently tardy in reflecting changing costs, recognized the upward trend in prices. In 1860, the college estimated annual board charges at between $58.50 and $97.50; in 1870, between $136.50 and $234. Since board charges accounted for over half of the estimated expenses of the college year, alumni, trustees, and students looked upon board as an area of particular challenge. In 1867 the trustees appointed a committee to inquire into the advisability of converting the old president's house into a boarding hall.[56] In 1870 a student proposed that the various local eating clubs be consolidated, in order to permit wholesale purchasing and a subsequent reduction in board costs.

In the meantime the alumni had attacked the problems of the college on other fronts as well. At their Williamstown meeting in June 1871 they appointed a committee of five to report at the next annual meeting on the propriety of admitting women students to the college. Another committee was asked to promote the endowment of class scholarships.[57] Its regular committees—a visiting committee which reported annually and a committee composed of alumni trustees—also were at work. In June 1872 the visiting committee recommended an increase in scholarships for needy students, the speedy erection of a low-cost boarding hall, improved public relations, an expanded library, and better living accommodations for the undergraduates. The trustee committee urged an increase in the general funds, further improvements "in the embellishment of the College grounds," and also acknowledged the desirability of a college dining hall.[58] Neither of these reports exhibited any particular indebtedness to the concept of education which James A. Garfield had presented to the alumni at their New

55. TR, 1, 172; Sept. 3, 1805.
56. Ibid., 460; July 29, 1867.
57. SOA Records; June 29, 1871. Williams Quarterly, 19 (1871), 33.
58. Vidette, 6 (July 6, 1872), 200–4.

York meeting in December 1871. Indeed, almost every new suggestion for improving Williams carried with it the sometimes not
very subtle rejection of Garfield's concept and of Hopkins' college.

Not every proposal was acted upon, and not all those that were
necessarily implied a turning away from the kind of college over
which Mark Hopkins had so long presided. There was something
very traditional, in fact, in the unexpected $75,000 appropriation
from the Commonwealth in 1868 and in the busy and desperate
exertions with which Hopkins and his alumni found another
$75,000 to match it. As for opening the doors of Williams to
women, the Society of Alumni agreed with Hopkins that there was
little sense in facing that problem until women applied. "This is
all very well and an easy way to dispose of a troublesome question,"
a student remarked, but the alumni took the easy way.[59] At their
June 1872 meeting a majority of three reported against the admission of women, observing that they were not convinced that
the wisdom of coeducation had been completely demonstrated. A
minority report from those stormy petrels, David Dudley Field
and John Bascom, urged the admission of women upon their fellow alumni as a Christian duty. Much to the satisfaction of Hopkins, the reports were tabled—for a year, the resolution said, but
apparently forever.[60]
Other solutions, however, reflected upon both Hopkins and the
college as he had administered it. In 1864 a provisional chapter of
Phi Beta Kappa was established at Williams, and despite the objections of the Hopkins brothers—suspicious of Greek letters—
this society dedicated to scholarly attainment was granted a charter in 1867.[61] The recourse to newspaper advertising in 1870 was
an admission that the reputation of Hopkins was not alone sufficient inducement to interest young men in Williams College.[62] The
new attention to college grounds and plant was an admission that
physical deterioration had been permitted to go too far. The request in 1869 that professors deliver their annual reports to the
trustees in person and the adoption the same year of the practice
of sending graded lists of class standings to all parents repre-

59. *Williams Review, 2* (1871), 3.
60. *Vidette, 6* (July 6, 1872), 1–11.
61. See E. B. Parsons, *Phi Beta Kappa, Gamma of Massachusetts, Williams College* (Syracuse, Moser and Lyon, 1887), p. 3; as well as penned notation of W. T. R.
Marvin on p. 7 of WCL copy, in which Marvin describes his efforts to obtain the
charter and the opposition of the Hopkins brothers.
62. TR, *3*, 29; June 27, 1870.

sented the ascendancy of a concern for discipline and standards
that Hopkins had never exhibited.[63] In 1869 eighteen freshmen
who bolted one of Franklin Carter's classes were sent away from
Williamstown for the remainder of the term.[64] In 1870, despite the
crisis in enrollment, applicants for admission were more carefully
screened than they had been in the past. Partial-course men—
those students who had been permitted complete freedom in the
selection of courses and excused from all examinations but who
received no degree—were brought under faculty control, subjected to examinations, and made liable to expulsion for poor
scholarship.[65] Although some alumni and parents protested against
these new assertions of faculty prerogative, the professors persisted
in challenging the casual and disinterested attention to discipline
and standards which had characterized the old Williams.

When Thomas Henry Day was dropped from the college for
poor scholarship in 1869, his father's request that he be permitted
to return to Williamstown as a special student under Mark Hopkins
was denied by the faculty. The father, a nongraduate of the Class
of 1838, asked Mark Hopkins what was to become of a college
which thus permitted its faculty to destroy "the affection and
sympathy of its own Alumni." [66] His anxiety was shared by Erastus
Cornelius Benedict, college trustee and eminent New York ad-
miralty lawyer, who complained to Hopkins in April 1871:

> I am quite sure that we have a most excellent Faculty. Perhaps
> that excellence may lead them . . . to think that the way to
> build up a college is to graduate only good scholars and that
> none should be allowed to enter but those who are well fitted in
> the preparatory studies and that a college that cannot succeed,
> on such a theory, ought to go down. [The true policy of the
> college] is to take in, all that can get in, and to make of them,
> all that you can make of them. . . . Why should we drive away
> the timid . . . the forgetful, the dull, or the lazy and unam-
> bitious . . . when we can do them great good with great ad-
> vantage to ourselves? . . . It can [do nothing but] injure us
> that we send back to their parents and to their schools young
> men to say "It's no use for any one but a first rate scholar to
> try to get into Williams College." [67]

63. *Ibid.*, 18; June 21, 1869. *Vidette, 4* (Nov. 6, 1869), 1.
64. *Vidette, 4* (Dec. 11, 1869), 2–3.
65. *Ibid., 5* (Nov. 26, 1870), 84–5. TR, *3,* 28; June 27, 1870.
66. Daniel Day to MH, Sept. 10, 1869; WCL, HP, *4.*
67. Apr. 21, 1871; WCL, Misc. MSS, *10.*

But even Erastus Benedict was guilty of succumbing to the new tendencies. At the commencement meeting of the board of trustees in 1871 he announced that he had established a fund that would provide for annual monetary prizes in Latin, Greek, French, German, mathematics, natural history, and history. And as an additional inducement to scholarly effort, he also provided for "The Benedict Prize for Prizes"—which was to be awarded annually to that undergraduate who had garnered the most prizes during the college year.[68] Benedict did not intend that his prizes should be a criticism of the manner in which Hopkins had conducted the college, although it is apparent that he hoped to facilitate the development of a competitive spirit in the classroom. But in the same sense that the trustees' decision to build a college commons and offer board at $2.50 a week signaled the end of many years of administrative neglect, his prizes announced that the neglect of scholarship had also come to an end.

As for the man on the end of the log, he, too, made his contribution to the changes which were taking place, as he had already contributed to the problems which some of the changes were intended to solve. At a special meeting of the board of trustees in Springfield on April 10, 1872, Mark Hopkins announced the greatest change of all when he tendered his resignation as president of Williams College.[69] He was to go on teaching until his death in 1887, but the last fifteen years of his life would also be spent in watching the college change under the guidance of new hands and the impulse of new forces. These forces, in fact, had already made their impact felt, and to a very large degree they had inspired the agitation and anxiety which clouded his last years as president. The material world, for instance, had already won its victory on the Williams campus. Athletic teams, Greek letter fraternities, and even books had left their fatal impact upon the old ways. A poor country boy, such as he once had been on the Williams campus, was no longer completely at home in a college that everywhere bore the impress of the new urbanism and new wealth. Williams men had once cared more for their souls than for anything else, and now they talked excitedly of tidying up the college grounds and putting a fresh coat of yellow paint on old West College. We must turn out scholars, the new members of the faculty insisted, as if scholarship could hold a candle to character.

Not everything was new—some things stayed as they were: the

68. TR, *3*, 38; June 26, 1871.
69. *Ibid.*, 44; Apr. 10, 1872.

old geographical headache, the low faculty salaries, the absence of any strong and remunerative denominational tie, the competition from new and more widespread colleges. Even the curriculum would be slow in feeling the force of the new tendencies. Mark Hopkins would continue to deliver his renowned lectures, and instruction in the Westminster catechism would survive at Williams long after it had been dropped elsewhere. But by 1872 the returns were really in, and change was the order of the day. The evidence was readily at hand—a glee club instead of a choir to sing the anthem at Sunday chapel services, a college dining hall for the poor boys and fraternity eating clubs for the others, great rejoicing because the president-elect commanded a reputation for business efficiency—and scarcely a word about his effectiveness as a preacher.

Yet Mark Hopkins was quite certain that the new president would be firm in his adherence to the old orthodoxy. For that reason, among others, he had prevailed upon the trustees to elect Paul Ansel Chadbourne, then president of the University of Wisconsin, to be his successor. Others had aspired to the post, including John Bascom and Franklin Carter, but no one, it seemed to Hopkins, showed better promise than Chadbourne of moving the college forward without excessive deviation from the past. In advising James A. Garfield on the mood in which to cast his welcoming address from the alumni at the new president's inauguration, Arthur Latham Perry wrote:

> I hope you will not be too "gushing." The fact, and especially the manner, of Chadbourne's election were very distasteful to the gentlemen here on the ground. It was a dark-lantern affair. . . . His fitness . . . could never abide a fair and full discussion. . . . There is not a particle of ill-will towards him, but only distrust and doubt. . . . It requires a man of broader shoulders, bigger feet, and steadier heart. . . . But he is a *good* man, and active, a good financier . . . and may be able to help the college financially. . . . We have more fears than hopes. He is irascible & egotistical.[70]

Mark Hopkins wrote to his old student, too, informing Garfield that he was satisfied that his own resignation was "best for the college, and I think you would say so if you knew the whole ground. The choice of my successor I think was a wise one." [71] Paul Chadbourne was in no sense a new broom, and although the college may

70. June 1, 1872; LC, Garfield Papers.
71. June 6, 1872; LC, Garfield Papers. For the election of Chadbourne see also Perry, *Williamstown and Williams College*, pp. 651–8.

have needed one, it had, after all, become comfortably accustomed to doing things a particular way for a very long time. The failure of the college to recover after the Civil War had impressed itself upon even Mark Hopkins, and he realized that he could not keep on being president of Williams forever. "Why do I resign my present position?" he asked in his farewell address at Chadbourne's inauguration on June 27, 1872. "One reason is, that it may not be asked why I do not resign." There were other reasons too—a sense of being no longer equal to the burden of presiding over a college whose problems seemed to multiply in every way, a suspicion that his own power to draw students to Williams had been greatly diminished by his age, and a respect for the wishes of friends—including his brother Albert—who had advised it.[72]

The commencement week of 1872—the week in late June when Hopkins delivered his last baccalaureate address and spoke to the college for the last time as its president, the week when Paul Chadbourne was inaugurated as his successor—resembled only superficially those similar occasions in the past that had meant so much to Hopkins. In contrast to the wagons of neighboring farmers which had clustered around the white-steepled Congregational meeting house when he had received his bachelor's degree in 1824, the streets now glittered with "dashing equipages." The watermelon carts, grog-stands, the little tents where visitors gorged themselves with ginger-bread and sweet cider—these carnival-like trappings of 1837, when Mark Hopkins first presided over a Williams commencement, were a far cry from the luxury of the Kappa Alpha and Sigma Phi "spreads" on Class Day in 1872. On the Hoosic the college crew rowed, and the seniors on the evening of class day now promenaded "long after midnight." [73] One cherished ornament of a Williams commencement was, however, unchanged, and that was Mark Hopkins' baccalaureate address, as moral, as hopeful, as reassuring as ever. And yet even the baccalaureate must recognize the changing of the guard, the passing of the old order. In this, his last farewell to a Williams graduating class, he could not avoid a backward glance and an allusion to the years and sense of aloneness which had come upon him:

> The finger of Time will begin to trace its furrows upon the brow . . . and his hand to scatter its frosts upon your heads. You will see another generation coming up to take your places,

72. *Inauguration of Pres. P. A. Chadbourne. July 27, 1872* (Williamstown, 1872), p. 5.

73. For the ceremonies at Hopkins' last commencement and Chadbourne's inauguration see *Vidette, 6* (July 6, 1872). *Williams Review, 3* (1872), 8–10.

and will think it wonderful how fast they come. You will begin
to be called old men, and be surprised at it; you will begin to
be old men, till one and another shall pass away and the last
man shall be left alone bending with years, and tottering upon
the brink of the grave. . . . As age comes on the ardor of the
passions will cool, the imagination will be chastened, and the
judgment will predominate more. . . . Your thoughts, your
feelings, your associations, your pursuits will run on in settled
courses that will not be easily broken up. . . . As the body
decays so will the mind, or seem to. . . . First, the perceiving
faculties will fail, then the memory, then the judgment, and
then second childhood will have come. Whether it is desirable
for any one to reach this point God only knows, but they are to
be pitied who do reach it, having earned no title to the respect
and love of those who come after.[74]

Whether it was desirable, God only knew, though the seniors
of 1872 and the visitors who heard his eloquent valedictory knew
that senility had not yet come upon Mark Hopkins. And as for
respect and love, the inauguration of Paul Ansel Chadbourne four
days later, on the twenty-seventh of June, was very much more an
inspired and devoted farewell to the retiring president than it was
a welcome to the new one. James A. Garfield went so far on that
day as to remark that for most Williams men Mark Hopkins would
still be the president of Williams College, a remark which time
would indeed confirm.[75] The twenty-seventh of June was *his* day,
and he took the opportunity to reaffirm the principles and beliefs
which had motivated his administration of the college.

The anxiety and agitation of the past few years were calmly
tossed aside. "Buildings, grounds, apparatus, funds, are but instruments" was his parting challenge to the men who had recently
spoken so vigorously of the need for new buildings, scientific laboratories, and carefully tended college walks. "There is a false impression in regard to the benefit to undergraduates of the accumu-
lation of materials and books, and of a large number of teachers"
was his retort to critics who spoke of better libraries, a more elective
curriculum, and the introduction of new subjects into the Williams
course of study. "I should say, also," he remarked, in referring to
what so many men considered the pressing problem of enrollment,

74. MH, "The Circular and Onward Movement," in *Teachings and Counsels* (New
York, Charles Scribner's Sons, 1884), pp. 360–1.
75. *Inauguration of Pres. P. A. Chadbourne,* pp. 22–3.

"that for the best ends of an undergraduate course, the average number of this College for the last twenty years is quite sufficient and better than more."[76] In his last speech as president of Williams College, Mark Hopkins did not invite the friends of the college to turn back, but he did in effect ask them to rally to the concept of the log—to the idea of a small unpretentious college, at which inspired teaching molded young men of good character rather than of accomplished scholarship. As the last of the great old-time college presidents—"the father, teacher, counselor, and guide"—he was conspicuously privileged to issue such a call.[77]

For Hopkins the changes of the next fifteen years were vastly overshadowed by the generous homage that was paid to an old man whose work was not quite done. He was asked if he would be willing to preside over the new graduate school at Boston University, and although he refused, he honored Boston—as well as Oberlin, Yale, Vassar, and the New Jersey College for Women—with lectures on the old themes. He accepted a temporary appointment as provisional professor of intellectual and moral philosophy at Bowdoin in 1874, and he wrote articles "disseminating the same old simple doctrines" for the *Princeton Review*.[78] He lived long enough to be the first American college president to see one of his students become President of the United States. At the reception for Williams alumni held at the White House after the inauguration of James A. Garfield in 1881, he—rather than the President—was the center of attraction.[79] Admiring letters from former students, the tremendous standing ovation at the Harvard exercises in 1886 where he was awarded an honorary degree, the obvious respect which was still accorded him at meetings of the American Board, the roomy white clapboard house which the college had built for him in Williamstown, the growing flock of grandchildren—old age was really not so painful.

"This is a new sensation; I think it must be death" were the calm words with which he turned to Mary Hopkins for the last time, early on the morning of June 17, 1887. The official eulogy was delivered at Williams College the following year by his old friend, David Dudley Field, who was lavish in his praises. But Mark Hopkins had already written his own best epitaph in a letter to Ray Palmer in 1872:

76. *Ibid.,* pp. 8–9.
77. Carter, *Mark Hopkins,* p. 14.
78. Jonas M. Libbey to MH, Jan. 5, 1881; HP, *8.*
79. See MH, "Memorial Discourse on President Garfield," in his *Teachings and Counsels,* pp. 375–95.

I have always been of the opinion . . . that my forte was teaching. The place I should have preferred would have been a teacher with no responsibility beyond the classroom. . . . I have made it a point to be present promptly at all recitations and have almost invariably filled the hours, and have hoped to make myself felt through the influence on the minds of the young men.[80]

80. David Dudley Field, *An Address Delivered before the Alumni of Williams College, in Love and Honor of Rev. Mark Hopkins, D.D., LL.D. Tuesday, June 26th, 1888* (New Haven, Tuttle, Morehouse, and Taylor, 1888), pp. 3–4. MH to Ray Palmer, Aug. 4, 1872; WCL, Palmer MSS.

Appendix

WILLIAMS COLLEGE 1793-1993: Three Eras, Three Cultures*

By Frederick Rudolph

Mark Hopkins Professor of History, Emeritus

In 1891 the Williams community was beginning to stir with anticipation of its forthcoming centennial celebration. A college that more than once had been given up for all but dead now looked at itself and felt rather good about what it saw. In this mood the editors of the senior yearbook, *The Gulielmensian*, decided to ask distinguished graduates what they thought of the college as it approached its centenary.

One they asked was Washington Gladden of the Class of 1859, author of *The Mountains,* eminent clergyman and social reformer, who had experienced the Williams over which Mark Hopkins presided with such skill that Hopkins's name was indelibly linked with the ideal of a small Protestant college fostering sound values and nurturing the aspirations of poor country boys. Gladden had been one of them. Now, in 1891, he surveyed the social landscape at Williams and expressed his alarm at the "luxury and extravagance" of student life, regarding it not simply as a development he disliked but as one that shut out young men of "narrow means."

Williams in 1891 had moved from one era into another. The new era so readily apparent to Gladden's critical eye lasted beyond his lifetime, reaching its last burst of legitimacy in the years between the two World Wars. Today, from a bicentennial perspective, it is clear that Gladden's Christian college had become a gentleman's college by 1891 and, in the years since World War II, something else: a more serious academic enterprise that more recently has taken on attributes of a consumer's college.

Three eras, three cultures, held together by continuities of time, place, and tradition, but three cultures nonetheless—that is the history of Williams. And, indeed, of American higher education and of the United States itself. Williams in its infancy shared the

Delivered in the Bicentennial Faculty Lecture Series, February 4, 1993.

Christian orientation of its sister institutions and of the nation that
nurtured them. As a gentleman's college, it may have been better at
it than some others, but all American colleges and universities and
the country their graduates took charge of in the late nineteenth
century were beholden to an emerging class of powerful gentlemen.
Today Williams and the whole network of American higher
education are vibrant instruments in translating the aspirations of
millions of student consumers into lives of civic and professional
consequence. This two hundred-year transformation has not been
limited to institutions of higher learning. The church, the military,
the medical and legal professions, among others, have experienced a
similar transformation. They shared the prevailing Christian world
view of the eighteenth and early nineteenth centuries; they then fell
under the direction of self-perpetuating elites—graduates of the
theological seminaries and the military academies, the governing
officers of the American Medical Association and the American Bar
Association and their branches. And now they, too, are paying more
attention to the needs and desires of consumers, exhibiting a greater
sensitivity to the people they are intended to serve, whether by eliminating Latin from the Mass, ordaining women pastors, accepting
homosexuals into the armed services, or by making access to legal
and medical skills more universal.

Underlying these changes is the movement toward equality of
condition that Alexis de Tocqueville regarded as the inevitable
democratic consequence of the discovery of America He did not
predict that Williams would be a consumer college but he did say
that turning over a virgin continent to the exploitation of the
American people would greatly accelerate human equality. He did
not predict universal medical insurance, but he would only be
surprised by how long it has taken to achieve it.

The past attaches itself to the present with such tenacity,
however, that what we were may sometimes mask what we have
become. Evidence abounds that Williams was once a Christian
college and later a gentleman's college and now is neither. Certainly,
too, Christian Williams and gentleman's Williams paid attention to
the nature of the market they served. All Protestant denominations,
not just Congregationalists, were welcome at Christian Williams,
just as poor boys who simply could not afford the appropriate style
were enrolled at the gentleman's college. They were proof that the
place was still Christian.

Much of the simple prescribed classical curriculum considered
necessary for Christian leadership survives from early Williams.
Freeing the Williams gentleman from the narrow confines of that

APPENDIX 241

classical course but also denying him elective license led to the pattern of concentration and distribution, sequence and prerequisites, that, although now seriously weakened, became the generally recognized props of a liberal education. The past lingers, but props and prescription have given way to the desires of student consumers, with the cooperation of an increasingly specialized and greatly expanded faculty. From a tidy cupboard to a somewhat elegant specialty shop to a quality supermarket in two hundred years is the story that leaps out from the 350-page course catalogue of consumer Williams.

Whether selective or eagerly grasping every applicant coming down the pike, all of American higher education is caught up in this era of student consumerism. How each institution responds to its competitive opportunities is, of course, a function of its own peculiar history, its leadership, its priorities, its ability and willingness to meet student expectations with imagination and adequate resources. Student consumers do not alone shape the life of Williams and other colleges, but nonetheless, just as the culture of Christian Williams and of the gentleman's college set the institutional tone and style, so the culture of student consumerism has in recent decades been similarly defining. To ignore this development or to deny it is to refuse to recognize the patterns that have given coherence to institutional life.

Christian, gentleman, and consumer are not pejorative terms, but in the rarefied atmosphere of the academy consumer has been thought of as a word freighted with somewhat distasteful content appropriate for the studies of Thorstein Veblen and J. Kenneth Galbraith and the misdirected energies of Madison Avenue. We may acknowledge our historic debt to Christians and gentlemen, but how could we possibly identify Williams with consumers?

Dividing the history of the college into three eras, three cultures, the first defined by a transcendent Christian purpose, the second by an almost obsessive cultivation of gentlemanly values, and the third by a zealous attention to the academic market and the student as consumer, delivers three sharp profiles. They convey a sense of the college as it revealed itself to the outside world and as it responded to the demands and expectations of that world. American colleges and universities have been the least ivory-tower of institutions. They have been so eager to be what was expected of them that even today, in the opinion of David Riesman and other astute observers of American higher education, there are no more than a few hundred colleges and universities, Williams among them, that can afford to be serious about their academic programs. That is why the history of American higher education is mostly about religious revivals, fraternities, and football, and less so about literature, science, and philosophy.

Williams has been first and foremost a *college* for two hundred years. That means it was not a church when it was Christian, nor a club when it was a gentleman's college, any more than it is simply a business today, even though in successive eras the pervading tone and style has been greatly informed by values and outlooks not essential to an academic enterprise.

Even in its geographic and demographic reach and the mode of transport by which students arrived at Williams, each era speaks with its own distinctiveness. Christian Williams drew its clientele from a limited neighborhood; poor boys of Calvinist upbringing who could not afford to go to Yale arrived by stagecoach, in the family wagon, and by foot from the hilltowns of southern Berkshire and adjacent counties. By the time of the college's centennial, Williams alumni were well-established in the urban centers of the East and Midwest; special trains carried their wealthy citified sons and their friends to New York for the Thanksgiving Day Yale-Princeton football game or home in special Pullmans to Chicago for Christmas. Today Williams is almost a classless and certainly a national institution going global; international airlines delivered more than 80 students from abroad in 1991, and nearly every state in the Union is represented in the student body.

If the Christian era spawned a temperance society and the gentleman's era a drinking society known as Kappa Beta Phi, the characteristic creation of a consumer college is the elaborate network of agencies coordinated by the Office of Health's "substance abuse specialist" to help students deal with alcohol. Mark Hopkins lectured students on the dangers of masturbation; at the gentleman's Williams, doctors warned against frequenting the brothels of Troy without condoms; today the college not only passes them out, but in 1991 the Williams faculty adopted a code governing faculty-student sexual relations, having refused to prohibit such activity as being a denial of student and faculty rights.

Students at Christian Williams who received financial assistance were known as charity students. At the gentleman's college in the 1880s rooms in Morgan Hall, the most luxurious dormitory on any American college campus and the first at Williams with indoor plumbing, were auctioned and awarded to the highest bidders, a practice that encouraged, at best, discomfort among the decreasing number of students then receiving aid. At today's Williams a need-blind admissions policy provides financial assistance for every admittee who needs it.

In the Christian era the leading private benefactor, Amos Lawrence, was drawn to Williams by his regard for the steady Christian faith and inspiring preaching of Mark Hopkins. In the gentleman's era the great benefactor was Frederick Ferris Thompson, who, as an undergraduate, had transferred from Columbia to Williams for the purpose of founding a chapter of his Greek letter fraternity and for whom he eventually built a great stone citadel of privilege at the crossroads of Williamstown, overlooking the rise on which the Congregational meetinghouse had once stood. The consumer's college may not have one benefactor as significant as Lawrence or Thompson, but its dependence on the collective generosity of alumni in annual fund drives and capital campaigns suggests that a college dependent on alumni as benefactors necessarily must pay attention to students as consumers.

Christian Williams approached nature in the firm knowledge that God had created heaven and earth for the benefit of man, but there was a sense of awe and respect with which Christian Williams accepted that gift. Gentleman's Williams reaped the rewards of a less tender and more exploitive approach to nature, as the natural resources of a virgin continent were translated into great private wealth. Francis Lynde Stetson, at the behest of his client, J. Pierpont Morgan, whose personal counsel he was, created the United States Steel Corporation. And then there was Stetson Hall! Consumer Williams, coming to terms with the naive message of *Genesis* and the rapacious assault on nature that it encouraged, created a Center for Environmental Studies.

A Jewish student entering Mark Hopkins's Williams quickly converted to Congregationalism, if he had not already done so. In the gentleman's era, anti-Semitism was practiced in many of the ugly ways that have been devised to express prejudice, hatred, and incivility. A Jewish freshman in 1938 lost his roommate a few weeks after the opening of college when his roommate's mother demanded that he be transferred away from "that Jew boy." In 1990, responsive to the desires and needs of Jewish students and faculty, as well as desiring to increase the pool of Jewish applicants for admission, the college built a Jewish Religious Center behind the old Phi Delta Theta house and across the street from the old Alpha Delta Phi house. (In the heady days of fraternities at Williams, the alumni fathers of Alpha Delta Phi anxiously debated whether the time had come to withdraw the charter of its chapter at C.C.N.Y. because of the tide of Jewish students transforming that institution. In the waning days of fraternities at Williams, Phi Delta Theta lost its national affiliation on pledging a Jew.)

And so it goes across the board. "The ideal college is Mark Hopkins on one end of a log and a student on the other," James A. Garfield is said to have assured an alumni gathering in 1871, at a time when the shortcomings of a simple country college were beginning to endanger its future. As the needs of educated gentlemen became ascendant, libraries, laboratories, and splendid fraternity houses were soon substituted for the log. Today the fraternities are gone, and so are many of the codes and styles and expectations that went along with what was understood as gentlemanly behavior. The ideal college could once be defined solely by extolling the classroom relationship between students and teacher. The ideal college today supports a black student union, a multicultural center that celebrates ethnic diversity, a bisexual-gay-lesbian union, a women's alliance, a Jewish Religious Center, and as a necessity, if it is to be responsive to consumer expectations, vegetarian dining halls.

In the era of the Christian college, challenges to academic freedom were inspired by departures from religious orthodoxy (John Bascom's sister warned Mark Hopkins against her brother's liberalism). In the era of the gentleman's college, challenges to academic freedom were inspired by departures from economic and political orthodoxy (Arthur Latham Perry's advocacy of free trade made him a constant target of alumni entrepreneurs, just as Frederick L. Schuman's alleged "softness" on Russia required that Phinney Baxter protect him even from some of the trustees). Today challenges to academic freedom are most likely to be inspired by departures from sexual, racial, and gender orthodoxy.

At Christian Williams, art was represented by Assyrian bas reliefs sent to Williamstown by a missionary alumnus. By the time the college was emerging as a gentleman's college, Richard Austin Rice of the history department was delivering extracurricular art lectures on what to see in Europe. Sensitive to the desire of students for creative opportunities in art, the college today offers a studio art major alongside a history of art major that in an earlier day had been judged adequate to the needs of young gentlemen.

Williams in its early years could not be anything but a small Protestant college, and there was little or nothing that might have been done to resist its transformation into a gentleman's college. Colleges do not so much define their world as they are defined by it. Williams does not choose to be a consumer's college. It is required to be a consumer's college, if it also chooses to be selective and competitive.

And being a consumer's college, it does what is necessary. There is no compulsory chapel, but there are Protestant, Catholic, and Jewish chaplains, as well as weekly Muslim and Baha'i services. A student body of self-conscious consumers expects much more of everyone and everything, and they get it: an athletic complex, for instance, that stretches the full length of Spring Street and beyond. At Christian Williams, climbing Mt. Greylock served the same purposes, until young gentlemen imported baseball and football and began to erect tennis courts adjacent to their fraternity buildings.

Attention to students as consumers requires an appropriate bureaucracy. Mark Hopkins and his small faculty allowed their students to chop their own wood, stoke their own fires, create their own boardinghouses, and take care of their own illnesses. Gentlemen, of course, expected more. Taking matters into their own hands, they turned their fraternities into facilities that echoed urban men's clubs. And they took over Morgan Hall as soon as it was available; the college rented rooms there to the highest bidders. A college infirmary opened in 1895.

Fifty years ago the director of health was also the director of athletics. In his medical capacity he was assisted by one doctor, two consulting and distant part-time psychiatrists, a surgeon on call, and an infirmary matron. As director of athletics he depended on the scheduling and policy skills of an assistant, who also operated the college's financial aid office, and on the coaching skills of a staff of six. Today the director of health has his own medical practice, and so do the eighteen physicians, gynecologists, surgeons, and radiologists who assist him, but their availability to the Williams student is a fundamental aspect of their practice. Seven nurses staff the health center, where students may consult five psychotherapists of one variety or another, one health educator, and one substance abuse specialist. On the athletic front, an administrative staff of eleven and a coaching staff of twenty do for today's student body of 2,000 what the assistant director and six coaches did fifty years ago for 800, almost doubling the ratio of staff to students.

Hopkins Hall has had to be greatly enlarged, in part, to accommodate ten deans and their eight secretaries and assistants. The library staff has tripled. Instead of the one-man admissions office of pre-World War II years, there are now eight admissions officers and eight in staff support. Instead of a superintendent of grounds and buildings, who headed a small maintenance program, now the director of physical plant supervises a staff of nineteen and a work force of more than a hundred.

Neither Christians nor gentlemen required the array of offices that serve today's consumers: an affirmative action office, an audio-visual center, an office of career counseling, a computing center, a duplicating center, a campus post office, a telephone switchboard, and instead of the lonely night watchman of a half-century ago, a security office (a director and an assistant director with a police force of thirteen). This administrative bureaucracy was not invented to create jobs, nor has it proliferated as a result of some mindless tendency of autonomous institutions. What is here described is an affluent college's recognition that today's college student is a customer who expects to be treated like an intelligent consumer.

The grounds of Williams College are considered an important asset in projecting an image of financial good health, institutional self-confidence, and community. These grounds and buildings require money and staff to maintain, but who would suggest returning to the Hopkins era when good Christians bemoaned expenditures for aesthetic pleasure and were happy to have so-called lawns cared for by roaming livestock? The gentlemen's clubs along Main Street symbolized by the Sigma Phi lawn, the Kappa Alpha pillars, the imposing stone lodge of St. Anthony designed by Stanford White and adorned with the work of John LaFarge and Augustus St. Gaudens bespoke a gentleman's college and did not cost the institution a penny.

If early Williams was Christian because that is what a college was, and if it became a gentleman's college because that is who went there, how did it become a consumer's college? How did it move away from being a gentleman's college? One way was to reverse the process by which students entered Williams. Until World War II students chose the college; after the war, the college increasingly selected the students.

In the years before World War II the admissions office was accepting applicants as late as a few weeks before the first day of classes. Whatever else was going on in those days, Williams was not a selective college. A four-year Latin requirement for admission, not abandoned until the entrance of the Class of 1938, effectively limited the applicant pool largely to Eastern private schools and a few select public high schools, thus confirming the college's willingness to be an institution whose ethos was patterned on the values of wealthy young gentlemen.

After World War II, the G.I. bill, a booming economy, and the enhanced value of a college degree as revealed to millions of enlisted men and women by the comforts and privileges and perhaps even the talents and self-assurance of commissioned officers, made going to college an attractive possibility for high school students who in an earlier day would have gone to work instead. The changing nature of the economy turned a college degree into a passport to specialized graduate training. The degree became a credential that before the war was not desired by most young men and women and not even taken too seriously by many young men at Williams for whom opportunities awaited in family businesses.

These developments created suburbs, high schools, and aspirations among young men and women in families that had never sent anyone to college. They required that Williams be selective, and they also challenged it to choose wisely and with regard to defensible criteria. Soaring applications and limited openings led to a phenomenon remarked upon by members of the faculty: The selected often came to think of themselves as having been anointed and therefore empowered, and the college came to regard with ambivalence the treasures they had recruited but who, for one reason or another, might have been lost to, or even have preferred, Amherst or Princeton or Duke or Stanford.

Out of this student self-confidence sometimes bordering on arrogance and this institutional nervousness sometimes bordering on extravagance (elaborate recruiting campaigns to enhance the quality of an already huge applicant pool, on-campus visits designed to woo the uncertain best and brightest, guaranteed financial aid for every needy accepted applicant) came a psychology that helped to define the student as consumer and the institution as a provider of services. And with it came the swollen bureaucracy and budget, the sensitivity to individuals and self-defined groups of all kinds, and, on the part of students, an awareness of their power as consumers.

What, it may be asked, have the abolition of fraternities, the admission of women, and more than doubling the size of the college had to do with all this? The answer is a great deal. Fraternities were the central institution of the gentleman's college; there young men could practice the conversational arts fueled by their courses in art history, English literature, and politics; there they learned how to hold their liquor, express ideals appropriate to their innocence, and swagger a bit in the knowledge that the world was their oyster. Fraternity members were instrumental in recruiting more of their kind from the best boarding schools; they advanced a code of ethics that found expression in the honor system on which examination procedures rested; and they rewarded what they considered their best with election to an honor society known as Gargoyle.

But there was also the flip side, and after World War II that was the side that mattered. The student body was larger and brighter, less homogeneous, more dependent on cars and road-tripping to women's colleges for social diversion. The fraternities and other adornments of extracurricular life lost some of their traditional attractiveness. In 1961, when Jack Sawyer followed Phinney Baxter into the presidency of Williams, there lay on his desk a petition from a group of student leaders asking that fraternity rushing be replaced by some system whereby the college itself distributed students among the fraternities.

As ludicrous as such a proposal looked to those for whom a fraternity was defined by whom it kept out, the proposal was both sincere and responsive to widespread discomfort among many students with a process that required them to make quick, superficial, even prejudicial judgments on their fellows in order to support a caste system that divided the college into exclusive enclaves and a rejected remnant. That remnant grew smaller as students devised ways to open wider fraternity doors, but the problem presented by the fraternity as an anachronism would not go away.

Williams was no longer a small, exclusive New England liberal arts men's college, class-bound, regional in its reach, essentially white Anglo-Saxon Protestant in its clientele. As the American high school replaced the New England boarding school as the primary source of students, a fresh breeze—democratic, tolerant, diverse—blew across the campus. And each year, as the admissions process delivered young men more serious, more sensitive, more oriented toward the college as a center of learning, the fraternity, while remaining a place to sleep and eat, no longer commanded the time, loyalty, and devotion, nor summoned up the mystique of an earlier day.

In the era of Williams as a Christian college, discipline was regulated by a rigid and rigorous code of laws imported from Yale, expressing in minute detail the moral expectations of the college and the conduct appropriate to aspiring Christians. There always would be college laws, but in time common sense and a degree of collegiality and community replaced both the strictures and penalties of the Yale code and the eagle-eyed professors who enforced it. This change was made possible as fraternities assumed responsibility for student discipline, a development that perhaps was not even recognized as it was happening. For their members, loyalty to fraternities meant a concern for the reputation of their fraternities, and that meant attention to their own behavior as it reflected upon their fraternities. Those badges worn so proudly and prominently may have been an assertion of superiority and of unabashed adolescence, but they also carried an obligation.

In the 1950s this obligation had all but disappeared. A notorious

Sunday milk-punch party on the Delta Psi lawn, where a nude girl is alleged to have cavorted in a bathtub of punch, stalled traffic around Field Park. Fraternity elders at Phi Gamma Delta were brought to their senses, if not catapulted out of them, when they learned of the call-girl operation with which their graduating seniors one year celebrated the end of classes and exams. And when some members of Sigma Phi entertained themselves by tossing a cat into the drier at a local laundromat, the era of the fraternity as an enforcer of student discipline could be said to have ended. A college security force of a dozen or more officers was on the way.

And so was coeducation. The same student body that revealed its discomfort with fraternities also found a single-sex college unnatural and, for most students, an experience that departed from their long years in the public schools. Fundamental to the demise of Williams as a male bastion were the same competitive concerns that had led Yale clumsily to court Vassar and, when rebuffed, hastily to open its doors to women.

Yale had been losing too many desirable candidates to Harvard, drawn there by the open secret that it had abandoned the fiction of Radcliffe as a coordinate institution and was, in fact, coeducational. Faced by Princeton's moves toward coeducation, Yale seems to have panicked itself into admitting women. Williams went about it deliberately, assessing its options, concluding that the ablest male American high-school graduates were unlikely to opt for an all-male college to cap twelve years of elementary and secondary school coeducation.

The college integrated slowly—first with exchange students, then with gutsy women transfers who later stood as self-confident role models for entering female freshmen—and did not accelerate the coeducational process until new dormitories, with adequate wattage for hair drying, were in place, nor until the entire campus offered equal restroom facilities. Thus, while the consumer college revealed itself as sensitive to the market in going coed, the style in which it went there was surely that of a gentleman.

As elsewhere in life, one thing led to another. The decision to greatly increase the size of the student body represented a reluctance to reduce the number of men at Williams, thus decimating athletic teams and alienating alumni. It also recognized that without a much larger student body the college could not support a large enough faculty and a sufficiently expanded curriculum to fulfill the expectations of its more talented student body or its obligation to the expanding world of knowledge.

Nearly doubling the size of the college encouraged attention to

the demographics of the future and to the process by which the
United States was accommodating diverse cultures, races, and
creeds even as a new and changing definition of American culture
was being written. Christian Williams justified itself and earned
support and respect and survival by training candidates for the
leadership class, the clergy and lawyers and doctors of a fledgling
nation. When that leadership moved to finance and business, the
gentleman's college responded with striking success.

The future leadership of the United States, the college now concluded, would be drawn to a great degree from ethnic and racial
sources not yet significantly tapped, just as certainly as that leadership was once nurtured in God-fearing New England villages and
then selected from the ranks of enterprising gentlemen. In recruiting aggressively among the ethnic minorities entering colleges in
greater numbers, in creating an environment where aspiring young
men and women of diverse backgrounds from all over the United
States can be comfortable and at home, Williams may indeed be sensitive to its function as a provider of services to new generations of
academic consumers. It is also being socially responsible and true to
its founding mission—the training of a governing elite. The style
with which that mission is carried out, with a regard for learning,
character, courtesy, and responsibility, says that, while the gentleman's college may be gone, its best and redeeming values survive.

Williams has always been a college of aspiration, where
ambition might be fueled and ability encouraged, but perhaps less
so in the gentleman's era, and more so today than ever before. In the
gentleman's era privilege tempered aspiration among many young
men whose lives had already been defined by family wealth and
position. In the present era, a college of diversity brings together
aspiring young men and women and rewards them with credentials
and passports to the meritocratic world that awaits them.

Williams between the two World Wars was a closer community
than it is today, even though the caste system imposed by the
fraternities was a source of divisiveness. It was smaller, the student
body was more homogeneous, a narrower course of study meant a
more common educational experience, everyone ate at the same
time, and the extracurriculum celebrated community ties. Yet the
price of community was the absence of those invigorating developments that today make Williams an intellectually and socially more
stimulating place. In becoming a consumer's college, Williams has
left behind its country-club image. As late as 1946, at the opening
assembly of the year the dean of the college instructed the student
body on procedures for registering airplanes and polo ponies. In

their absence, Williams has become more an institution of learning. How has this happened?

Perhaps the first indication that it would happen at all was the imploring letter that Ebenezer Fitch, soon after arriving in Williamstown in 1791, sent to a friend in New Haven urging him to find someone to open up a bookstore in the intellectually barren frontier of Western Massachusetts. Another was the founding of student literary societies, a tradition imported from Yale soon after the college opened. In those societies and their libraries, debates, exhibitions, and literary exercises, an extracurriculum grew alongside the prescribed course, the difference being that the literary societies engaged their members in the issues and events of the day (slavery, social inequality, prisons) and made available to them such authors as Cooper, Dickens, and Hawthorne, who could not find their way into the narrowly defined college library.

Ralph Waldo Emerson was their guest more than once. When denied the use of the college chapel for a series of Emerson lectures on "American Life" in 1865, his student sponsors procured the Methodist meeting house, the largest assembly hall in town. Looking out of the window of one of his student hosts, Emerson caught a glimpse of the college chapel and asked rhetorically how many faiths there were in Williamstown. Emerson's own quick answer was persuasive enough to induce the student host to become his personal secretary after graduation: "Three thousand five hundred people; three thousand five hundred faiths in the village of Williamstown! Let yours not come from tradition . . . widen the circle, so as to admit ventilation."

This intellectually liberating message was more ventilating than the college was prepared to endorse, but the message was heard because students recognized it as an invitation to make a vital connection between self and opportunity in an unfolding America, one that their Lyceum of Natural History, in its expeditions, collections, and meetings, had already extended. Emerson at Williams was a call to action instead of a call to prayers.

Strange as it now may seem, one student enterprise after another advanced the intellectual life of the college by providing attractive alternatives to the prevailing climate of piety and the prescribed course of study. College students often may be turned off by what goes on in the classroom, but their exertions, at Williams and elsewhere, moved belles lettres, natural science, history, and literature out of limbo into their societies and journalistic endeavors and eventually into the formal curriculum itself.

Franklin Carter was the college's first scholar-president.

His election to the Williams presidency in 1881 coincided with his election as the founding president of the Modern Language Association. His first faculty appointments invigorated the academic life of the college; the gifts of the Thompson science laboratories in the 1890s elevated science instruction from embarrassing neglect; and the transformation of the library from a sleepy repository of unused books to a vital and central element of academic life moved the college closer than ever to being an institution of learning.

Even for someone as determined and qualified as Carter, it was not easy to make formal learning central to the Williams experience; the academic "core" remained peripheral. The young gentlemen at Carter's Williams were devoted to their clubs, teams, and other extracurricular activities with such intensity that Carter's academic innovations stood in stark contrast to the life of the playing fields, the fraternity dining rooms, and the literary journals and student newspapers that tested both the gentlemanliness and the future success of Williams undergraduates. An abiding concern of the student newspaper during the Carter presidency was whether Williams men were lapsing from gentlemanly standards in the style with which they cheered their athletic teams.

Carter's successors found other ways to insinuate a regard for learning into a not readily receptive environment. One artifact of the gentleman's college was the "gentleman's C"—a totem of student indifference to academic demands but at the same time a reminder that the faculty knew the difference between a C and a B or an A. If at Harry Garfield's Williams it sometimes seemed that gentlemanliness edged toward stuffiness and dilettantism, Garfield himself advanced the intellectual life of the college by putting structure and focus into the departmental major and went further on the road to academic seriousness by importing from Swarthmore the opportunity for advanced work leading to an honors degree.

Tyler Dennett's three brief years, 1934-1937, set the direction of the college for the rest of the century. His faculty appointments and those of his successor, Phinney Baxter, so strengthened the teaching staff that Williams was regarded in the years before World War II as possessing the liveliest college faculty in New England. Dennett's profoundest contribution to learning at Williams, however, may have been his attack on the stultifying homogeneity of the student body, his insistence that young men could not learn from each other if in matters of class, income, and geography they were all the same. His trumpet call for diversity, which singled out Williams fraternities as an impediment to change, may have helped him to lose his job, but no one in the decades that followed has failed to hear it.

When Jack Sawyer arrived in 1961, the prospects for intellectual revitalization and curricular reform depended on sustaining these
trends and opening up the campus by abolishing fraternities. Until
social life at Williams was freed from their domination, the faculty
was not going to trust the student body sufficiently to reform
the curriculum in ways appropriate to the quality of students that
selectivity was delivering.

The end of fraternities allowed the faculty to recognize students
as serious partners in an academic enterprise and inaugurated a
time of trust and common endeavor on which Sawyer's successors,
John Chandler and Frank Oakley, would build with such success
that in 1991 and 1992 Williams was ranked by *U.S. News and World
Report* as the best liberal arts college in the United States. That
designation benefited from the quality of a student body for most of
whom the B.A. degree was not terminal, but it also recognized the
multicultural amplification of the curriculum, the introduction of
Asian languages, the first college environmental studies program,
the transformation of Jesup Hall into a computer center, the
existence of a Williams program at Oxford, and the beginnings of
tutorial instruction, all of them developments intended to help the
college maintain its competitive edge as an institution of learning.

The Christian era slipped into the gentleman's era not without
some breakage. Athletic practice collided with compulsory evening
prayers; athletics prevailed. The gentleman's era slipped into the
consumer's era with similar results; now, while there may be
prayers of many persuasions, Thompson Memorial Chapel is no
longer the place where the *college* gathers for prayer. If there were
blacks or Jews at early Williams, they and the college looked the
other way. As eager as he was to diversify the student body, Tyler
Dennett advised his admissions officer to dissuade blacks and
Jews from applying to a fraternity college where they could not be
happily accommodated. A consumer's college, on the other hand,
welcomes diversity and encourages the assertive demonstration of
difference, sometimes in acts and styles painful beyond belief for
observers who love the college but who knew it in, for them, a more
comfortable time when it was possible to deny women and blacks
and gays and all the ethnic minorities who arrived too late to claim
Plymouth Rock instead of a slave ship or Ellis Island as their
American point of entry.

A remarkable fulfillment of the democratic promise of America
is in the process of reshaping this country, as well as its colleges and
universities. Williams is being responsive to that process even as it

contributes to it, having played its role in the continuous redefinition of American culture for two hundred years.

In becoming a consumer's college, Williams has shared freely and openly in a movement that David Riesman referred to as early as 1980 as "an era of rising student consumerism." Clark Kerr considered the rise of the student consumer and the consequent decline of faculty dominance of institutional life as "one of the two greatest reversals in all the history of American higher education." In participating in these developments Williams and other colleges and universities have revealed how much they are shaped by forces and expectations visited upon them by society. Moreover, in creating the bureaucracy and infrastructure that allows it to be the best consumer-oriented liberal arts college in the country, Williams has consciously fulfilled its obligations to society.

Three eras, three cultures, held together by continuities of time, place, and tradition, and by singularity of purpose—the training of a governing elite—*that* is the history of Williams.

Now, as the college and the nation move inevitably, imperceptibly beyond the era of the collegiate consumer and the ethos of consumption, another era beckons, beyond these nervous times that suggest an overripeness in the nation's social and economic practices, beyond the deficient responses of our political institutions to compelling national needs. As Williams enters its third century, there will be a good deal of looking back and some looking forward. The old college of Mark Hopkins will be revered by some, the loss of the leisurely era of young gentlemen will be lamented by others, and consumer Williams will be moving on, making way for the as yet undefined next era in the college's history.

Bibliographical Essay

HISTORIANS who undertake studies of American higher education are well advised to make use of everything they can lay their hands on. The proper questions will lead to obvious sources, but the answers may be found in unlikely places. Because so much of the work already done has been the inspiration of worshipful alumni and publicists—both of whom lead useful lives but usually not as historians—the serious researcher interested in American educational institutions must frequently break new ground. In addition to the sources used in the preparation of *Mark Hopkins and the Log,* therefore, this bibliographical note attempts to indicate the kind of sources historians of other educational institutions and movements might find useful.

1. BIBLIOGRAPHICAL AIDS

John Adams Lowe, *Williamsiana: A Bibliography of Pamphlets & Books Relating to the History of Williams College, 1793–1911* (Williamstown, Trustees of Williams College, 1911) is a serviceable check list of published materials, but it was compiled almost a half century ago. Although it is not complete, *Publications of the Presidents and Professors of Williams College, 1793–1876* (North Adams, James T. Robinson and Son, 1876) is a useful listing of the literary output of the Williams faculty. The Williams College Library maintains a separate card file for its Williamsiana materials, which on the whole are also housed separately. This catalogue of manuscripts, archives, and published matter pertaining to the college is invaluable. New sources for Williams and for Hopkins material were uncovered with the help of notices which appeared in various metropolitan and regional newspapers.

2. MANUSCRIPTS AND OTHER UNPUBLISHED MATERIAL

To a large extent reliance has been placed upon manuscript material unavailable to or overlooked by earlier students of Mark Hopkins and Williams College. When the repository of the manuscripts is not indicated, they are located in the Williams College Library.

Mark Hopkins

The major collection of Hopkins letters is in the Williams College Library. This collection includes a group labeled "Hopkins Letters," in six portfolio volumes, consisting of approximately 500 letters, most of them written by Hopkins to members of his family but including some letters by Albert Hopkins and other members of the family. These letters span the years from Hopkins' life as an undergraduate through his retirement from the presidency of the college; they permit an insight into his nonofficial life which is nowhere else available. Williams also possesses a collection known as "Hopkins Papers," in eleven portfolio volumes, a group of approximately 750 letters, some from Hopkins to his wife and the family but most of them to Hopkins in his capacity as president of the college; this collection is particularly useful in exploring aspects of Williams history heretofore neglected, in part because of inadequate sources.

The Massachusetts Historical Society has a large collection, "Hopkins Family Papers," including approximately forty letters of Mark Hopkins, largely written to his mother between 1828 and 1853. These letters are full of details of family life. No collection is more useful than the "Amos Lawrence Papers," also at the Massachusetts Historical Society; these include approximately fifty letters written by Hopkins to Lawrence, 1844–52, as well as four copybooks of the complete correspondence between Hopkins and Lawrence during those years. In his letters to Lawrence, Hopkins was a faithful reporter of college affairs—during a period when there was no undergraduate newspaper—and the correspondence as a whole is unquestionably one of the most revealing demonstrations extant of the nurture of the gospel of wealth.

The "James A. Garfield Papers" in the Library of Congress include twenty-five letters from Mark Hopkins, 1854–81, as well as important letters from John Bascom and Arthur Latham Perry. The letters demonstrate Hopkins' continuing interest in Garfield after his graduation, and taken with Garfield's letters to Hopkins, which are in the "Hopkins Papers," they help to explain the conviction with which Garfield defended Hopkins at Delmonico's in 1871. At the Oberlin College Library are a few letters in the sporadic correspondence between Hopkins and Charles Grandison Finney, as well as ninety-five letters, mostly on religious themes, written in an almost illegible hand by John Morgan of the Class of 1826 to Hopkins. The Garfield and Oberlin materials are available at Williams in photostat or microfilm.

Forty-three letters from Hopkins to Ray Palmer, written 1861–63 and 1870–74, are in the Williams library; they deal frequently with religious matters, but they are also some of the most introspective letters which Hopkins wrote. Mrs. Henry Hopkins of Shaftsbury, Vermont, widow of one of the Hopkins grandchildren, permitted the use of approximately twenty letters in her possession, most of them from Hopkins and his wife to their son Henry.

Charles Scribner's Sons, New York, has in its files approximately two hundred letters from Hopkins dealing with the publication of several series of his lectures. Although this book is not concerned with Hopkins' relations with the American Board of Commissioners for Foreign Missions, note should be made of the fact that fifty-two letters from Hopkins to the Board are on deposit in Houghton Library, Harvard University.

Efforts to locate other collections of Hopkins letters were unavailing. His letters to John Morgan would have been useful, and there must have been Hopkins letters in the papers of David Dudley Field. Some Palmer letters to Hopkins are in Hopkins Family Papers, Williams College Archives. I was also unable to locate the manuscript diary kept by Albert C. Sewall, ed., *Life of Prof. Albert Hopkins*, New York, Anson D. F. Randolph, 1879.

Williams College, General

Two useful collections of Williams College manuscripts are in the college library. In the "Durfee Papers" are several hundred letters and assorted items collected by Calvin Durfee in the preparation of his pioneer studies of the early history of the college. "Williams College Miscellaneous Manuscripts" consists of fourteen portfolio volumes that include probably a thousand or more letters. This collection has served as a catch-all for small bundles of undergraduate letters and for stray items not easily categorized. A more systematic arrangement of these manuscripts would be useful, but they are well preserved and carefully catalogued.

A volume of minutes of faculty meetings, 1821–71, is located in the vault in the office of the registrar, Hopkins Hall. These records are not as revealing as the historian would like, for meetings were irregular and routine and the keeping of minutes perfunctory. More complete but also frequently frustrating are the trustees' records. The minutes of the board, located in the vault, office of the director of admissions, begin with the incorporation of the free school in 1785; three volumes covering the years to 1898 are well indexed. Minutes of the annual meetings of the Society of Alumni, beginning in 1821, are in the society's office, Jesup Hall. Of these official records, those of the faculty are the least useful; those of the trustees are essential for matters involving finance and policy; and the Society of Alumni minutes provide a clear record of the ascendancy of alumni influence in the life of the college. Records of the Church in Williams College, the college church, beginning in 1834, are also in the vault, office of the director of admissions.

Student Letters and Diaries

The following collections of undergraduate letters reveal aspects of Williams life that might otherwise have been impossible to ascertain: Samuel Chapman Armstrong, Class of 1862, approximately twenty-five letters to his family, and Helen W. Ludlow, ed., "Personal Memories and Letters of General S. C. Armstrong," a compilation made in 1898 that includes many of Armstrong's undergraduate letters and that is now in the possession of his daughter, Mrs. Arthur Howe, Plymouth, N.H.; Derick Lane Boardman, Class of 1844, twelve letters to his father; Alonzo Calkins, Class of 1825, and Lyman D. Calkins, Class of 1867, four letters of the former and thirty-six of the latter, now in the possession of Miss Marion Douglas, Westfield, N.J.; Samuel Warren Dike, Class of 1863, forty letters to his family; Ezra Jones Peck, Class of 1851, approximately 150 letters written to Peck by his contemporaries during college vacations and soon after his graduation; William Dwight Whitney, Class of 1845, over 100 letters to and from Whitney, in the "Whitney Family Papers," Sterling Memorial Library, Yale University.

Special mention must be made of the Armstrong, Peck, and Whitney collections. Armstrong was a keen and prolific correspondent, reporting on life at Williams to his missionary family in Hawaii; it seems as if nothing escaped the attention of this young man who became the founder of the Hampton Institute. The Peck collection is unusual in the degree to which it reveals early fraternity life. Peck's correspondence, like Whitney's, has the benefit of consisting to a large extent of letters between college undergraduates.

There must certainly be in existence more Williams undergraduate diaries than have come to light during the preparation of this study, but use was made of all that were available. Of special value were those of Samuel E. Elmore, Class of 1857, who kept a journal of the expedition of the Lyceum of Natural History to Florida, Feb. 19 to Apr. 26, 1857; Marshall J. Hapgood, Class of 1872, whose diary for 1868–69 is in the Wilbur Library, University of Vermont, and in typescript at Williams; William W. Hayden, Class of 1861, whose diary for 1860 is in the Collection of Regional History at Cornell University, and in photostat at Williams; Edward Payson Hopkins, Class of 1864, who kept a journal of the expedition of the Lyceum of Natural History to Greenland, June 27 to Aug. 27, 1860; and Arthur Latham Perry, Class of 1852, whose recollections and diaries are in two typescript volumes, prepared and edited from manuscripts in the possession of the family by Bliss Perry and made available to me by Lewis Perry.

College professors have often suspected that their students' lecture notes reveal very little about the actual lectures. Such seems largely to be true of the notebooks of Alfred Clark Chapin, Class of 1869, Chapin Library, Williams College; Allyn S. Kellogg, Class of 1846; and Francis W. Tappan, Class of 1837.

Student Organizations

The minute books of undergraduate organizations give a revealing impression of the enthusiasms and interests of selected groups of students. Of course, no use was made of the records of the various secret societies, although the Peck letters, previously noted, serve as an excellent substitute.

The career of evangelical religion can be accurately traced in the minute books of the Society of Inquiry, 1818–20; Mills Society of Inquiry, 1820–49; Theological Society, 1829–49; and Mills Theological Society, 1849–73. These organizations nurtured religious activity among Williams students until the appearance of a chapter of the Y.M.C.A. in 1873, and their records are an excellent source of information on attitudes and interests.

Although the origin of the two literary societies is apparently coeval with the founding of the college, records of Philologian and Philotechnian go back only to 1817, earlier records having been lost by fire. In the lengthy minutes of equally lengthy meetings are revelations of undergraduate political and social thought, as well as evidence of the declining importance of the societies after the birth and growth of the secret societies.

Minutes of the Lyceum of Natural History, 1835–1914, are particularly revealing for the years covered in this study; an understanding of the role of the Lyceum in popularizing science on the Williams campus would be impossible without them. A less successful but equally important effort at popularization is recorded in the minutes of the Art Association, 1858–70.

In the days when college classes were integral to undergraduate life and government, there were frequent class meetings, of which records were kept. The only class minute book at Williams is that for the Class of 1856, covering the years 1854–1906. A whole set of similar records would be a mine of information on undergraduate life; that for the Class of 1856 is itself extremely revealing.

3. PUBLISHED MATERIAL

Not all published material used in the preparation of this study is considered here, but attention is given to the most important sources of information.

Writings of Mark Hopkins

The writings mentioned by no means constitute a complete bibliography of Hopkins' works. They are, however, the materials which are most useful in exploring his thought.

Basic, of course, are the volumes which contain the four series of lectures he delivered at the Lowell Institute. In *Lectures on the Evidences of Christianity, before the Lowell Institute. January 1844* (Boston, T. R. Marvin, 1846), Hopkins proved the supernatural origin of Christianity and demonstrated that the future belonged to it and not to competing religions. *Lectures on Moral Science* (Boston, Gould and Lincoln, 1862) contain the lectures on ethics and philosophy "without essential alteration" (p. vii) which Hopkins began delivering at Williams in 1830. Hopkins' views on moral philosophy as a science and his outlook on political and economic questions are best understood from *The Law of Love and Love as a Law: or, Moral Science, Theoretical and Practical*, New York, Charles Scribner, 1869; the relationships between body and soul are explored in *An Outline Study of Man; or, the Body and Mind in One System*, New York, Scribner, Armstrong, 1873. In presenting these lectures in Boston, Hopkins pioneered in the use of the blackboard.

Hopkins' other writings fall into two categories, sermons and addresses; he wrote little of significance that was not first presented before a public audience. Most of these sermons and addresses can be found in four volumes of collected writings: *Miscellaneous Essays and Discourses* (Boston, T. R. Marvin, 1847), which covers the years 1828–47 but does not include any baccalaureate sermons; *Baccalaureate Sermons, and Occasional Discourses* (Boston, T. R. Marvin, 1862), which covers the years 1850–62; *Strength and Beauty: Discussions for Young Men* (New York, Dodd and Mead, 1874), which consists of slightly altered versions of some of his baccalaureate sermons; and *Teachings and Counsels: Twenty Baccalaureate Sermons with a Discourse on President Garfield* (New York, Charles Scribner's Sons, 1884), which covers the years 1850–82. The sermons and addresses included in these volumes were also published separately as pamphlets, which were consulted for this study and are considered below.

While the subject matter of Hopkins' baccalaureate sermons varied, these popular and renowned features of Williams commencement activities were essentially guides to material and spiritual success. The success theme is best studied in *Choice and Service: A Baccalaureate Sermon, Delivered at Williamstown, Ms. July 31, 1864,* Boston, T. R. Marvin and Son, 1864; *Eagles' Wings: A Baccalaureate Sermon, Delivered at Williamstown, Ms. August 1, 1858,* Boston, T. R. Marvin and Son, 1858; *Faith, Philosophy, and Reason: A Baccalaureate Sermon, Delivered at Williamstown, Ms. August 18, 1850,* 2d ed. Boston, T. R. Marvin and Son, 1859; *Higher and Lower Good: A Baccalaureate Sermon, Delivered at Williamstown, Mass. August 4, 1857,* Boston, T. R. Marvin and Son, 1857; *Life: A Baccalaureate Sermon, Delivered at Williamstown, Mass. June 26, 1870,* Boston, T. R. Marvin and Son, 1870; *Nothing to Be Lost: A Baccalaureate Sermon, Delivered at Williamstown, Ms. July 29, 1860,* Boston, T. R. Marvin and Son, 1860; *Self-Denial: A Baccalaureate Sermon, Delivered at Williamstown, Mass. August 3, 1856,* Boston, T. R. Marvin and Son, 1856.

Hopkins' views on education are scattered throughout his writings, but a study of his educational ideas should begin with *An Inaugural Discourse, Delivered at Williams College, September 15, 1836,* Troy, N. Tuttle, 1836; this address is an eloquent defense of the liberal arts college. Also important for a record of Hopkins' outlook near the end of his life are "Inaugurating Address," *Inauguration of Pres. P. A. Chadbourne, July 27, 1872* (Williamstown, Williams College, 1872), pp. 5–11; and *A Dis-*

course Delivered at Williamstown June 29, 1886 on the Fiftieth Anniversary of His Election as President of Williams College, New York, Charles Scribner's Sons, 1886. His attitude toward popular and practical education is contained in "Address," *Public Exercises at the Laying of the Corner Stone of the People's College, at Havana, N.Y. Thursday, September 2d, A.D. 1858* (New York, John F. Trow, 1858), pp. 18–30. *An Address, Delivered at the Dedication of Williston Seminary, at East-Hampton, Mass. December 1, 1841* (Northampton, J. H. Butler, 1841) reveals his views on the proper role of secondary schools; of equal value on female education is *An Address, Delivered in South Hadley, Mass. July 30, 1840, at the Third Anniversary of the Mount Holyoke Female Seminary,* Northampton, John Metcalf, 1840. The relationship of higher education to social stability is explored in *Colleges and Stability: A Discourse, Delivered in Marietta, Ohio, Nov. 8, 1868, at the Quarter-century Anniversary of the Society for the Promotion of Collegiate and Theological Education at the West,* "Reprinted from the proceedings of the society," n.d. Hopkins discussed the recruitment and training of an educated ministry in *An Address, Delivered in Boston, May 26, 1852, before the Society for the Promotion of Collegiate and Theological Education at the West,* Boston, T. R. Marvin, 1852.

His construction of the gospel of wealth is best stated in *Receiving and Giving: A Baccalaureate Sermon, Delivered at Williamstown, Mass. August 15, 1852,* Boston, T. R. Marvin, 1852; *A Discourse Commemorative of Amos Lawrence, Delivered by Request of the Students, in the Chapel of Williams College. February 21, 1853,* Boston, T. R. Marvin, 1853; and *Fruit in Old Age: A Discourse, Commemorative of Nathan Jackson, Delivered by Request of the Students, in the Chapel of Williams College. May 17, 1863,* Boston, T. R. Marvin and Son, 1863.

On the idea of progress two addresses are important: *An Address, Delivered before the Society of Alumni of Williams College, at the Celebration of the Semi-centennial Anniversary. August 16, 1843* (Boston, T. R. Marvin, 1843) and *The Law of Progress: A Centennial Discourse, before the Alumni of Williams College,* North Adams, James T. Robinson and Son, 1876. Hopkins' introduction to Emerson Davis, *The Half Century: or, a History of Changes that Have Taken Place, and Events that Have Transpired, Chiefly in the United States between 1800 and 1850* (Boston, Tappan and Whittemore, 1851), pp. xiii–xxiii, also touches upon progress.

The problems involved in reconciling science and religion attracted Hopkins' interest throughout his life; the career of his thought on this subject can be charted in *Religious Teaching and Worship: A Sermon, Preached at the Dedication of the New Chapel, Connected with Williams College. Sept. 22, 1859*, Boston, T. R. Marvin and Son, 1859; *Science and Religion: A Sermon, Delivered in the Second Presbyterian Church, Albany, on Sabbath Afternoon. August 24, 1856*, Albany, Van Benthuysen, 1856; *The Bible and Pantheism: A Baccalaureate Sermon, Delivered at Williamstown, Ms. July 29, 1866*, Boston, T. R. Marvin and Son, 1866; *The Body the Temple of God: A Baccalaureate Sermon, Delivered at Williamstown, Ms. June 25, 1871*, Boston, T. R. Marvin and Son, 1871; *The Circular and the Onward Movement: A Baccalaureate Sermon, Delivered at Williamstown, Ms. June 24, 1872*, Boston, T. R. Marvin and Son, 1872; and *Influence of the Gospel in Liberalizing the Mind: An Address, Delivered before the Porter Rhetorical Society of the Theological Seminary, at Its Anniversary. Sept. 5, 1837*, Andover, Gould and Newman, 1837.

Hopkins was never reconciled to the existence of the Roman Catholic Church; his opposition to what he and many of his contemporaries called "Popery" is recorded in *A Sermon, Delivered at Plymouth, on the Twenty-second of December, 1846*, Boston, T. R. Marvin, 1847; *A Sermon, Delivered before the Pastoral Association of Massachusetts, in Park Street Church, Boston. May 30, 1843*, Boston, Tappan and Dennet, 1843; *The Sabbath and Free Institutions: A Sermon, Delivered before the American and Foreign Sabbath Union. May 1847*, Boston, T. R. Marvin, 1847; *God's Provisions and Man's Perversions: A Discourse, Delivered before the Congregational Library Association in the Tremont Temple, Boston. May 29, 1855*, Boston, T. R. Marvin, 1855; and *The Central Principle: An Oration Delivered before the New-England Society of New-York. December 22, 1853*, New York, E. French, 1854.

Many of Hopkins' anti-Catholic sermons and addresses also reveal a skepticism about popular government, but probably the most useful statement of his attitude toward democratic governments and electorates is *A Sermon Delivered before His Excellency Edward Everett, Governor, His Honor George Hull, Lieutenant Governor, the Honorable Council, and the Legislature of Massachusetts, on the Anniversary Election. January 2, 1839*, Boston, Dutton and Wentworth, 1839. *The Sabbath and Free Institutions: A Paper Read before the National Sabbath Convention, Saratoga.*

Aug. 13, 1863 (New York, Edward O. Jenkins, 1863) is also revealing, while *Memorial Discourse on President Garfield Prepared at the Request of the Trustees of Williams College* (Troy, H. Stowell, 1882) is Hopkins' tribute both to the dead president and to what he considered a democratic political career at its best.

Hopkins felt that his own training and that of his students placed too little emphasis upon aesthetics; his views on the relationship between aesthetics and morality are contained in *Strength and Beauty: A Baccalaureate Sermon, Delivered at Williamstown, Ms. August 17, 1851* (Boston, T. R. Marvin, 1851) and *The Connexion between Taste and Morals: Two Lectures*, Boston, Dutton and Wentworth, 1841.

Tendencies of the age which Hopkins particularly feared and warned against are the subject of three sermons given between 1845 and 1867: *A Sermon, Preached before the Annual Convention of the Congregational Ministers of Massachusetts, in Boston. May 29, 1845* (Boston, T. R. Marvin, 1845), which attacks materialism; *Liberality—Its Limits: A Baccalaureate Sermon, Delivered at Williamstown, Mass. July 28, 1867* (Boston, T. R. Marvin and Son, 1867), which challenges relativism; and *The Temple of God: A Sermon Delivered at the Dedication of the South Congregational Church, Pittsfield, Mass. Nov. 13, 1850* (Pittsfield, Dodge and Hubbard, 1850), which warns against secularism. Reformers come in for sharp treatment in *Burdens to Be Cast upon the Lord: A Sermon before the American Board of Commissioners for Foreign Missions, at the Thirty-sixth Annual Meeting, Brooklyn, N.Y. Sept. 1845*, Boston, Crocker and Brewster, 1845.

Advice on preaching is contained in *The Object, Subject, and Manner of Preaching: A Sermon, at the Ordination of Mr. Charles M. Hyde, at Brimfield. August 19, 1862*, Boston, T. R. Marvin and Son, 1862; on the conduct of missions, in *The Promise to Abraham: A Missionary Sermon*, Boston, T. R. Marvin and Son, 1858; and on the efficacy of prayer, in *Prayer and the Prayer-Gauge: A Discourse in the First Presbyterian Church, Troy, N.Y. December 15, 1872*, Albany, Weed, Parsons, 1873.

Writings about Mark Hopkins

The two biographies of Hopkins are useful. Franklin Carter, *Mark Hopkins* (Boston, Houghton, Mifflin, 1892), is by a former student, colleague, and successor in the presidency of Williams. Published five years after Hopkins' death, it was written at a

time when it was believed that few Hopkins letters had survived;
it is the most informative work on Hopkins' relationship with the
American Board of Commissioners for Foreign Missions. A grand-
son of Hopkins, John H. Denison, provides the best treatment of
Hopkins' background and youth in *Mark Hopkins: A Biography*,
New York, Charles Scribner's Sons, 1935. Although based on
more manuscripts than the Carter biography, in many ways it is
less satisfactory, suffering from an excess of adulation. *Early
Letters of Mark Hopkins* (New York, John Day, 1929) is a collection of Hopkins family letters, edited and interwoven with com-
mentary by Hopkins' daughter, Susan S. Hopkins. The manuscripts from which this collection was taken are now in the
Williams College Library and were consulted in the preparation
of the present study. On the whole, Miss Hopkins did a faithful
job of editing, although she did not always indicate the possibly
embarrassing excisions.

Two revealing reminiscences of Hopkins by former students and
colleagues are John Bascom, "Mark Hopkins," *Collections of the
Berkshire Historical Society*, *3* (1899), 169–88, and Leverett W.
Spring, "Mark Hopkins," *op. cit.*, *2* (1894), 124–50. M. A. De
Wolfe Howe's chapter on Hopkins in *Classic Shades; Five Leaders
of Learning and their Colleges* (Boston, Little, Brown, 1928), pp.
81–120, is a good example of the Hopkins legend.

For an appraisal of Hopkins as a philosopher nothing matches
James Bissett Pratt, "Mark Hopkins as a Philosopher," which is in
manuscript in the "Pratt Papers," Williams College Library. Delivered as a lecture at Williams in 1936, this paper properly should
be listed with manuscript sources, but its inclusion here may place
it in a more useful context. Professor Pratt, who held the Mark
Hopkins Professorship of Intellectual and Moral Philosophy, de-
molishes the notion that Hopkins can or should be treated seriously
as a philosopher.

Histories of Williams College

There are four general histories of the college. David Ames Wells
and Samuel H. Davis, *Sketches of Williams College* (Springfield,
H. S. Taylor, 1847) is the work of two undergraduates who conceived a venture typical of 19th-century student life. Their study
has been superseded, but it is still a pleasant book to read. Calvin
Durfee, *A History of Williams College* (Boston, A. Williams,
1860) is now valuable both as a document and as a pioneer study
based upon manuscript sources. From the point of view of the

present, the book perhaps suffers from an antiquarian outlook, but Durfee's diligence in collecting the materials on which his study was based has rewarded all successors in the field of Williams history; the chapters on the religious history of the college, by Albert Hopkins, alone make it an important document.

Arthur Latham Perry, *Williamstown and Williams College* (Williamstown, privately printed, 1899) is a monumental and controversial work that is more trustworthy than has often been supposed. Although his judgment of many of his contemporaries was sometimes harsh, and although he made some factual errors, Perry wrote a sweeping history of over 800 pages that is a basic book to a student of the college. A prolix style, lack of documentation, and an inadequate index militate against it, but I have been many times impressed by the frequency with which my own researches led to the discovery of documentary evidence to support what I had supposed to be questionable portions of Perry's narrative. The most recent full study of the college is Leverett W. Spring, *A History of Williams College* (Boston, Houghton Mifflin, 1917), which is shorter and more readable than Perry but makes very little contribution of its own.

Published Documentary Material on the College

Catalogues, annals, and published records constitute a prime source of educational history, for while they may not be as revealing as unpublished records, they do provide the material on which statistics can be based and against which facts can be checked. And they save a great deal of time.

Catalogue of the Officers and Students of Williams College has been issued annually since 1796, although the title and place of publication vary. Williams College Library does not have numbers for 1797, 1807, 1808, 1816, 1820, and 1821, in which years none may have been issued. This series of catalogues is essential in charting the changing curriculum, the size and origin of the student body, and the personnel of the faculty.

Probably the single most useful compendium is the *General Catalogue of the Officers, Graduates, and Non-Graduates of Williams College 1930*, Williamstown, Williams College, 1930. The series of general catalogues, issued triennially until 1874, began in 1799. The first number to be written in English, rather than Latin, was issued in 1880. The 1920 edition is the last to indicate alumni clergymen; the 1930 edition is the most recent and also the first to catalogue graduates and nongraduates in the same volume; there are earlier numbers of general catalogues for both groups.

The changing character of crime and discipline can be traced in *The Laws of Williams College*, issued eleven times, with varying places of publication, between 1795 and 1873.

Biographical information on Williams alumni can be located in Calvin Durfee, *Williams Biographical Annals*, Boston, Lee and Shepard, 1871; it contains sketches of the presidents, trustees, faculty, benefactors, and graduates through the Class of 1865. Unfortunately it does not include information on nongraduates. Since 1875 the college has published a series of obituary records which carry on the purpose of the *Annals*. The earliest are Calvin Durfee, *Williams Obituary Report, 1865–75* (North Adams, James T. Robinson and Son, 1875) and Calvin Durfee, Lewellyn Pratt, and Eben B. Parsons, *Obituary Records of Williams College, 1875–85*, Baldwinsville, N.Y., Gazette Book Print, 1885.

The contents of the Williams library were recorded in published catalogues on nine occasions between 1794 and 1875, the title and place of publication varying but the customary title being *Catalogue of Books in the Library of Williams College, Williamstown, Mass.* There are also catalogues of the literary society libraries, which were in many ways more important and useful to the students than was the college library during the Hopkins period: *Library Catalogue and Constitutions and By-Laws of the Philologian Society of Williams College, 1862* (Williamstown, the Society, n.d.) and *Library Catalogue and the Constitution and By-Laws of the Philotechnian Society of Williams College. 1861*, Williamstown, the Society, 1861. There is also a Philotechnian catalogue for 1867.

Catalogue of the Lyceum of Natural History of Williams College, Instituted A.D. 1835 (Williamstown, Lyceum of Natural History, 1852) provides an excellent index to the activities and interests of the students who popularized science at Williams. Washington Gladden, ed., *Songs of Williams* (New York, Baker and Godwin, 1859) is the first collection of Williams songs.

Undergraduate and Alumni Periodicals

Five student periodicals existed at Williams during the period from 1831 to 1873. The earliest, *Adelphi* (1831–32), combined news and literary and political essays, but this semimonthly pub-

lication, operated for a time by the literary societies, could not be
sustained. The next effort, *Williams Monthly Miscellany* (1844–
45), was of similar character and met a similar fate. The most impressive and successful of the periodicals was *Williams Quarterly*
(1853–72) ; it provided news and comment on undergraduate life,
but its larger function was as an outlet for undergraduate essayists
who contributed papers on a remarkable range of subjects. *Williams Review* (1870–74) was a monthly, and *Vidette* (1867–74)
appeared in several forms during its short existence; neither of
these publications attained the stature of the *Quarterly*, although
they are sometimes more useful for current news.

The history of the college yearbook begins in 1853, with the
publication of the *College Index*, which became the *Gulielmensian*
in 1857. In its early days, the college annual provided very little
information that was not available in catalogues of the fraternities
and other organizations whose membership it listed.

Williams Alumni Review (1909–   ) carries occasional articles
of historical interest.

Autobiographies, Biographies, and Diaries of Williams Alumni

The careers of Williams alumni may be studied in Calvin Durfee,
Williams Biographical Annals and, for the most notable, in the
Dictionary of American Biography. Many Williams men have told
their own stories or been the subjects of biographies, but not all
these books shed light on the history of the college. Those which
do, however, are worth noting.

The most useful autobiographies are John Bascom (Class of
1849), *Things Learned by Living*, New York, G. P. Putnam's
Sons, 1913; S. G. W. Benjamin (Class of 1859), *The Life and
Adventures of a Free Lance*, Burlington, Vt., Free Press, 1914;
Keyes Danforth (Class of 1846), *Boyhood Reminiscences*, New
York, Gazlay Bros., 1895; Washington Gladden (Class of 1859),
Recollections, Boston, Houghton Mifflin, 1900; G. Stanley Hall
(Class of 1867), *Life and Confessions of a Psychologist*, New York,
D. Appleton, 1923; and Timothy Woodbridge (Class of 1812),
*The Autobiography of a Blind Minister: Including Sketches of the
Men and Events of His Time*, Boston, John P. Jewett, 1856.

Biographies which give more than passing treatment of their
subjects' careers at Williams are Edith Armstrong Talbot, *Samuel
Chapman Armstrong* [Class of 1862] : *A Biographical Study*, New

York, Doubleday, Page, 1904; Ethel M. McAllister, *Amos Eaton* [Class of 1799]: *Scientist and Educator*, Philadelphia, University of Pennsylvania Press, 1941; Theodore Clarke Smith, *The Life and Letters of James Abram Garfield* [Class of 1856], 2 vols. New Haven, Yale University Press, 1925; Horace E. Scudder, *Life and Letters of David Coit Scudder* [Class of 1855], *Missionary in Southern India*, New York, Hurd and Houghton, 1864; Clyde K. Hyder, [Francis H.] *Snow* [Class of 1862] *of Kansas*, Lawrence, University of Kansas Press, 1953; and Roswell Ward, *Henry A. Ward* [Class of 1855]: *Museum Builder to America*, Rochester, Rochester Historical Society, 1948.

Albert C. Sewall, *Life of Prof. Albert Hopkins* [Class of 1826] (New York, Anson D. F. Randolph, 1879) contains so many selections from Hopkins' diary that it should not be considered a biography; Increase Tarbox, ed., *Diary of Thomas Robbins, D.D. 1796–1854* [Class of 1796] (2 vols. Boston, Beacon Press, 1886–87) is one of the earliest records of Williams life.

Regional History

The most useful history of Berkshire County continues to be David Dudley Field, ed., *A History of the County of Berkshire, Massachusetts*, Pittsfield, Samuel W. Bush, 1829. Histories published later in the 19th century are less trustworthy and informative and more promotional than this early work, but there is some utility to Josiah Gilbert Holland, *History of Western Massachusetts* (2 vols. Springfield, Mass., Samuel Bowles, 1855) and J. E. A. Smith, ed., *History of Berkshire County, Massachusetts, with Biographical Sketches of its Prominent Men*, 2 vols. New York, J. B. Beers, 1885. An early travel guide that documents the period of its publication is Washington Gladden, *From the Hub to the Hudson: with Sketches of Nature, History, and Industry in Northwestern Massachusetts*, Greenfield, Mass., E. D. Merriam, 1870.

Collections of the Berkshire Historical and Scientific Society (3 vols. Pittsfield, 1892–99) contains articles relating to the history of the college. Robert R. R. Brooks, ed., *Williamstown: The First Two Hundred Years, 1753–1953* (Williamstown, McClelland Press, 1953) is a cooperative venture which supplements Arthur Latham Perry, *Origins in Williamstown* (New York, Charles Scribner's Sons, 1894), both of which are better local histories than most communities can boast.

Educational History

I had hoped to provide this account of the Hopkins story with more comparative data on other colleges, but the nature of existing studies in the field of educational history did not permit. The difficulty in this area is best demonstrated by what happened when I attempted to assemble comparative statistics on endowment: finding most published histories inadequate, I turned to the treasurers of the various colleges. Some graciously provided the desired information; one warned that I was not to publish the figures he gave me; and some confessed they were unable to make sense of their old records. A great deal of research remains to be done on specific institutions before any meaningful comparative study can be made. Charles F. Thwing, *A History of Higher Education in America* (New York, D. Appleton, 1906) is still the best general study.

Many existing studies, however, are extremely useful. Some of a general nature which make important contributions are Frank W. Blackmar, *The History of Federal and State Aid to Higher Education in the United States*, Bureau of Education Circular of Information, Herbert Baxter Adams, ed., *Contributions to American Educational History*, Washington, Government Printing Office, 1890; George P. Schmidt, *The Old Time College President*, New York, Columbia University Press, 1930; Louis Franklin Snow, *The College Curriculum in the United States*, New York, Teachers College, Columbia University, 1907; and Donald G. Tewksbury, *The Founding of American Colleges and Universities before the Civil War, with Particular Reference to the Religious Influences Bearing upon the College Movement*, New York, Teachers College, Columbia University, 1907.

Two histories in particular deserve to be considered as models, and no student can read them without realizing the vast potential which exists in American higher education as a respectable area of study: Robert S. Fletcher, *A History of Oberlin College, from Its Foundation through the Civil War*, 2 vols. Oberlin, Oberlin College, 1943; and Thomas Le Duc, *Piety and Intellect at Amherst College, 1865–1912*, New York, Columbia University Press, 1946. Although it covers a later period than the Hopkins era, George W. Pierson, *Yale: College and University, 1871–1937* (2 vols. New Haven, Yale University Press, 1952–55) is a painstaking and monumental achievement.

Some colleges and universities have been better served by historians than others. Some of the better college histories are Arthur C. Cole, *A Hundred Years of Mount Holyoke College: The Evolution of an Educational Ideal*, New Haven, Yale University Press, 1940; E. Merton Coulter, *College Life in the Old South*, 2d ed. Athens, University of Georgia Press, 1951; Merle Curti and Vernon Carstensen, *The University of Wisconsin, 1848–1925*, 2 vols. Madison, University of Wisconsin Press, 1949; Claude M. Fuess, *Amherst: The Story of a New England College*, Boston, Little, Brown, 1935; Samuel E. Morison, *Three Centuries of Harvard, 1636-1936*, Cambridge, Harvard University Press, 1946; Frederick C. Waite, *Western Reserve University: The Hudson Era*, Cleveland, Western Reserve University Press, 1943; and Thomas J. Wertenbaker, *Princeton, 1746–1896*, Princeton, Princeton University Press, 1946.

If there are any retired college and university treasurers or presidents who are casting about for a project, they could perform a great service by following in the footsteps of President Stanley King, whose *A History of the Endowment of Amherst College* (Amherst, Amherst College, 1950) is a unique and welcome contribution.

Special Articles

The best guide to articles in undergraduate and alumni periodicals is the footnote citations in the present volume, but special mention must be made of the series of short histories of the various departments at Williams which appeared in the *Williams Alumni Review*: Herdman F. Cleland, "Geology at Williams," *17* (1925), 245–9; Carl S. Hoar, "Biology at Williams," *17* (1925), 331–6; Orie W. Long, "The Department of German in Williams College," *19* (1927), 165–72; Brainerd Mears, "Chemistry at Williams," *18* (1925), 113–24; and Theodore Clarke Smith, "History at Williams," *18* (1926), 220–6. An equally useful study is Charles J. Bullock, "The History of Economic and Political Study in Williams College," *Education*, *24* (1904), 532–7.

Essential to an understanding of the religious history of the college are the two articles of Albert Hopkins which appeared as "Revivals of Religion in Williams College," *Quarterly Journal of the American Education Society*, *13* (1841), 341–51, 461–74. Carroll A. Wilson, "Familiar 'Small College' Quotations, II: Mark

Hopkins and the Log," *The Colophon*, new ser. *3* (1938), 194–209, brilliantly pursues the aphorism of the log and develops its career from the Delmonico banquet of 1871 into the 20th century.

Miscellaneous

Since a bibliography should not be autobiographical, no useful service would be performed by listing here all other books that may have had something to do with the preparation of this study. For general and specific matters of American social history there are excellent bibliographies in the various volumes of Arthur M. Schlesinger and Dixon Ryan Fox, eds., *A History of American Life*, 13 vols. New York, Macmillan, 1929–48. Merle Curti, *The Growth of American Thought* (New York, Harper and Brothers, 1943) and Ralph H. Gabriel, *The Course of American Democratic Thought* (New York, Ronald Press, 1940) are the best guides to American intellectual history.

The footnotes contain much bibliographical information; for instance, the chapter on fraternities provides data on fraternity catalogues consulted; there seems little reason to repeat this and similar information here. Some stray items, however, do deserve special mention in a Williams bibliography. William R. Lawrence, ed., *Extracts from the Diary and Correspondence of the Late Amos Lawrence; with a Brief Account of Some Incidents in His Life* (Boston, John Wilson and Son, 1855) helps toward an understanding of Lawrence's philanthropy. Willis I. Milham, *Early American Observatories: Which Was the First Astronomical Observatory in America?* (Williamstown, privately printed, 1938) and *Meteorology in Williams College* (Williamstown, privately printed, 1938) are responsible studies of early American science. And Charles J. Woodbury, *Talks with Ralph Waldo Emerson* (New York, Baker and Taylor, 1890) is a delightful account of conversations between Emerson and Woodbury which occurred at Williams in 1865, during Woodbury's senior year.

Index